The Image of the Middle Ages in Romantic and Victorian Literature

Kevin L. Morris

CROOM HELM
London ● New York ● Sydney

©1984 K.L. Morris
Croom Helm Ltd, Provident House, Burrell Row,
Beckenham, Kent BR3 1AT

Croom Helm Australia, 44-50 Waterloo Road,
North Ryde, 2113, New South Wales

British Library Cataloguing in Publication Data

Morris, Kevin L.
    The image of the Middle Ages in Romantic
    and Victorian literature.
    1. English literature—18th century—
    History and criticism   2. English literature
    —19th century—History and criticism
    3. Middle Ages in literature
    I. Title
    820.9'358   PR448.M4
    ISBN 0-7099-3511-0

Reprinted 1987

Printed by Antony Rowe Ltd, Chippenham, Wiltshire

THE IMAGE OF THE MIDDLE AGES IN ROMANTIC
AND VICTORIAN LITERATURE

CONTENTS

CONTENTS

"So they are all a single people with a
single language!" said Yahweh. "This is
but the start of their undertakings!
There will be nothing too hard for them
to do. Come, let us go down and confuse
their language...."

Genesis 11, 6-7.

history may become / A travelling voice
of prophecy ...

F.W. Faber Sir Lancelot (1844).

... there will be only one flock, and one
shepherd.

John 10, 16.

PREFACE

Eighteenth and nineteenth-century medievalism was
part of an agitated quest for a new outlook on life,
a new diagnosis of man's ills and a new cure. One
writer has said : "considering the strength ... of
the Gothic revival in architecture, the overtly
religious strain in nineteenth-century medievalism
was curiously weak";[1] and another supposed that
eighteenth-century medievalists had merely "an
antiquarian interest in the curious and old-fashion-
ed",[2] while Dean Inge thought Romantic medievalism
a failure, no more than "a matter of sentimental
antiquarianism".[3] But religious medievalism - that
aspect of literary medievalism which refers especially to the medieval Church in a religious or quasi-
religious manner - was strong and seldom solely a
matter of dilettantism, nostalgia, escapism or
aestheticism; rather, it was serious and genuinely
religious.
     Little has been written on the theme, while
other aspects of medievalism have received due
attention : Chandler's A Dream of Order deals chiefly
with the socio-political aspect, Girouard's The
Return to Camelot explores the ideal of the gentleman in relation to chivalry, Merriman's The Flower
of Kings concerns the revival of the Arthurian legend
and two unpublished American Ph.D. theses by Kegel
and St. Louis deal with socio-political medievalism
with reference to a small number of writers. The
Pre-Raphaelites - seldom religious in their medievalism - have received much attention.
     This work asks the question "how serious, how
important was post-Enlightenment literary religious
medievalism?" It demands a range of answers in areas
fraught with imponderables, so no dogmatic answers
or neat schemas are possible. The best one can hope
to achieve is to look at a wide variety of examples

1

and draw tentative conclusions, always aware that the inductive principle leaves much to be desired, especially in literature. Of course, few medievalists were exclusively medievalist, and their significance should not be exaggerated.

Religious medievalism frequently had at its core a perception of the problem of man's sense of alienation, and unselfconsciously and implicitly suggested a model or myth of reconciliation.This work suggests, then, that religious medievalism was not a superficial cultural phenomenon; that the romantic spirit, with which it was (at least) chronologically connected, was intimately associated with the metaphysical, and so naturally acted as mid-wife to this 'cultural' expression of essentially metaphysical yearnings. The work seeks to elucidate the post-Enlightment relationship between aesthetic culture and 'aesthetic' religion, romanticism, medievalism and religious trends. The first five chapters examine the range and development of attitudes, while the following two analyse the range of medievalist attitudes in relation to art.

I must thank Dr.A.W.Bower and Prof. J.A.V. Chapple of Hull University for their advice, the University of Hull for its grant to me, Dr.Eamon Duffy of Cambridge University for his ruthless criticism, Dr.Louis Leuridan of Louvain University for advice on philosophical points, Mr.Gerard de Lisle of Quenby Hall for supplying me with copies of manuscripts, Mr.Michael Dormer for putting me in contact with Mr.De Lisle, Mr.J.M.Farrar of Cambridgeshire County Record Office for help with manuscripts, Mr.Trevor Kaye for giving me access to documents in Trinity College Library Cambridge and Brenda Parry-Jones for the same service in the Library of Magdalen College Oxford. I have also made considerable use of the John Rylands Library Manchester, Manchester Reference Library, Hull University Library and the library of Quarr Abbey, and for the help of these bodies I am very grateful.

Notes:

1. J.A.W.Bennet RES XXIII (1972) 376-8.
2. Herbert H.Coulson "Medievalism in the Modern World" The Catholic Historical Review XXVI (1940-41) 421.
3. William R.Inge Outspoken Essays. Second Series (1933) 199.

ABBREVIATIONS

BS II.	Kenelm Henry Digby The Broad Stone of Honour (1823).
BS V.	Kenelm Henry Digby The Broad Stone of Honour (1876-7).
C.	Kenelm Henry Digby Compitum (1848-54).
Chandler	Alice Chandler A Dream of Order.
C.U.P.	Cambridge University Press.
CW	Complete Works of John Ruskin ed. Cook and Wedderburn.
DNB	Dictionary of National Biography.
DR	Dublin Review.
ed.	editor / edited by / edition.
ER	Edinburgh Review.
Fairchild	Hoxie Neale Fairchild Religious Trends in English Poetry.
FM	Fraser's Magazine.
H.	Charles Kingsley Hereward the Wake.
LM	Charles Kingsley : His Letters and Memories of His Life ed. Fanny Kingsley 2v. (1878).
MC.	Kenelm Henry Digby Mores Catholici (1831-42).
Memoir	Bernard Holland Memoir of Kenelm Henry Digby (1919).
MLR	Modern Language Review.
NCBEL	New Cambridge Bibliography of English Literature.
NCF	Nineteenth-Century Fiction.
n.d.	no date
no.	number.
O.U.P.	Oxford University Press.
P	Charles Kingsley Poems (1902).
P. & P.	Thomas Carlyle Past and Present (George Routledge & Sons, (1893).
PMLA	Periodical of the Modern Language Association of America.

ABBREVIATIONS

PQ	Philological Quarterly.
pub.	published.
qu.	quote(d).
RES	Review of English Studies.
rev.	revised, review.
R.R.	G.K. Chesterton The Resurrection of Rome Ist. ed. (1930).
ser.	series.
TLS	Times Literary Supplement.
U.P.	University Press.
UTQ	University of Toronto Quarterly.
v.	volume(s).
VNL	Victorian Newsletter.
VP	Victorian Poetry.
VS	Victorian Studies.
Whibley	Charles Whibley Lord John Manners and His Friends 2v.(1925).

Chapter I

THE CUCKOO'S EGG : ROMANTICISM AND RELIGIOUS
MEDIEVALISM

Antiquity! thou wondrous charm, what art
thou? that, being nothing, art everything!

Charles Lamb "Oxford in the Vacation"
The Essays of Elia

It is evident that in the Europe of the second
half of the eighteenth century confidence in the
cultural, intellectual and spiritual status quo of
the Enlightenment weakened, with the result that many
abandoned ship in quest of new norms. Some looked to
the Middle Ages for a scale of values, and the medieval Church became a theme significant, but fraught
with ambiguity, duality, paradox and irony, all set
within a frame of imponderables, so that a tentative
discussion of relevant contemporary ideological
currents is necessary to gain angles of vision and
points of perspective.

The broad impression given by literary and
religious historians is that the Catholic Revival
was part of the Romantic Movement; which implies
that religious medievalism (an aspect of the Catholic
Revival), the Gothic Revival and Catholicism (both
Anglo- and Roman) are romantic, or more romantic than
classic. (This would seem to suggest that Protestantism is more "classic", especially in view of its
claimed rationalism.) In 1833, in Die Romantische
Schüle, Heinrich Heine completely identified
Catholicism, the Catholic Revival and religious
medievalism with romanticism. Henry Beers echoed
Heine's approach in his histories of eighteenth and
nineteenth-century English romanticism. More
recently, Friedrich Heyer wrote that "from Romantic
sources came a passion for anything associated with
the Middle Ages : pilgrimages, processions ... Marian
devotion",[1] a statement which is substantially true,

5

but by implication misleading. Heine's categoriza-
tion is much too vague to be true. By way of clarif-
ication, two things will be suggested in this chapter : the first is that while religious medievalism
was not originally inspired in England by a desire
to return to Catholicism, and was always in one sense
or another romantic, it was not simply a product and
aspect of the Romantic Movement; for, in so far as it
was Catholic, it was anti-romantic, and might even be
regarded as nearer to the classic. In this respect,
religious medievalism was a radical romanticism because it strained away from the important - one might
say central - romantic syndrome, namely faith in
progress, faith in man and individualism. The second
point is that religious medievalism issued reasonably
and naturally from romanticism because romanticism is
itself a largely religious phenomenon, a religious
quest, and not merely a cultural, political or
aesthetic phenomenon. This chapter goes some way,
then, towards explaining in what sense the Catholic
Revival (in so far as it was Catholic) and religious
medievalism could be anti-romantic, and, correlatively, how romanticism could give birth to such an
anti-romantic enthusiasm : it indicates how the
cuckoo's egg of religious medievalism could be laid
in the nest of romanticism.

English religious medievalism was not an
isolated phenomenon, and was invigorated by the more
defined religious medievalism of the Continent. The
first seeds of the romantic revolt floated from
England to the Continent, rather than vice versa,[2]
and the work of Percy, Hurd and Macpherson turned
many European minds to the distant past. In the
1780s - a traumatic decade in which people began to
look seriously for alternative structures - German
Romantics began to see the Middle Ages as an age of
faith, as a cultural, political, social and religious
scale of value by which the present could be condemned and healed. The first of the following two
sections deals with this Continental context, with
reference to the Enlightenment and the Romantic
rebellion against it; while the second elaborates
the relationship between religion and medievalism,
within the context of romanticism.

The Continental Context

By the second half of the eighteenth century
the ideological monopoly of the rationalist Enlightenment was being eroded, perhaps through boredom, but
also because of the realization that man cannot live

by reason alone.[3] This insight is the essence of the
eighteenth-century crisis of anxiety which, though
frequently manifested in cultural terms, was at root
metaphysical. Because of dissatisfaction with Enlightenment norms and standards, the bases of individual conduct collapsed, so that the anxiety erupted
in the sense of alienation of the individual from
community and from self. This resulted in the revitalized quest for a rationale of duty, community
and God.

The Enlightenment was anti-Christian: in the
twenty years prior to the French Revolution, 400 new
anti-religious publications were issued in France.
It was especially anti-Catholic: even Alexander Pope,
privately a Catholic, projected a deist persona.
Diderot and D'Alembert produced the Encyclopédie ou
Dictionnaire Raisonée (1751-72), with its basically
secular morality, holding human happiness as the
object of life: a happiness which was to be encouraged by education in the right secular knowledge.
There was a secularized sense of the orderliness of
creation, with the "great chain of being", and the
individual as an integral part of an orderly society,
in which community the individual fulfilled himself
through duty. Reason, the new "inner light",
facilitated and promoted this commitment, and entail-
ed a rejection of external authorities (as Kant
explained in his essay of 1784, "What is Enlightenment"). Reason was the substance of the optimistic
theory of progress, based on Locke and Newton.
Enlightenment progressivism continued into the
Romantic period with the Marquis de Condorcet's
Esquisse d'un tableau historique des progrès de
l'esprit humain (1793); but a symbol of the breakdown of this system is the effect of the Lisbon
earthquake of 1755, which destroyed Voltaire's
optimism and prompted Candide (1759), with its message of the deficiency of all philosophic systems, the
unattainability of absolute truth and the proposal
that man's duty is simply "to cultivate his garden".
But why? Kant believed that reason prescribed the
course of duty; yet many did not believe in the
objectivity of his categorical imperative. This
breakdown was addressed by romanticism, which P. van
Tieghem fittingly characterized as "dissatisfaction
with the contemporary world, restless anxiety in the
face of life, and sadness without cause".[4]

Enlightenment concerns continued into the Romantic period, though with imagination replacing reason
as the panacea: "intuition," as Hugh Honour has so
felicitously expressed it, "was called in to solve

the problems which empiricism had brought to the surface".[5] Rousseau was a "bridge" between the periods, and exemplifies the secular search for new structures to overcome alienation. His Du Contrat Social (1762) proposed a civil religion, "étatisme", with citizens avowing the sanctity of the contract and laws, whereby the individual surrenders his will to the community, to the infallible "General Will", which is greater than the sum of its parts. But this is only good for primitive society uncorrupted by civilization, in which man's now-latent, natural, infallible goodness flourishes. He had taken the Enlightenment notion of the providential harmony of man with nature and transformed its inner light of reason into the inner light of the moral sense, which he took from Calvinism. This presented a virtual deification of the individual (to match a divine state),a theme pregnant for Romantics. Other roman- tic optimists who proposed in the nineteenth century the virtual worship of humanity as the cure for alienation included Marx, Feuerbach and Comte. Utilitarianism, pantheism and secularized Protestan- tism were also attempts to establish a lost harmony.

Rousseau exemplifies the shift from society to individual and from reason to feeling; a shift not so dramatic, since the Enlightenment had its own individualism, rooted in the rationalist, self-con- fident conscience, and its own equivalent to feeling in the Lockean, empirical tradition of sensual impression and personal experience of life as an evaluative and perceptional base. But such schemes as Rousseau's were felt by some Romantics to be unfaithful to contemporary experience, by maintaining too much of the Enlightenment and by too surely in- voking new systems: they felt the age to be one of anxiety and atomization, and wished to reflect that. One Enlightenment school had doubted the doctrine of the providential order of nature, and this gave a lead to those who turned back to the "older Christian view of nature as a battlefield and of man as a creature torn between duty and self-interest".[6] These, such as the German "Sturm und Drang" pre- Romantics of the 1770-78 period, took an angry del- ight in their alienation, and celebrated their individualism; indeed, "the majority of Romantics appear to have been in some degree alienated from their fellow men".[7] But the Victorians could not so celebrate individualism, for by then the Industrial Revolution had deepened the anxiety of loneliness and isolation.

"Belief in the alienation of the individual from

contemporary society was inseparable from the cult
of primitivism";[8] many who were not content with
self-indulgence and protest alone looked to the past,
and the primitive age was often identified with the
rude Middle Ages.[9] The Enlightenment, which had
failed for so many, had been anti-Christian and especially anti-Catholic; so what more natural rebellion than to turn to the reviled Age of Faith? This
impression was reinforced by the belief that Enlightenment atheism, in promoting the reconciliatory
vision of scientific empiricism and rationalism, had
ousted the medieval reconciliatory order of theism.
If the Enlightenment mentality said "the affirmation
of God constituted an estrangement and alienation
from the inner dynamism of man's most decisive
achievement, namely, a truly scientific mentality",[10]
and since this view was held by romantics to have
failed, then the situation had to be inverted:
rationalism had to be abandoned and God had to be
reinstated.[11] "Once everything has been run through
- whither is one to run then? ... Would one not have
to come back to faith? Perhaps to a Catholic faith?"
mused Nietzsche in a later period.[12] Hence the
search for a re-integrating, authoritative world-
view which could answer the crisis of alienation, the
sense of lost social purpose and the individual's
loss of faith in life itself. Alienation is the
sense of a breakdown in understanding, characterized
by atomization, by the failure to see, or to have
faith in, the relationship of one thing to another,
and by the individual's feeling of estrangement from
self, society and cosmos; and all accompanied by an
oppressive sense of foreboding.[13] "Alienation"
originally meant progressive insanity; and C.G. Jung
said that insanity was the consequence of a loss of
myth, and that sanity was based on the achievement of
a psychic harmony between the self and the world.
Perhaps, then, the conquest of alienation involves
the holding of a myth (which is a means of perceiving
truth). Catholic Christianity, especially as it had
appeared in the Middle Ages,was for some such a myth.
    De Maistre, Chateaubriand, De Bonald and the
Abbé Barruel, who dissented from current norms, saw
the French Revolution and its evils as the product of
the Enlightenment, and condemned both. So did the
German Idealists; and both groups split from mainstream romanticism in their objection to individualism, which they - paradoxically, but correctly - took
to be the issue of the Enlightenment. One may call
such Romantics radical romantics, because they looked
for a new system and were anti-individualist, as were

the religious medievalists by implication. Friedrich
Schleiermacher (1768-1834), another rebel, exemplifies the radical romantic. In 1799, while a member of
a Romantic group, he opposed the status quo by
stressing mystery, imagination and feeling, in On
Religion: Speeches to its Cultured Despisers. The
Christian Faith (1821-22, 1830-31) suggested religion
was a sense of complete dependence on God, and sin
was the attempt to be independent and free of God,
thereby denying the essence of rebellious romanticism. This in itself suggests that Christianity at
its deepest level is opposed to romanticism at its
deepest level.

Benedetto Croce commented on the metaphysical
anxiety of the romantics and their attempt to resolve
this anxiety. He pictures romantics as in between
faiths: they "dreamed of returning to religious
transcendence and the peace that it seemed to promise", and of submitting to an authority which would
release them from the responsibility of finding their
own solutions. "The highest expression," he says,
"of this sort of transcendence and of this imperative
ruling was the Catholic faith". In the same place he
notes the historiographical developments of the period, which gave such people a new and vivified view
of the Middle Ages, the result being that they made
what he calls a "religion of the Middle Ages".[14]
The implication is that the coincidence of anxiety
and historiographical developments led to religious
medievalism in Continental Romanticism. Certainly,
few people during the Enlightenment had had an
opportunity to appreciate the Middle Ages because of
the historiographical despotism of the "enlightened":
"it was only towards the end of the century that
sympathy for the Middle Ages came in with Johannes
Müller and the Romantic movement".[15] Indeed, Lord
Acton judged it had been the "mission" of the
Romantics to make the Middle Ages "intelligible to a
society issuing from the eighteenth century".[16]

The development of historicism was a crucial
factor in the growth of medievalism.[17] Historicism
supposes that the truth and value of phenomena are
best perceived in the light of the immediate historical context, and, sometimes, in the light of an
alleged historical development, involving entities
such as Culture, National Spirit, Humanity or Reality. Before this development, it was usually assumed
that human nature was constant; but with the shift
from the mechanistic and static picture of creation
to the organic and dynamic, the idea that human nature changed with time and circumstances came to be

10

respected. With the growing respect for individuality, it was fitting that different ages should be
valued for their own sakes, and that people living in
them should be viewed in relation to their contexts.
This meant that people were more sympathetic to past
ages, and the way was opened for medievalism.[18]
Novalis's Die Christenheit oder Europa (1799) was one
fruit of historicism in its organic view of history
as a theodicy in which the medieval civitas dei would
be restored in an improved form. It should be noted,
however, that historicism gave rise to certain ideas
out of sympathy with Christianity, such as relativism
and the notion that the study of history should help
uncover laws of development which determined the
"flow" of history and society. Such determinism is
associated with meliorism which, paradoxically, in
the nineteenth century gained converts from Christianity. Meliorism often presupposes that man is
subject to external forces of history, society and
environment, and that if these can be changed for the
better, men will be changed for the better. This
position contradicts Catholic Christianity, which
says that men are fundamentally free and not determined.
     This Romantic historiography was more myth-
making and propaganda, a reflection on its own age,
than history. For example, the notion of medieval
unity became an obsession: "those were fine, magnificent times when Europe was a Christian country,
when one Christendom inhabited this civilized continent and one great common interest linked the most
distant provinces of this vast spiritual empire....
one sovereign governed and united the great political
forces," said Novalis in Die Christenheit oder
Europa.[19] Unity - spiritual, intellectual,aesthetic,
social - was necessary for salvation. Such beliefs
were political and religious at the same time, as was
Friedrich von Schlegel's, expressed in Philosophie
der Geschichte (1829), that in the Middle Ages
principle had been predominant, now only opinion,
that then there was greatness, now only decay. Even
the Saint-Simonians - progressivists though they
were - believed in the 1820s that the Middle Ages had
been an "organic" age of creativity, and that the
modern age (beginning with the Reformation) was a
"critical" age of negation - a view of history which
was, according to John Stuart Mill, "the general
property of Europe, or at least of Germany and
France".[20] Tieck criticized Protestantism for its
dry ritual and theology, while Chateaubriand turned
in disgust from the modern world: "imagination," he

said, "is rich, abundant, wonderful; existence is
poor, arid, without magic. One lives with a full
heart in an empty world."[21] To remedy this, he
looked back, in Le Génie du Christianisme,[22]to the
Middle Ages, the age of spiritualized imagination -
a faculty which had been destroyed by rationalism -
and dwelt on them in a mélange of narrative, emotional religiosity and Catholic apologetics, dwelling on
the outward forms of Catholic Christianity. Thirty
years later in England, Kenelm Henry Digby was re-
producing his ideas,[23] as was Frederick Ozanam in
France;[24] and Montalembert, the historian of medieval
monasticism, expressed the feeling that the religious
were embattled by atheism, opposition to individualism and the analytical spirit, and the wish to return
to the Middle Ages to find the opposites: faith,
community and sympathetic emotion.[25] Also, Michelet
wrote the "most romantic of portraits of the Middle
Ages, an idealized study of crusades, a reverent ...
portrait of St.Thomas Aquinas, a Puginesque glorying
in the religious nature of earlier Gothic art and
architecture".[26] Allied spirits included Clemens
Brentano, Joseph von Eichendorff, Joseph Görres,
Werner, Schütz, Carové, Adam Müller, Gries, and
Auguste von Schlegel. Blankenagel sums up German
Romanticism thus: "Romanticism's penchant for
medieval Catholicism was rooted on the esthetic element, mysticism, and the fondness for unity".[27] In
fact, these elements - aestheticism, mysticism and
unity - were interrelated.
    One can see in these examples how the cultural
crisis was also a spiritual one, since the attempt
to enrich the cultural scene and to cure the political one also readily palliated metaphysical anxieties.
One may take as a symbol of the relationship between
romantic art and religion the curious - but then
widely held view - of Heinrich Heine, that romanticism was religious because it was a rebirth of medieval art, which was itself essentially religious, even
when ostensibly secular.[28] The obsession with the
collapse of artistic standards, shared by neo-class-
icist and Romantic alike, and manifested by such as
Hurd in England, Chateaubriand, Rousseau and the
students of Jacques-Louis David in France, and the
Nazarenes, Winckelmann, Herder and Friedrich von
Schlegel in Germany, was so powerful, so morally
inclined and so pervasive that one is persuaded to
view it as a metaphysical obsession, indeed as a
correlative of the age's spiritual anxiety.[29] John
Keble was to note the metaphysical responsibility of
the Romantic poets, which consisted in repairing the

rift between man and his natural surroundings caused
by rationalist philosophy, with the revelation of
"natural supernaturalism". For Keble, rationalism
meant disintegration, while poetry meant participation and reintegration.[30] Heine isolated division of
aims as the vice of the age, a division caused by
poets no longer being absorbed by a single faith or
enthusiasm, an idea developed by Matthew Arnold.
"Once," said Heine, "the world was whole, in antiquity and the Middle Ages; despite external conflicts,
there was an all-embracing unity, and the poets were
also whole."[31] He also said, when speaking of the
medieval arts, that "at that period all manifestations of life harmonised most wonderfully".[32] When so
many eighteenth and nineteenth-century intellectuals
looked to the "Age of Faith" for solutions to contemporary problems, we must at least consider that the
quest could have been metaphysical.
     The question may be asked why all Romantics did
not find this reconciling power in Protestantism,
since many were Protestant, Protestantism was dominant and Romanticism had more in common with Protestantism than with Catholicism. Novalis, looking at
the medieval Church, came to the conclusion that "its
omnipresence in life, its love for art, its profound
humanity ...its delight in poverty, obedience and
loyalty ... make it unmistakable as the true religion".[33] By permeating every aspect of life, the
medieval Church made sense of it by unifying and
integrating it: it was the universally adhered-to
matrix and template of life. But now there was no
universally accepted orthodoxy and Protestantism was
seen to be the very author of, and monument to, disintegration and alienation. It propagated sects and
allied itself with discredited orthodoxies such as
rationalism, deism and pantheism. Romantics perceived the Reformation to have been, in Chadwick's
phrase, the "baptism of the secular world".[34]
Novalis said in Die Christenheit oder Europa that the
total Protestant emphasis on the letter, rather than
the spirit, of the Bible militated against supernatural understanding and revelation (while promoting
Reason): "the history of Protestantism, therefore,
records no more splendid manifestations of the supernatural ...", while "secular power began to rule" and
the unity of Christendom was lost.[35] Ronald Taylor
emphasizes the point that to Novalis this led "to the
centuries of Rationalism and Enlightenment, by which
time, in his eyes, the disintegration, and with it
man's disgrace, was utter".[36] In losing the all-
embracing and unifying faith, Europe had lost its

13

grip on the transcendent, which was of central
importance to the Romantics. Therefore, in recovering the medieval Church they were also recovering
transcendentalism, and thereby a myth of integration.
Also, present Protestantism did not appeal to the
Romantics as much as past Catholicism because, as
Blankenagel points out,

> Romantic longing for the infinite finds
> its reflex in an interest in the distant
> past and in distant regions. At a distance,
> said Novalis, everything becomes poetic,
> everything becomes romantic. The magic power
> of the imagination is freed from the limitat-
> ions of time, space, and actuality both in the
> the past and the future.[37]

The Romantics felt they could not idealize Protestantism because it was a phenomenon of the modern age,
without a long, glorious past and temporally distant
zenith; and, moreover, without appeal to the imagination. In addition, Protestantism was observed to be
an ally of modernism,[38] and so suffered from the
impact of criticism of the latter.
    Why then did not all Romantics become Catholics?
It is possible that some Romantics remained Protestant because they were not sufficiently sensitive to
the crisis to require them to look beyond Protestantism for a solution. From the above, it would seem
reasonable to suppose with Schenk that Romanticism
is "intrinsically anti-Protestant",[39] that Catholicism - or medieval Catholicism - is the ideal milieu
for the Romantic. People are more variable than
theory would suggest, however, and as Schenk himself
says,[40] Catholicism was only one of the potentialit-
ies latent within Romanticism, along with nihilism
and other beliefs. Indeed, it is amazing that there
could be a Catholic revival, since anti-Catholic
propaganda in Protestant Europe had been so prepond-
erant and was still very lively; consequently it is
not surprising that many Romantics could not overcome
inertia and remained Protestant. And, as will be
illustrated, Protestantism and Romanticism held
certain fundamentals in common. Furthermore, a
completely different interpretation of the Reformation could be more readily entertained by people
inclined to Protestantism. For example, according to
Wallace K. Ferguson, Hegel favoured the Renaissance
as both the antithesis of the Middle Ages and as the
forerunner of the Reformation, and saw medieval
feudalism as combining with the Church to destroy

freedom and to barbarize and debase the spirit.
Hegel, he says, was summarizing an old German view
which identified the Renaissance "with the ideas of
reaction against medieval transcendentalism and of
the reassertion of man's self-consciousness, his
moral and intellectual autonomy, and his spiritual
reconciliation with this present world",[41] a view
with which Heine sympathized.[42] It is a view which
David DeLaura describes as "in the broadest sense
'Protestant'"[43] : it is also romantic. This is
virtually to say that Protestantism has a this-wordly
bias, albeit a type of reconciliatory power. The
Hegelian/Germanic view gives credence to the notion
that the Protestant Weltanschauung was horizontal and
immanentist, and to a limited extent secularizing,
whereas many Romantics wanted to restore the vertical
and transcendental, the axis of which could extend to
the depth of being. Yet some Romantics - in England,
certainly the majority - were undoubtedly satisfied
with the Hegelian view and so continued to despise
the Middle Ages as their Enlightenment forbears had
done.
        How seriously should one take the Catholicism of
these romantic medievalists? The importance to them
of such "romantic" factors as medieval Catholicism's
aesthetic/imaginative qualities, its slightly exotic
nature, its temporal distance, its "primitiveness"
and its organic unity only emphasizes their neglect
of Catholic theology. In a sense, they were attracted by the appurtenances of Catholicism rather than by
its essence - they themselves would have insisted
they were attracted by its spirit, the Catholic idea
- although it is vital to realize that one could
argue that to be attracted to its appurtenances is to
be indirectly attracted to its essence, and is to
move in the direction of Catholicism. It may be that
Catholicism was only a totem for their romanticism.
Grierson implied that the cult of medieval Catholicism was only a fashion when he said it was "only a
phase of the spiritual element in the [romantic]
revolt", and there is some truth in this view.[44]
Fairchild asks if the Catholicism of Chateaubriand's
Génie du Christianisme and of Novalis's Heinrich von
Ofterdingen is genuine, and wonders if it "merely
adds the beauty of mystery and tradition to an essentially non-Catholic type of religious experience".[45]
This is not to deny, however, that their experience
was genuinely religious.[46] On the other hand, Schenk
charitably realizes that distance lends enchantment
and uses this to explain why "genuine admiration for
the piety of medieval man so often tended to

degenerate into Schwärmerei"; though he admits that
sometimes "the Romantic-Catholic alliance ... seemed
indeed precariously based on aesthetic values".[47]
Heine said that German religious medievalism was
merely a patriotic response to Napoleonic conquests,
an anodyne for the trauma which they occasioned.[48]
He also believed that religious medievalists were in
search of their native pantheism, so their Catholicity was suspect; and he noted that when the Catholicity of medievalism became clear, its reputation was
"severely damaged in public opinion".[49] Croce supposed that many of the Catholic converts never became
true Catholics, being too consumed by Catholic
externals and aesthetics, and seeking too great a
change within the Church.[50] Grierson believed that
romantics who revived medieval Catholicism knew they
were "dreaming", so that there was something religiously false in their medievalism, even though the
"dream" was a myth rather than a lie.[51] The real
reason, however, why one should be suspicious of the
Romantic Catholic revival is that Catholicism and
Romanticism are fundamentally opposed (a point
developed below). Nevertheless, it is equally vital
to remember that Romantic literary exertions on behalf of the Church did aid the nineteenth-century
Catholic revival, because they seemed completely
sincere and valid, as even a "real" Catholic like
Nicholas Wiseman observed in 1833:

> I have of late felt a keen interest in the
> great movement of modern literature and
> philosophy, which seems to me ... trying
> once more to fly into the purer, Christian
> ether of Dante or Chaucer, there to catch
> and bring back upon this chilly world a few
> sparks of chivalrous enthusiasm and religious
> devotion. ... the exertions of such men as
> Schlegel, Novalis, Görres ... Manzoni,
> Lamennais, [and] Lamartine ... do show a
> longing after the revival of Christian
> principle as the soul and centre of thought,
> and taste and feeling.[52]

Another question is why the Continental medievalists did not have more influence on England than
they did. Some English romantics may have thought
that to embrace Catholicism - even medieval Catholicism - would mean compromising their nationalist,
romantic (and Protestant) individualism, their tendency to humanism and pantheism. Pantheism in particular seemed to fulfil the rôle of reconciler and

integrator in Romantic England, played in Germany
largely by religious medievalism. France and England
were more attracted to German Sturm und Drang, to
Goethe, Schiller and Bürger, than to the Jena group
and Catholic writers. Carlyle, the chief interpreter
of German thought to the English, was, for example,
the first to write of Novalis (as late as 1829); but
even he took notice of Novalis's Kantian and Fichtian
discipleship rather than his religious attitude. And
in writing of Catholics, like Werner and Schlegel, he
virtually never mentions their religion.[53] Another
factor is that England was an almost completely
Protestant nation, and therefore resistant to Catholic propaganda even of a romantic nature. For
example, Friedrich Schlegel's influence outside
Germany was impaired by his conversion to Roman
Catholicism in 1808.[54] And H.V. Routh notes that
while the French and German medievalists came to
regard the Roman Catholic Church as the zenith of the
old world, the English were simply slower in respond-
ing to Catholicism.[55]

Religion, Medievalism and Romanticism

Commentators seem agreed on the basic cultural-
ideological development : that

> the romantic revival was a movement of
> the heart and imagination, a passionate
> quest for a more adequate and satisfying
> conception of life, something that had
> been lost with the disappearance of the
> great Catholic Faith and Philosophy of
> the Middle Ages and the disintegrating
> progress of physical science, the dis-
> placement of St. Thomas and Dante by
> Locke and Newton.[56]

So the Romantic/Classic conflict was fundamentally
religious. Indeed, for Beers romanticism was "a
reaching out of the human spirit after a more ideal
type of religion and ethics than it could find in
the official churchmanship and the formal morality of
the time".[57] Similarly, Owen Chadwick believes that
with the coming of romanticism, common sense was
rejected as shallow, in favour of beauty and truth,
so that "religious men wanted poetry of heart in
their hymns, sacramental sensibility in their worship, recovery of symbolism in art and architecture".[58] As romanticism had religion very near its
heart, and since the dominant ethos was Christian, it

17

was natural that some romantics should look for a
specifically religious form of expression in historical Christianity. The alternatives, then, were the
early Church and the medieval, and the latter took
precedence because of its romantically exotic colour
and because of the wider prevailing medievalist amb-
ience. Modern Catholicism was out of the question
because of deeply ingrained prejudice and fear; while
medieval Catholicism had a more national flavour.
"For some strange reason," wrote G.K. Chesterton,
"man must always ... plant his fruit trees in a
graveyard. Man can only find life among the dead."59
The fruit ripened in the 1820s when, as Raymond
Chapman testifies, "Romantic enthusiasm for the
Middle Ages brought an exaggerated but encouraging
notion of a society in which faith was universal and
the Church powerful".60
     The above comments tend to confound romanticism
with Catholicism simply by neglecting to distinguish
them; and it is important to appreciate that Catholicism is essentially anti-romantic, so that one
may appreciate that religious medievalism, far from
being merely a fanciful expression of the romantic
spirit, was, potentially and at its heart, a radical
revolt, not only from the Enlightenment, but also
from Romanticism, which had much in common with the
Enlightenment. It is a mistake - a mistake arising
from the romantics themselves - to assume that the
romantic causes behind the taste for Gothic are
exactly the same as the causes of attraction towards
Catholicism, and that therefore the taste for Catholicism is to be unequivocally equated with romanticism
: one must distinguish between the romantic perception of Catholicism and the thing itself, thus avoiding any "inevitable" connection between it and romanticism. For example, though Catholicism was often
used by romantics to beat mechanistic rationalism, it
does not follow that Catholicism itself is irrational.
     Romanticism is the quest for metaphysical
stasis, and is therefore dynamic, expanding, in a
state of becoming.61 Temporary relief from the
anxiety of questing is found when an authority is
newly recognized : such as rationalism, pantheism or
religious medievalism. When these authorities are
accepted, a stasis, or resolution or "classicism" is
achieved. Romanticism is characterized by the overthrow of preceding authorities,62 and consequently by
diversity of belief and individualism. Just as the
romantic society or the Romantic movement is "becoming", so the true Romantic is "becoming" or expanding

into his "higher self", to use Novalis's phrase.[63]
Indeed, Paul Frankl sees "becoming" as the central
characteristic of romanticism : romantic poetry is,
he says, quoting F.W. Schlegel, "a progressive,
universal poetry", and while "other types of poetry
are completed ... romantic poetry is still in process
of becoming, indeed its real nature is that it can
forever only become, never be completed";[64] a phenomenon which accounts for the frequent indefinity and
incompleteness of romantic creations. Honour notes
that Coleridge liked Gothic architecture because for
him "Gothic was perpetually in a state of becoming,
like Romantic poetry, aspiring to ideals ...".[65]
Heath-Stubbs provides the corollary : "Romanticism is
dynamic, the movement towards the clear integrated
whole; it belongs to the world of Becoming, rather
than of Being". In contrast, he says, "the Classical
vision is the most complete, rounded, and perfected
of which the limited human mind is capable; it is
life ... seen steadily, and seen whole. In a sense,
we must all ultimately attempt to be Classicists, but
we have to be Romantics first of all ...".[66] In this
sense, Catholicism can be equated with the classical
vision, the systematic, rounded, infallible, dogmatic
and integrated view of life. Grierson believed that
the Church, with its reasoned dogma and comprehensive, synthesized world-view, represented the classical spirit in the Middle Ages.[67] At least Catholicism can sensibly be regarded as lying nearer to the
classical than to the romantic pole, and the acceptance of its authority represents a resolution of the
inner struggle, the achievement of 'classical'
repose. In other words, there is a conflict between
Catholicism - and thereby partly also with medievalism - and romanticism.

Some romantics could be religious medievalists
while remaining true romantics because they saw in
medieval Catholicism what they wanted to see, and
used from it what their romanticism would allow.
Some of these would identify with the Middle Ages or
medieval Catholicism and then realize that it was
antagonistic to their outlook : such were Heine,
Michelet, Hugo and even, to some extent, Pugin. In
one sense romantic religious medievalism was a
mistake, because some romantics either misinterpre-
ted, or only partially interpreted, their subject :
they mistook it for something else; or perhaps one
may say that they were not truly themselves, not
truly romantic. (Similarly, anti-medievalism was
largely a mistake, for it was based usually on
prejudice, ignorance and an unhistorical attitude.)

So the common alignment of the Catholic sphere with romanticism is an oversimplification. Indeed, Catholicism might even be associated with the classic, and romanticism with Protestantism, where "classicism" and "romanticism" are viewed as expressions of human characteristics or tendencies rather than as historical phenomena. (It should be made clear that this alignment of romanticism with Protestantism is not original, and that some points in the following discussion owe their origin to Fairchild.)[68] The uneasiness of the supposed relationship between romanticism and Catholicism is exemplified by William George Ward of the Oxford Movement, who left behind his romantic medievalism when he became a Catholic.[69] Some Catholics did, however, retain their romanticism to some extent, and remained medievalists; and this was possible because religious medievalism was a radical type of romanticism, capable of becoming properly Catholic.

The cultural alliances of Catholicism and Protestantism can be further explored to give perspective to the problem of romantic Catholicism. Fairchild sees "no inevitable connection between Catholic belief and classical style",[70] and one would not wish to identify creed with style. Jerome Bump is correct when he sees the opposition between religious and secular medievalisms (ie. the courtly love tradition) as a reflection of the Victorian debate between Hebraism and Hellenism: he also notes Ruskin's opposition between religious medievalism and "Classicalism" and "Modernism",[71] and one would not wish to associate these opposites. "Classical" is intended here in much the same sense as Thorlby uses it when discussing Romanticism's destruction of norms : "the classical perspective may have become inaccessible to us with the loss of any certainty that standards of excellence and truth do really abide".[72] This type of classicism should be associated with "standards", while relativism should be linked with romanticism : the objectivism of classicist Arnold and the relativism of romanticist Pater support this scheme.[73] The question of relativism is one of the more important distinctions between "classic-Catholic" and "romantic-Protestant", and Isaiah Berlin has singled out relativism - the notion that "truth is not an objective structure, independent of those who seek it" - as the constant element in the writings of Romantic thinkers.[74] The Catholic Modernist George Tyrrell, who was expelled from the Jesuits for his views, identified the medievalists (ie. orthodox Catholics) with a static, final,

authoritarian view of the truth, and the modernist
with a relative view;[75] and credal relativism is to
be identified more with Protestantism than with
Catholicism, since the Protestant emphasis is on
quality of belief, rather than on content. Fairchild
encapsulates this when he says that "creeds, rules,
logical formulas, sharp distinctions, external
controls of every sort, are repugnant" to the liberal
Romanticist, and that "shunning the permanent and
normative elements of life, he revels in spontaneity,
diversity, uniqueness, individual expansiveness".[76]
Recognizing that the "liberal Romanticist" is the
child of Low Church Anglicanism, and that "creeds,
rules, logical formulas," etc. are typical of
Catholicism and classicism (Fairchild's context is
that of Tractarian anti-romanticism), he implicitly
provides support for the correlation of Catholicism
with classicism.

   Relativism was one aspect of the new, elevated
view of man, which placed considerable emphasis on
feelings. Both relativism and this emphasis began
in the Enlightenment : relativism was born of
Enlightenment scepticism, and rationalist faith in
man issued in respect for his feelings. Feeling and
reason came to be commonly opposed only late in the
century. Sentimentalism strengthened as it combined
with the Enlightenment view of nature and deism, with
its preference (which often resulted in scepticism)
for rationalism and natural religion over faith and
revelation, and more often with latitudinarian
Christianity, which embraced a less emphatic rationalism than deism. "Nature" was understood as the
universe plus man, so deeply infused with the spirit
of God that it was fundamentally good : hence the
righteousness of sentimentalism, and hence the passing of the salvation initiative from God to man. In
the literary sphere, salvation often appears in the
guise of developing a sense of taste which is both
aesthetic and moral : hence the metaphysical
dimension of the eighteenth-century aesthetic crisis.
The optimistic aspect of seventeenth-century Calvin-
ist Puritanism - that of assured personal salvation -
was sustained, while the theology decayed, resulting
in the decline of the transcendent God and the
exaggerated rise of the immanent. To clarify the
line of descent, Fairchild suggests the metaphor of
"a road leading from Low-Church Anglicanism and Non-
conformity, through latitudinarianism, to sentimental
deism and on to romantic pantheism", and claims "the
tendency of Protestantism to collapse into pantheism".[77] But due to theological laxity, the

descendant is often to be found side by side with the
ancestor, so that the sentimentalist or romantic is
often also the Protestant. The connection between
sentimentalism and the secularizing, progressivist
and natural-supernaturalist movements is obvious,
especially in the light of the growth of the romantic
notion that feeling is a religious faculty : "the
feelings, the feelings alone, provide the elements of
religion" declared F.E.D. Schleiermacher,[78] while Mme
De Staël believed that "the only true atheism is
coldness".[79]
     The more purely religious equivalent of senti-
mentalism is generally called enthusiasm. Enthusiasts were Christians who tried to be less worldly than
the norm and pay more attention to the directly-felt
guidance of the Holy Spirit. For them, religion was
not necessarily a matter of forms and ordinances or
of intellect, but essentially a matter of personal,
emotional contact with God.[80] Enthusiasm was a
romantic phenomenon in its individualism, revolutionary fervour, high emotionalism, anti-authoritarian-
ism, inspirationalism and anti-rationalism. Knox
completes the picture of romantic religion by remark-
ing the anthropocentric bias of enthusiasm, in its
preoccupation with personal salvation rather than
God's glory.[81] The sentimentalist-enthusiasts were
against Catholic emphasis on theology because they
relied on the anti-theological "inner light", which
complemented the sentimentalists' and pantheists'
faith in nature. Nevertheless, Catholicism was often
charged with being enthusiastic, especially in its
medieval form; yet it was, by and large, divorced
from enthusiasm, being essentially communal,
conservative, rational, authoritarian, and with
little anthropocentric bias. Hence Catholicism
cannot easily be classed with romanticism; so it
seems an unlikely proposition that a Protestant, and
often secular, atheistic, and pre-Romantic society
should have produced religious medievalism.
     As the Enlightenment venerated man's intellect,
so romanticism revered his non-rational dimension,
and the stage was set for the spiritual and emotional, as well as intellectual, shift from God to man.
While romanticism had a strong religious element, its
main thrust was of the demythologizing species, submitting to the modern notion that traditional theism
is a source of alienation. In opposition to romanticism, Christianity maintains that man is fallen and
preaches self-sacrifice, while the romantic rejection
of religious authority is antagonistic to Catholicism, with its special emphasis on conformity with the

Church's teaching. This rejection springs from what
is virtually a counter-theology of the ego and faith
in man. This theology appears in Mrs. Ward Camp-
bell's belief that romance is somehow about faith in
man, a faith made possible when Christ raised the
value of humanity. So she can say "the lamp of love
and hope, with its faith in the divinity of man,
inspired all the middle ages. The romance of the
middle ages was the romance of Christ."[82] She
virtually equates the Middle Ages, Christ and faith
in man. There emerged an overlap or confusion between romanticism, with its profound optimism about
man as man, and Protestantism. Fairchild produces a
great mass of evidence indicating that "the quasi-
religious beliefs and feelings associated with
romanticism are much more closely related to the
Protestant than to the Catholic tradition".[83] His
thesis reveals the generative connection between
seventeenth-century Protestantism (particularly
Puritanism), eighteenth-century sentimentalism and
the religious aspects of the Romantic movement.[84]
For him, romanticism is the "way of expressing the
basic psychological motive which unites the varieg-
ated cultural manifestations of human pride", and is
therefore in conflict with orthodox Christianity
which posits man's insufficiency and God's transcendence. It is faith in the goodness of human powers,
and its "taproot" is man's desire to trust, express
and expand himself.[85] The "flower" springing from the
taproot is the concentration upon the emotions
arising from the interfusion of natural and supernatural, finite and infinite, man and God. The
romantic emphasis is away from the Christian notion
of an external, obejctive, and absolute divine law,
since the individual man becomes the measure of all
things. Romanticism gravitates towards the pole of
deifying man : "the beginning, middle, and end of
Religion is MAN", said the quintessentially romantic
philosopher Ludwig Andreas Feuerbach.[86] It is interesting to note, as Fairchild does, that Feuerbach
believed that his doctrine of the man-centredness of
religion had been more grievously perverted by
Catholicism than by Protestantism, an opinion one
might anticipate in the light of Fairchild's thesis
that Protestantism was a compromise with the romantic
spirit. The romantic Christian John Middleton Murry
exemplified this alignment, for he believed that the
great divide is between "the great classical and
Catholic dogma of original sin" and "the great
Romantic dogma of man being born equal and perfect"[87]
that Christian rebirth is re-integration through

individual divinization and that this religion is the
substance of "modern Romanticism".[88]
    According to M.H. Abrams, the general tendency
of Romanticism was "to naturalize the supernatural
and to humanize the divine",[89] thereby attempting to
heal the alienation begun in the modern age in a
special and intense way by the Cartesian revolution,
which separated thought and feeling and ultimately
separated man from the world by helping to destroy
his faith. J. Robert Barth disagrees with this
interpretation, saying that Carlyle's point (in the
chapter in Sartor Resartus called "Natural Supernaturalism") and Coleridge's is directly opposite to
Abrams' thesis : "that the natural is supernaturali-
zed, the human is divinized".[90] There is truth in
this; but "natural supernaturalism" is easily
inverted. The religious aspect of romanticism was
corroded and gave rise to the secularizing theology
of a Kingsley, the totally secular "religion" of a
George Eliot, radical twentieth-century Protestant
theology, humanism, Marxism and Fascism : concepts
which feed on the myth of man's fundamental, natural
goodness,[91] and propagate the idea of heaven on
earth. In the eighteenth and nineteenth centuries,
certain Protestant groups aided unconsciously this
collapse of the genuinely religious spirit into a
divinized secularism. (Similarly, Herbert Butterfield associated post-Reformation Protestants with
secularization and individualism, though he also believed that secularism was the result of innumerable
subtle shifts and changes not directly attributable
to Protestantism.)[92] Religious medievalists tended
to support traditional religion and opposed secularization. As the search for reconciliation intensif-
ied with romanticism, it was not entirely extraordinary for a section of a nominally Christian world to
seek a specifically Christian model of reconciliation
to oppose to the more secular versions.
    Nevertheless, the Catholic boom is puzzling, for
the above-mentioned reasons, and because Romanticism
was in many ways a re-enactment of the period of the
Renaissance and Reformation - that is, of the "anti-
medieval" period. Certain features of Romanticism
were not, however, antagonistic to religious medievalism : "feeling", in so far as it was a religious
emphasis, to some extent found satisfaction in the
medieval Church; renewed emphasis on the metaphysical also helped, while romantic indefinity, non-
conformity and exploratory spirit paved the way for
Catholicism or neo-Catholicism. New attitudes to
authority and art were further contributory factors.

The romantic attitude to authority is ambiguous,
for the romantic in search of authority is divided
against himself, since he is an individualist in search of conformity, a rebel in search of submission,
a dynamo in search of stasis, a traveller questing
for home : he is tired of romanticism and looks for
a radical, reconciling romanticism which will resolve
his struggle in a standard or authority - in a sense,
a new classicism. In contrast, according to Irving
Babbitt, the pure romantic throws off Christian and
classical disciplines and conventions in favour of
the expression of his own genius, setting his ego
above any supposedly transcendent pattern.93 A.W.
Schlegel perhaps saw further when he said that
Romantic poetry "is the expression of a secret longing for the chaos which is perpetually striving for
new and marvellous births"94 : religious medievalism
was one of these "marvellous births". What appeal,
asks Alfred Cobban, more suitable than "from an age
of rebellion and self-assertion to the age of subor-
dination and caste, from an age of the breaking of
all bonds and loosening of all ties - social, moral
and religious - to the age of fixed feudal hierarchy
and unalterable law?"95 Those who made such an
appeal wanted the re-establishment of what they
believed to have been the medieval order, with God,
the prime authority and ground of all authority,
bestowing authority on monarchs via the pope.96
(Romantic absolutism ought to be distinguished from
the idea of authority in the Catholic Church.97)
Protestant writers like Southey and Coleridge would
have nothing to do with the papacy; yet they wanted
a social order fully integrated with and based on
religion, and they were duly drawn to the medieval
Church.
     Developments in this period regarding imagin-
ation, the sublime and myth-making were aspects of
the romantic quest for deeper perception, and they
led some to review the medieval faith. These
developments gave the mainstream cultural sense a
profundity to which it was unaccustomed; and the
profounder aesthetic meant that "aesthetic" medievalism had a more-than-aesthetic inspiration. For
the pre-Romantics and Romantics, imagination was a
religious power, for it enabled men to perceive the
transcendent and their relationship to it. This was
true for Coleridge,98 and Blake said "Imagination ...
is the Divine Body of the Lord Jesus" (<u>Jerusalem</u> 5.
58-9), while Digby, the arch-medievalist in England,
who constantly spoke of the medieval Church as food
for the imagination, believed that "imagination soars

above the limits of the present life, and the sublime
in every subject is a reflection from the Divinity"[99]
The sublime, which could be perceived and appreciated
through the imagination, was the incarnate transcendent; and such a religious concept might be expected
to find expression in religious subject matter, such
as the medieval supernatural ethos. Thomas Warton
hinted this when he said in the 1770s that, in relation to the Middle Ages, "ignorance and superstition
... are the parents of imagination".[100]
 The search for new modes of expression, which
the developing "theology" of imagination helped to
bring about, resulted in the requisitioning of a
variety of novel images and myths, some related to
the Middle Ages. "Myth" is here meant in the sense
of a centre of reference, a rallying point, a symbol
by which a whole range of feelings and beliefs could
be expressed concisely.[101] To a certain extent,
writers extracted material from the Middle Ages to
give form to whichever idea they wanted to express :
they all thought they were being historically accurate, but in fact they were myth-makers. Myth is a
way of conveying the experience of intangibles and
imponderables :
 ... still the heart doth need a language,
 still/Doth the old instinct bring back the
 old names.[102]

This search for new myths was necessitated by the
shifts in eighteenth-century thought. The Victorian
critic David Masson made the point :

 as astronomy has felled the old physical
 images to which men attached their ideas
 of heaven and hell, so in a thousand
 other directions has the thought of man
 felled the ancient images to which ideas,
 morally as everlasting as these, had their
 sensible attachment.[103]

Present images were felt to be inadequate, so new
ones were taken up, and these turned out to be old
images - classical and medieval - newly dressed.
Myth-making is ultimately an attempt to say something
about, or to evoke, the eternal, heavenly and
spiritual, through the temporal, earthly and physical
: which is to say it is sacramental. Though difficult to prove, it is probable that the Protestant
England of the later eighteenth century, heavily
influenced by enthusiasm, with its Lockean and
Platonist divorce of reason from religion and its

divorce of the understanding of God from symbolism or analogies, came to feel a need for the restoration of the Aristotelian <u>mise en scenè</u> of traditional Christianity and its sacramental world-view, and edged towards it in religious medievalism. Catholic sacramentalism and reliance on externalism (images,ritual, traditions), sanctioned by the theology of the invasion of the physical world by the Transcendent in the Incarnation, appealed to romantics in their confused search for the transcendent, especially since Catholic "externalism" paralleled the romantic exploration of imagery, symbolism and myth. This search for the image to embody spirituality should be constantly recalled in discussion of medievalist "aestheticism".

Romantics searched for the sublime, which was associated with the mystical and the transcendent.[104] This search for transcendence was also a search for "depth", a word used by radical theologians like Paul Tillich as a synonym for God. Herbert L. Stewart makes the point that Romanticism, in its "sense of the mysterious depth of being in the human soul and in the natural world" was "an important factor in the history of religion".[105] The transcendent includes the depth of things : in seeking the depths, in exploring the Freudian id, the romantics were questing for the transcendent, and tried to objectify it in myth, symbol and "archetypal" image. It may be that imagination, as the waking form of sleep, the faculty of conscious dream, was for them the tool of reconciliation, not only of man with his id, but of man with the transcendent : "the Imagination," said Keats, "may be compared to Adam's dream - he awoke and found it truth".[106] It may also be that they needed exotic "dream" worlds in which, or by which, to exercise this sacred imagination. The Middle Ages provided such a dream world, and it was particularly suitable because it represented the "id" - the primitive, instinctual stage - of modern Europe, while appealing to the concern for unity (or reconciliation), sacramentalism and transcendence.[107]

But this medievalist dream was for mainstream romantics a nightmare, for they travelled further along the Enlightenment path, with its faith in man and belief in progress. In the sense that they rebelled against this tendency to divinize the secular and find the fulcrum of meaning in man, the religious medievalists were seeking a radical alternative to the dominant ethos, which they felt had developed from the Renaissance and Reformation. Medievalist ranks were also split, for some followed their interest to its logical conclusion and became

Catholics (or neo-Catholics), while others did not.
Non-Catholic religious medievalists were at odds with
themselves : their ids, attracted by Catholicism,
lost the fight against their super-egos, so they look
like typically romantic dabblers in exoticism. Even
their "aesthetic" medievalism was usually serious in
the sense that they genuinely delighted in aspects
of medieval spirituality. These divided allegiances,
which are a function of the fact that no individual
and no movement fits perfectly into any category, led
to much paradox and ambiguity, exacerbated by the
ambiguities inherent in literary expression. Divided
allegiances, mixed motives and overlap of categories
form the substance of the difficulty in speaking
generally about the relationship between one movement
and another. No single or simple model will cover
all cases.

    While the romantic ranks were divided, romanti-
cism itself was a bridge between Protestantism and
Catholicism. The romantic ethos was a catalyst,
sometimes stimulating non-Catholics to a new,
sympathetic and even empathetic, view of the Catholic
world, and helping individuals from one set of norms,
through turbulence and energetic questing, to a new
or modified set of norms. But it is too much to say
that in this period the romantic spirit was the
direct progenitor of the Catholic Revival (which can
even be viewed as classic) : it is nearer the mark
to say they were fish swimming in the same river -
the unfathomable river of ideological change.[108]
Catholicism is not romantic,[109] though the perception
of it may be. This is not to deny that religious
medievalism had romantic aspects, or that romanticism, because of its strongly religious, exploratory
and experimental dimensions, helped to pave the way
for such medievalism and Catholic renewal, but to
preserve the integrity of the notion of religious
medievalism as a radical romanticism - indeed, as a
romanticism which denies, or tends to deny, mainstream romanticism.

    This chapter has attempted to explain, by
reference to the Enlightenment, Continental medievalism, religious aspects of romanticism and anti-
romantic aspects of Catholicism, how some elements
of spiritual change in the pre-Romantic and Romantic
period articulate vis à vis the Catholic revival
(broadly understood). Or - returning to the opening
metaphor - it has shown that the cuckoo's egg exists,
and has explored the principles of its natural
history. A cuckoo's egg is remarkable by virtue of
its being both alien and not alien, and religious

medievalism was remarkable in the same way - just as was Romanticism itself. Chapter II explores the embodiment of these principles in the incubation and hatching period.

NOTES

1.   Heyer The Catholic Church From 1648 to 1870 (1969) 144.
2.   See Hoxie Neale Fairchild "The Romantic Movement in England" PMLA LV (1940) 23;   Lilian Furst agrees : Romanticism in Perspective (1969) 44.
3.   Cf. Norman Hampson The Enlightenment (Harmondsworth, 1968) ch.6 "The Inner Voice".
4.   From Le Romantisme dans la littérature européenne (1948): given in Anthony Thorlby The Romantic Movement (1966) 22.
5.   Romanticism (1979) 18.
6.   Hampson The Enlightenment 189.
7.   Thorlby The Romantic Movement 7.
8.   Hampson The Enlightenment 208.
9.   See R.G. Collingwood The Idea of History (Oxford at the Clarendon Press, 1946) 86-7.
10.   Patrick Masterson Atheism and Alienation (Harmondsworth, 1973) 17; and see all ch.I.
11.   H.G. Schenk interprets Romanticism, and particularly medievalism, as an attempt to recover Christianity: eg. The Mind of the European Romantics (1966) 39.
12.   Ibid. 243-4.
13.   Ibid. ch. V. "Forebodings and Nostalgia for the Past".
14.   History of Europe in the Nineteenth Century translated by Henry Furst (1934); given in Romanticism: Problems of Definition, Explanation and Evaluation ed. John B. Halstead (Boston, 1968) 54-5.
15.   G.P. Gooch History and Historians in the Nineteenth Century (1928) 11.
16.   Acton, Inaugural Lecture Lectures on Modern History (1970) 38.
17.   See Thorlby The Romantic Movement 83-98; R.G. Collingwood Ruskin's Philosophy (Chichester, 1971) 15-19.
18.   Yet Friedrich Meinecke, the scholar of historicism, believes that "Romantic" historicism in its medievalizing and Catholicizing tendencies was an aberration: see Thorlby The Romantic Movement 85.
19.   This work pub. 1826. Translation from H.S. Reiss The Political Thought of the German Romantics

1793-1815 (Oxford, 1955) 126-7.
20. Autobiography of John Stuart Mill (New York 1964) ch. V 125.
21. Qu. Thorlby The Romantic Movement 147 from Le Génie du Christianisme.
22. Pub. 1802; 1st. English ed. 1813: The Beauties of Christianity ... Translated ... by Frederic Shoberl. With a preface and notes by the Rev. Henry Kett 3v. In the second half of the century there were several more English eds.
23. Eg. Mores Catholici (1831) v.I, 8.
24. Monsignor Louis Baunard Ozanam in His Correspondence (Dublin, 1925) 145.
25. Count de Montalembert's Letters to a Schoolfellow 1827-1830 translated by C.F. Audley (1874) 132.
26. Owen Chadwick The Secularization of the European Mind in the Nineteenth Century (1975) 154.
27. John C. Blankenagel "The Dominant Characteristics of German Romanticism" PMLA LV (1940) 4.
28. Die Romantische Schule in The Prose Writings of Heinrich Heine. Edited, With an Introduction, by Havelock Ellis (London, n.d., "The Scott Library") 73, 76-77.
29. For an account of how this cultural anxiety gave rise to medievalism see Ernst Gombrich "The Turn of the Tide" The Listener v. 101 no. 2599 (22 Feb. 1979) 279-81.
30. W.J.A.M. Beek John Keeble's Literary and Religious Contribution to the Oxford Movement (Nijmegan, 1959) 90-7.
31. Italien (1828-9). Die Bäder von Lucca Kap. IV; qu. H.V. Routh Towards the Twentieth Century (C.U.P.,1937) 136.
32. Die Romantische Schule in The Prose Writings of Heinrich Heine 79.
33. Die Christenheit oder Europa in Reiss Political Thought of the German Romantics 140.
34. The Secularization of the European Mind in the Nineteenth Century 8.
35. Reiss Political Thought of the German Romantics 131.
36. The Romantic Tradition in Germany : An Anthology ed. Ronald Taylor (1970) 133.
37. "The Dominant Characteristics of German Romanticism" PMLA LV (1940) 6. Cf. Digby Mores Catholici v.I, 8.
38. In 1863 Matthew Arnold observed the case to be so (although he did not condemn it): "Eugénie de Guérin" Essays in Criticism - First Series in The Complete Prose Works of Matthew Arnold III 97.

39. The Mind of the European Romantics 155.
40. Ibid. 96.
41. The Renaissance in Historical Thought - Five Centuries of Interpretation (Cambridge Mass., 1948) 171, 172.
42. Die Romantische Schüle in The Prose Writings of Heinrich Heine 80-81.
43. Hebrew and Hellene in Victorian England (Texas U.P., Austin & London, 1969) 347 : a view held by Heine in Die Romantische Schüle, Prose Writings 116-117.
44. Herbert Grierson "Classical and Romantic : A Point of View" in The Background of English Literature. Classical and Romantic (1962) 277.
45. "The Romantic Movement in England" PMLA LV (1940) 25.
46. Cf. Schenk The Mind of the European Romantics 37, 39.
47. Ibid. 39, 95-6.
48. Die Romantische Schüle in The Prose Writings of Heinrich Heine 89-92.
49. Ibid. 100-101.
50. Romanticism : Problems of Definition, Explanation, and Evaluation ed. Halstead 54.
51. Op. cit. 290.
52. Wilfrid Ward The Life and Times of Cardinal Wiseman 2v. (1897) I, 136.
53. L. Furst Romanticism in Perspective 24, 44; and Peter Le Page Renouf rev. of Carlyle's Past and Present DR XV (Aug.1843) 197.
54. René Wellek A History of Modern Criticism: 1750-1950. The Romantic Age (1955) 5.
55. Towards the Twentieth Century 46.
56. Grierson "Blake and Gray" in The Background of English Literature. Classical and Romantic 252-3; cf. Graham Hough The Romantic Poets (1968) 27, John Heath-Stubbs The Darkling Plain (1950) 48.
57. Henry A. Beers A History of English Romanticism in the Eighteenth Century (1926) 32; cf. C.M. Bowra The Romantic Imagination (1963) 23.
58. The Victorian Church 2v. (1966) I, 174.
59. What's Wrong With the World (1910) 29.
60. Faith and Revolt (1970) 27.
61. Cf. Harold Bloom The Ringers in the Tower: Studies in the Romantic Tradition (Chicago and London, 1971) 3, Alice Chandler A Dream of Order : The Medieval Ideal in Nineteenth-Century English Literature (1971) I. Henceforth cited as Chandler.
62. Cf. Honour Romanticism "Introduction".
63. Qu. Hoxie N. Fairchild The Romantic Quest (Philadelphia, 1952) 143. Cf. Carlyle on romantic

individualist expansionism in "Jean Paul Friedrich
Richter".
    64. The Gothic : Literary Sources and Interpre-
tations through Eight Centuries (Princeton, New
Jersey, 1960) 449.
    65. Romanticism 158.
    66. The Darkling Plain x.
    67. The Background of English Literature 283,
284-5.
    68. The chief references to H.N. Fairchild's
thesis are "The Romantic Movement in England" PMLA
LV (1940) 20-6, Religious Trends in English Poetry
5v. (1957-64) II, Introduction, Conclusion; v. IV,
Introduction; "Romanticism and the Religious Revival
in England" Journal of the History of Ideas v. II
(1941) 330-38. Those who would agree with Fairchild's basic position include Vernon F. Storr The
Development of English Theology in the Nineteenth
Century 1800-1860 (1913) 255, and Yngve Brilioth
The Anglican Revival : Studies in the Oxford Movement
(1933) 57-8.
    69. Raymond Chapman Faith and Revolt 51.
    70. Religious Trends in English Poetry v. IV,
11, n.15. Henceforth cited as Fairchild.
    71. "Hopkins' Imagery and Medievalist Poetics"
VP XV (1977) 100. The Ruskin ref. is from "Pre-
Raphaelitism" ... Works of John Ruskin ed. E.T.
Cook and Alexander Wedderburn (1903-12) XII, 134-60,
139. This ed. henceforth cited as CW.
    72. The Romantic Movement 3.
    73. See Walter E. Houghton The Victorian Frame
of Mind 1830-1870 (1974) 15-17.
    74. Preface to Schenk's The Mind of the
European Romantics xv, xvi.
    75. In Medievalism (1909); qu. J. Lewis May
Father Tyrrell and the Modernist Movement (1932) 242.
    76. "Romanticism and the Religious Revival in
England" Journal of the History of Ideas v. II
(1941) 337.
    77. "The Romantic Movement in England" PMLA LV
(1940) 21, 23.
    78. Über die Religion; qu. Thorlby The Romantic
Movement 146.
    79. Loc. cit., from Corinne.
    80. Ronald Knox Enthusiasm : A Chapter in the
History of Religion (1950) 1-2.
    81. Ibid. 3; see 19 for enthusiasm's
individualism.
    82. Qu. W.R. Inge Modernism in Literature :
The English Association Presidential Address 1937.
    83. Fairchild IV, 8.

84. Espec. ibid. III, 10-18. He points out
(ibid. IV, 9) that Bertrand Russell makes the same
correlation as himself between pride, emotion,
romanticism and Protestant individualism, in his
History of Western Philosophy.
85. Fairchild IV, 3. Honour isolates individualism as the keystone of Romanticism : Romanticism
"Introduction".
86. Fairchild IV, 6; qu from The Essence of
Christianity translated from 2nd.German ed. by
Marian Evans (New York, 1855) 25.
87. Murry Things to Come (1938) 263.
88. Ibid. 271, 99 respectively.
89. Natural Supernaturalism (New York, 1971)68.
90. The Symbolic Imagination : Coleridge and
the Romantic Tradition (Princeton U.P., 1977) 118.
91. Albert Guerard thinks that the belief in
man's natural goodness was one of the chief Romantic
myths: "Prometheus and the Aeolian Lyre" Yale Rev.
XXXIII (1943) 484.
92. The Whig Interpretation of History (Harmondsworth,1973) 45, 40-1.
93. Romanticism : Problems of Definition,
Explanation, and Evaluation ed. Halstead 11 : qu.
from Babbitt's Rousseau and Romanticism.
94. Thorlby The Romantic Movement 2.
95. Edmund Burke and the Revolt Against the
Eighteenth Century (1962) 264-5.
96. Cf. ibid. 266.
97. Heyer The Catholic Church From 1648 to
1870 132-33, especially 133 n.I.
98. See Barth The Symbolic Imagination ch. I.
99. The Broad Stone of Honour 2nd.ed. (1823)
149-50.
100. The History of English Poetry 4v. ed.
Richard Price (1824) III, 284-5. 1st ed. 1774-81.
101. Cf. E.M.W. Tillyard Some Mythical
Elements in English Literature (1961).
102. From Coleridge's expanded translation of a
passage in Schiller's Die Piccolomini; qu. M.H.
Abrams The Mirror and the Lamp (1971) 293.
103. "Pre-Raphaelitism in Art and Literature"
The British Quarterly Rev. XVI (1852) 197-220; given
in Pre-Raphaelitism : A Collection of Critical Essays
ed. James Sambrook (Chicago & London, 1974) 82.
104. See Clarence DeWitt Thorpe "Coleridge on
the Sublime" in Wordsworth and Coleridge ed. Earl
Leslie Griggs (New York, 1962) especially 205-7, and
Thomas Weiskel The Romantic Sublime (Baltimore and
London, 1976) 12.
105. A Century of Anglo-Catholicism (1929) 57.

106.   Letter to Benjamin Bailey 22 Nov. 1817.
107.   Cf. F.L. Lucas The Decline and Fall of the Romantic Ideal (1963) 29-47.
108.   Cf. Chadwick The Victorian Church I, 174.
109.   Piers Brendon disagrees : Hurrell Froude and the Oxford Movement (1974) xvii, 28, 203 n. 14.

Chapter II

RELIGIOUS MEDIEVALISM?   1750-1825

> The modes and fashions of different times
> may appear, at first sight, fantastic and
> unaccountable. But they, who look nearly
> into them, discover some latent cause of
> their production.

> > Bishop Hurd Letters on
> > Chivalry and Romance

        In eighteenth-century England, Roman Catholicism
and the Catholic Middle Ages were despized by the
rationalist, Anglican, patriotic establishment of the
Enlightenment, and this hatred was almost universal.
But by 1825 the works of non-Catholic writers had
begun to undermine anti-Catholicism. How could this
happen? This chapter supports the thesis that
aesthetic, fantasist, dillettantish, antiquarian and
political medievalisms often had a truly religious
dimension hidden under the secular mask; a dimension
which deepened as Romanticism became more profound
and universal, and developed the "theology" of imagination. This movement resulted in increased empathy
with the medieval Church, even while sympathy with
Catholicism would have been denied. The movement was
generated by a European crisis of spiritual anxiety,
which found expression in a cultural turmoil, itself
the subconscious search for new reconciliatory ideologies. Consequently, culture had the rôle of play-
ground on which new systems could be safely tested
and vicariously experienced.

Aesthetics and Religion in the Eighteenth Century

        The traces of this agitation can be found as
early as Allan Ramsey's Ever Green collection (1724),
with interest in the primitive and the titillation of

fancy. In the first half of the century popular
literature in the form of chap-books fed a taste for
tales of medieval romance, saints and magic;[1] among
them a Life of Saint Winifred (1743) by Thomas Gent
(or Ghent), who apologizes for his theme by protest-
ing the story's wealth in Christian practice and
precept. A High Churchman, he was a sympathetic medievalist, safe in the belief that such saints were of
his own Church. (Either this or he wore a mask so
complete that it extended into his notes.) He entered the medieval spirit so fully that his praise of
the saint is unstinting, the nobility are shown to
be pious,he argues that miracles happen, celibacy is
approved, and supernatural value is attached to
dreams.[2] Also unconsciously eroding anti-medievalism
were several later-eighteenth-century historians,
discovering political, social and cultural glimmer-
ings of light in the "dark ages".[3]

As Patricia Meyer Spacks has concluded, "the
bulk of allusion to the supernatural seems to have
increased steadily as the century progressed",[4] and
it is out of this interest that the pre-occupation
with the medieval supernatural, and hence with the
medieval Church and its spirituality, grew, leading
to its use as a myth or totem of unfamiliar, and
therefore fresh and powerful, spirituality. James
Beattie (1753-1803) exemplifies the genre in The
Minstrel (1771,1774). In the cold light of On Fable
and Romance, he condemns the Middle Ages; but he
exploits the licence of poetry to express a quasi-
religiosity, to which the far-distant and superstitious Middle Ages, with all its supernatural paraphernalia, is especially appropriate.

In parallel, the majority of Gothic fiction
makes use of Catholic elements for their dramatic
value and emotional appeal. Some novels, usually by
deists, are anti-Catholic on rationalist grounds,
others on political ones.[5] The gothic mode exemplifies the sense/sensibility split on anti- and pro-
Catholic lines.[6] Monasticism is explored as a rallying point of either psychotic evil or disciplined
faith. Devendra P. Varma summarizes the dialectic
reflected in Gothicism, itself reflecting the
dialectic of religious medievalism:

> these novelists were seeking a frisson
> nouveau, a frisson of the supernatural.
> They were moving away from the arid glare
> of rationalism towards the beckoning
> shadows of a more intimate and mystical
> interpretation of life, and this they

> encountered in the profound sense of
> the numinous stamped upon the archit-
> ecture, paintings,and fable of the
> Middle Ages.[7]

But there was no Damascus-like conversion to Catholicism, and the English literary love affair with
medieval spirituality was rarely consummated until
the Victorian age.

Ambrose Phillipps de Lisle said in his Notes of
his Conversion to the Catholic Church that "a fondness for antiquity and for romance" aided his conversion because they presented an impression - perhaps
"visionary or false" - of a perfect age from which
man is fallen, and which touches the heart. The
statement is revealing because it acknowledges the
disjunction between medievalist writing - whether of
the eighteenth or nineteenth century - and reality,
while still testifying to its effect: in short, the
cultural can be transmuted into the religious, myth
can strike the heart. "It is not," he continues,
"the recollection of the valiant knight, the devout
defender of the Holy Land, - nor the mournful musing
amidst ancient ruins, that makes the soul forgetful
of her God, or disinclined to devotion."[8] His
coupling of "antiquity" and "romance" is pregnant for
what follows in this chapter, since history - or
rather mythified history - and legend are symbiotic
elements in the growth of empathy with the medieval
Church.

Thomas Percy (1729-1811) was a classicist,
Anglican antiquarian, and therefore not a gullible or
romantic medievalist.[9] But it is almost certain that
his very popular Reliques of Ancient English Poetry
(1765) brought a vital picture of medieval Catholicism to the attention of the middle-class. In his
introduction to "On the Death of King Edward the
First" he regrets that "according to the modes of
thinking peculiar to those times, the writer dwells
more upon his devotion, than his skill in government;
and pays less attention to the martial and political
abilities of this great monarch ... than to some
little weaknesses of superstition, which he had in
common with all his contemporaries."[10] Like it or
not, this is typical of the material he presents to
his audience.

According to Richard Hurd (1720-1808), whose
Letters on Chivalry and Romance (1762) signposts the
cultural crisis,[11] "what we have gotten by this
revolution [the Enlightenment], you will say, is a
great deal of good sense. What we have lost, is a

37

world of fine fabling...."[12] The word "fabling",and
his use of "marvellous", are important, since both
connoted the supernatural. James Beattie elaborates
Hurd's ideas in On Fable and Romance (1763), where
he says, "it is owing ... to the weakness of human
nature, that fable should ever have been found a
necessary, or a convenient, vehicle for truth".[13]
Possibly Hurd regarded fable in the same light. But
in the Letters he rebukes Spenser for "pretending"
to give moral substance in the clothes of romance in
The Faerie Queene (151-2). Thus speaks classicist
Hurd; but his concept of fabling is ambiguous.
    In On the Idea of Universal Poetry he notes the
supernatural and quasi-divine aspect of poetry, and
suggests that medieval religion is suited to the
poetic creation of the marvellous. In his Letters,
he thinks that the ascendancy of reason decided
Milton against composing an Arthurian epic, in favour
of Paradise Lost, where, "instead of Giants and
Magicians, he had Angels and Devils to supply him
with the marvellous, with greater probability" (153).
In other words, Milton exchanged one "marvellous"
epic for another which was plainly religious, the
motive being merely "greater probability" and not a
preference of genre. Equating the marvellous with
the supernatural and associating it with romance
means that it is fair to interpret fabling as myth-
ologizing rather than mere story-telling. The significance of "marvellous" may be gleaned from the
O.E.D. definition: "of poetic material: Concerned
with the supernatural". It also quotes Pope's Iliad
Preface: "fable may be divided into the probable,the
allegorical, and the marvellous.... The marvellous
fable includes whatever is supernatural...." Hurd
is the paradigm of his age's transitional ambiguity,
unprepared to distinguish between "fable", "marvellous", "superstitions" and "supernatural". "The
marvellous of romance," says Arthur Johnston, "was
thought of [at that time] as a product of the superstitious attitude engendered by Roman Catholicism";[14]
and Hurd makes no attempt not to confuse the real
medieval religion and the supernatural extravagances
of romance. While condemning the "supernumerary
horrors" of medieval "Christian superstition" (165),
he supposes that had Homer known feudal times he
would have preferred the "superior solemnity of their
superstitions" to those of his own day (108). The
medieval supernatural (legendary and Catholic) was
good poetic material, "amusing" and "awakening" to
the imagination (109-10).This harnessing of the super
-natural to art is the fulcrum of Hurd's position and

sets a trend; but he also confusedly sensed there
was more to medieval story than aestheticism, though,
asked, he would have denied it. Effectually he says,
"what we have lost is a world of fine myth-making".
    Hurd accepted that the Middle Ages were an age
of faith: "no institution of a public nature could
have found credit in the world, that was not consec-
rated by the Churchmen, and closely interwoven with
religion"; and he testifies to the intensity of this
faith and its essential place in chivalry (91-2). He
seems most sympathetic to medieval religion when he
writes of the Saracen attacks on the Christian world
(91). He submerges his Protestant antagonism in the
presence of the Saracen, identifying "the faith" and
"the Christian world" with medieval Catholicism,
elsewhere condemned as "superstitious". Religion is
here envisaged as enlisting chivalry as its aid, in
contradiction to his assumption that chivalry was a
purely feudal product (83) and that the religious
element was only incidental (104). His extraordinary
duality allows him to idealize it at the same time in
a way typical of a later age: "PROWESS, GENEROSITY,
GALANTRY, and RELIGION" were the "peculiar and
vaunted characteristics of the purer ages of Chivalry" (92). In the light of such statements it almost
seems that Hurd, in advocating the Gothic period for
poetic use, was giving the cachet of scholarly
approval to medieval spirituality via the medieval
marvellous.
    His duality is mirrored in his approach to
truth. In essence, he advocates the pretence of believing in medieval supernaturalism, thinking that
this is imaginatively rewarding. His medievalist
sympathy is imaginative. He makes the Aristotelian
distinction between poetic truth - which is self-
consistency - and philosophical truth, or empirical,
natural truth(136-7). Making this distinction, the
poet can have "Gods, and Faeries, and Witches at his
command", so that in his world "all is marvellous and
extraordinary" (138). Such is imagination: it is
able to appreciate the supernatural, while reason is
not. "Sublime and creative poetry" (139) succeeds in
making poetic truth credible to the imagination. It
is not far removed from this to say that the sublime
is the revelation of the transcendent, and imagination is the faculty of perceiving the supernatural: a
strikingly proto-Coleridgean concept. Imagination,
he says, "loves to admire and to be deceived" in the
quest for touching the affections and interesting the
heart (139). This notion accords with the sensibilitarian cult of feeling which was loosely connected

in the romantic mind with the transcendent. He
concludes his discussion of poetic truth by affirming
that the fictions of the romancers were "of that kind
of creditable deceits, of which a wise antient pro-
nounces with assurance, 'That they, who deceive, are
honester than they who do not deceive; and they who
are deceived, wiser than they who are not deceived'"
(144). This suggests that poetic truth, which is
deception, is more important than philosophical
truth. Apply this dictum to the religious "deceivers" and "deceived" of the Middle Ages, and we have
the final piece in a jigsaw of imaginative empathy
with - if not actual belief in - medieval supernaturalism.

In helping to rehabilitate medieval legend, Hurd
inadvertently helped to rehabilitate the medieval
religion, from which he failed to distinguish it.
Beattie reinforced this error.[15] Sir Walter Scott
added to the confusion: "the gloom of superstition...
added a wild and dismal effect to the wonders of the
minstrel; and occasionally his description of supernatural events amounts nearly to sublimity." The
Gothic seems to have been regarded as a channel to
the religious or quasi-religious; so it is not
surprising when, in the same place (a review of
Ellis's and Ritson's work), he says that in medieval
literature, religion metamorphozed into "mythological
fable", thereby informing our understanding of Hurd's
and Beattie's use of the word.[16] It is only one step
from reverencing, though not believing in, the Gothic,
to reverencing, though not believing in, medieval
Catholicism, with which it was identified, especially
since, as Scott affirms, fable was the child of the
medieval religion.

Without undervaluing the contemporary prevalence
of "good sense, good taste, and good criticism",[17]
Thomas Warton (1728-1790) regretted the loss to the
poetic community brought about by the age of reason;
and in striking parallel to Hurd's sentiment on
deception, he proclaimed that

> we have lost a set of manners, and a
> system of machinery, more suitable to
> the purposes of poetry, than those which
> have been adopted in their place. We
> have parted with extravagancies that are
> above propriety, with incredibilities that
> are more acceptable than truth, and with
> fictions that are more valuable than
> reality.[18]

This is a translated desire for a more spiritually
vital milieu, where reason takes an inferior place
to faith, where "deception" becomes the means of
communicating the deepest truths, "extravagancies"
the norm, "incredibilities" the most credible, and
"fictions" acutely perceived reality.

Religion was peripheral to Warton's History of
English Poetry (1774-1781), but it contains a view
of medieval religion and supernaturalism. Fairchild
says: "nothing in his type of High Churchmanship
would give him any real sympathy with [medieval
Catholicism], but something in its flavor appealed
to his imagination."[19] Imagination, however, was of
the greatest importance to Warton. In Observations
on the Faerie Queene of Spenser (1754) he justified
the use of those aspects of marvellous fiction that
"rouse and invigorate all the powers of imagination",[20] those powers including the appreciation of
the sublime. Clearly, he recognized that "if we take
a retrospect of English poetry from the age of
Spenser, we shall find that it principally consisted
in visions and allegories";[21] but he nevertheless
occupied himself with that era.

In the History, Warton is surprisingly fair to
Catholicism. This fairness is a consequence of his
dominating desire to see ancient poetry in its proper
historical perspective: "in reading the works of a
poet who lived in a remote age, it is necessary that
we should look back upon the customs and manners
which prevailed in that age. We should endeavour to
place ourselves in the writer's situation and circumstances."[22] This means that he identifies more
closely with medieval religion than his predecessors.
His empathetic power bestows a certain equilibrium on
his judgement, which emerges in his discussion of the
mendicant friars, of whom he has a very high opinion.[23]

Warton, who shares Hurd's views, made the point
that medieval supernaturalism was conducive to the
work of the imagination:

> the customs, institutions, traditions, and
> religion, of the middle ages, were favourable
> to poetry. Their pageaunts, processions,
> spectacles, and ceremonies, were friendly
> to imagery, to personification and allegory.
> Ignorance and superstition, so opposite to
> the real interests of human society, are
> the parents of imagination. 'The very
> devotion of the Gothic times was romantic.
>   (III, 284-5)

He is unwilling to differentiate between medieval
religion and superstition: both stimulate the
imagination. He rigorously differentiates between
philosophical and poetic truth; but there is a
conflict here, for one moment he criticizes Rome
which had "carried ceremonies to an absurd excess"
(III,280), the next he applauds the poetry of
ceremony. He defends imagination, so ceremonies,
"Gothic" devotion and superstition, which are the
"parents" of imagination, cannot justly be called
"opposite to the real interests of human society",
unless he wishes also to say that imagination is
opposite to those interests. His cultural duality
goes pari passu with his religious division of
allegiance. In Freudian terms, empirical truth
appeals to his reality principle, Anglicanism appeals
to his super-ego, and imagination, fed by medieval
supernaturalism, appeals to his id. In his poetry,
the id occasionally achieves dominance. Warton
continues:

> the catholic worship, besides that its
> numerous exterior appendages were of a
> picturesque and even of a poetical nature,
> disposed the mind to a state of deception,
> and encouraged, or rather authorized, every
> species of credulity: its visions, miracles,
> and legends, propagated a general propensity
> to the Marvellous, and strengthened the
> belief of spectres, demons, witches, and
> incantations. (III, 285).

The question is, is this "deception" the deception
of those who are more honest than those "who do not
deceive", and is this "credulity" to be equated with
"incredibilities that are more acceptable than
truth"? The answer is surely affirmative, just as
the "Marvellous" is the same as the medieval
marvellous which Hurd admired. "The genius of
romance and of popery were the same," and "the
dragons and the castles of the one, were of a piece
with the visions and pretended miracles of the
other".[24] At times Warton seems to say that medieval
religion is only important in so far as it stimulates
the literary imagination, from which it would seem
that medieval Christianity is inferior to the cause
of literature. But since the "genius of romance and
popery" are the same, they are at least on a par.
His lack of clarity allows for a measure of self-
deception or intellectual dishonesty. Clearly,
religion is not merely the tool of literature, but

literature can be the vehicle of religion or religious feelings. In view of all that has been said in
Chapter I of the relationship between religion,
romanticism, medievalism, sublimity, myth and imagination, it is not unreasonable to suggest that
Warton's conception of imagination was one aspect of
the romantic shift towards the numinous, and that
"imagination" was a cultural analogy of faith. If
this is so, his defence of imagination can be interpreted as a kind of religious plea.

Warton was one of the first to associate monasticism with the cult of pensive melancholy established
by Milton, who divorced it from its debilitating
associations and united it with wisdom, poetry,
philosophy and saintliness. The Pleasures of
Melancholy describes the solemn glooms and twilight
cells "where thoughtful melancholy loves to muse".
Francis Gallaway points out that such melancholy was
thought in the eighteenth century to be "propitious
to love, to religion, and to art".[25] The combination
of religion and melancholy is epitomized in the
"Inscription in a Hermitage" (1777), where he uses
the mask of a devout hermit:

> At eve, within yon studious nook,
> I ope my brass-embossed book,
> Pourtray'd with many a holy deed
> Of martyrs, crown'd with heavenly meed:
> Then, as my taper waxes dim,
> Chant, ere I sleep, my measured hymn ...
>
> (11.25-30)[26]

In this almost Pre-Raphaelite verse the slowing metre
vivifies not only encroaching fatigue, but also
solemnizes action. Its earnestness is unmistakable,
especially when the hermit later laments the indifference of the secular world to his religious life.
"Written at Vale-royal Abbey in Cheshire" (1777)[27] is
not written with a mask, and consequently must -
while expressing regard for the benefits bestowed by
monasteries (11.13-80) - be seen to be critical, with
an obsequious affirmation of the establishment view
of the dichotomy between fancy and reason (11.81-4),
ending with praise for modern, enlightened institutions. This coda (11.81-92) is unconvincing and hangs
unnaturally on the end of the poem. Fancy and Superstition are self-consciously disowned and Science is
rather routinely lauded. Compare this with Fairchild's saying that "Warton has no religion which can
firmly be seperated from 'fancy'".[28] The distinction

43

between fancy and imagination was not current in his
day, and his "fancy" is more recognizable to a post-
Coleridgean as "imagination". This clarifies its
importance to him and makes his rejection of it unconvincing.[29] His image of modern religion is light
(1.91); but this is also his image for medieval
religion (1.59). Consequently, the advantages of the
modern age look like an anti-climax: does he really
see Religion spreading her "warmth divine" in the
context of "More useful institutes, adorning man"
(1.86), "Manners" (1.87), "civilities" (1.87) and
"social plan" (1.88)? The Augustan in him affirms
these things, but the main body of his poem would
seem the more likely context for such an elysium.
After 64 years there was a significant change: John
Mason Neale, fellow Anglican clergyman and Gothic-
enthusiast - but free of classicism - condemned the
poem for its anti-medievalism.[30]

The chief substance of "The Crusade" (1777) is
a victory song anticipating the Saracens' defeat.
The picture of an abused Palestine corresponds in
numerous particulars to the picture of derelict
medieval Christianity in "Vale-royal", a Christianity
brought low by the Reformation. Both poems describe
abused Christian sites and both end with the triumph
of Christianity. Both sites elicit his sympathy;
though in one the destructive force is identified as
the Saracen, while in the other the corresponding
force is unnamed, though implicit. It is almost as
if he unconsciously and implicitly criticizes the
perpetrators of destruction in "Vale-royal" by
creating a parallel scene in "The Crusade" with
verbal and imagistic reverberations. His approval of
the Christianity of "The Crusade" can be transferred,
with the affidavit of the many correspondences, to
"Vale-royal". This is supported by the enumeration
of the monastery's virtues - hospitality, art and
learning - in the latter.

His interest in the Middle Ages was at least, to
use Fairchild's phrase, "quasi-religious",[31] though
inhibitions and pressures prevented him from openly
sympathizing with, or understanding, medieval Catholicism. His purpose is elusive. He probably believed,
like Hurd, that poetry's function was to give pleasure, not to instruct. He certainly did not wish to
convert people to Catholicism. It is equally
obvious, however, that, through the catalyst of a
novel historicism, the medieval religious milieu was
for him a successful, satisfying embodiment of
religious feeling, if not of religion itself (if the
two can be distinguished). The consequences of this

attitude were probably widespread: "one may legitim-
ately argue that such affection for the Middle Ages...
ultimately helped to break down anti-Catholic prejudices and thus paved the way for the Oxford Movement".[32]

Warton, Johnson,[33] John Scott[34] and others[35]
were engaged by the monastic theme, which greatly
progressed with influential Thomas Chatterton (1752-
70),[36] whose empathy for religious medievalism in the
Rowley and Canynge poems was total. It may be argued
that he had to assume an empathetic position as the
condition of his deception, and that by disowning
responsibility, he did not have to apologize for
anything he said; but whatever the motive, he
produced completely empathetic poetry, the absolute
correspondence between form and content making
Chatterton's medievalism an outstanding example of
interest in the medieval religion. His personae,
William Canynge and Thomas Rowley are religious men,
one in religious orders, the other a monk.

He had reservations about Catholicism like all
the other eighteenth-century writers.[37] In one
"Elegy"[38] he refers to "the sons of Superstition",
and in another writes

> Now thro' the gloomy cloister's length'ning
> way,
> Thro' all the terror superstition frames...[39]

though this looks like a self-consciously assumed
eighteenth-century pose when compared with Rowley,
who is neither gloomy nor superstitious. In his
"Articles of the Belief of Me Thomas Chatterton" he
proclaims his anti-dogmatism: "That God being incom-
prehensible: it is not required of us to know the
mysterys of the Trinity &c.", yet also: "The Church
of Rome (some Tricks of Priestcraft excepted) is
certainly the true Church". While he criticizes an
abbot's inhumanity and pride (in "An Excelente Balade
of Charitie") and the Church's willingness to accept
wealth (in the "Prologue made bie Maistre William
Canynge" to "Goddwyn. A Tragedie"), it should not be
read as eighteenth-century anti-Catholicism, but as
medieval anti-clerical satire. The ridicule of
priestcraft in "Happiness. A Poem" is balanced by the
evocation of pure piety in "On Happienesse by William
Canynge". He epitomizes eighteenth-century duality,
professing atheism, yet carrying his "creed" about
with him like a talisman. Rather than suggesting
(biographically) belief followed unbelief, it is more
satisfactory to suppose that both were contemporan-

eously aspects of his personality. Rowley was the
atheist's alter ego expressed, with a striking
reverence for churchmen, church buildings and Catholicism.

He presents few miracles or enchantments, for he
is not interested in creating amazement, but in
presenting the reality of the medieval world. The
religious aspect of the Middle Ages he presents is
basically amiable. He wrote to Robert Dodsley of his
wish "to convince the world that the monks (of whom
some have so despicable an opinion) were not such
blockheads as generally thought...."[40] Laymen too
are shown in their generosity, endowing churches and
chantries.[41] The earthly spiritual home is so beautiful that Elle's sprite laments its loss:

> To heare the Chauntrie Songe sounde ynne
> myne Eare;
> To heare the Masses to owre holie Dame....[42]

The crusades are depicted in "A Knyghte Templar's
Spryte speeketh" as a holy war, purifying the Holy
Land. He cannot be said to have been a "mainstream"
poet, for he had no direct successors or predecessors. But he was a weather-vane of the imponderable
undercurrents of cultural and religious society, and,
paradoxically, a rebel in trying to present a favourable picture of medieval faith.

He and his Protestant contemporaries are enabled
to use the religious Middle Ages at all because they
have, as it were, put on a mask, and, as Sensibilt-
arians, look for stimulating - that is, necessarily
novel and apparently superficial - spiritual categories, which predominantly happen to be medieval
Catholic. As medieval religion gave birth, according
to Scott, to the fantastic, the fantastic now
fostered a new religious sensibility. The eighteenth
and nineteenth-century fascination with all medieval
supernaturalism was not a naive delight in the
extravagant, but the achievement of a catharsis, and
the expression of a deep-seated desire to witness and
partake of a more exciting, enthusiastic and "romantic" religious experience than was commonly available
to them in the Anglicanism of the restrained and
decorous Enlightenment. This dimension largely
escaped attention in the latter half of the century,
because of the residual inhibitions and formalities
of the previous age, and the fact that it takes time
for the true nature of a metaphor to reveal itself.
Only in the nineteenth century was the pebble seen to
be a pearl.

46

History and Religion in the Romantic Period

While some came to be concerned with the
religious aspect of the Middle Ages through the
medium of aesthetics, others approached the medieval
Church along the path of socio-political concern;
and since history then was not empiric or objective,
the question of medievalist empathy arises also with
the Romantic historians: in retrospect we can say
that at that time the dividing-line between history,
myth and (still) poetry was unclear.

Edmund Burke was a profoundly religious man, a
Protestant who campaigned on behalf of Catholics,[43]
a politician whose political actions rested on
religious principles. In his belief that society and
its working are divinely ordained and governed, he is
at once medieval and representative of his age,[44] and
an influence on the Lake Poets. Though Alice Chandler ignores Burke's religious world-view, it should
be remembered when reading his lament for the passing
of chivalry in Reflections on the Revolution in
France (1790), where sophistry, economy and calcul-
ation are set against generosity, pride and dignity[45]
He is aware of the full significance of chivalry and
openly reveres the medieval past explicitly for its
spiritual generosity and nobility, not merely for the
picturesque. Chivalry was in large part a religious
cult, according to Burke, combining "the spirit of a
gentleman, and the spirit of religion"; and it was on
this combination "that our manners, our civilization,
and all the good things which are connected with
manners, and with civilization, have, in this European world of ours, depended for ages...." (173). The
coda of the eulogy on chivalry is explicitly moral
because of his religious outlook, which pervades the
Reflections. For Burke, man is a "religious animal"
(187), and as religion is the basis of civil society,
he passionately affirms the necessity of a religious
reverence for the unity of Church and State.[46] He
concurred with the medieval Thomist view that the
just social order and hierarchy was divinely ordained, and saw in the medieval structure a valuable and
spiritually acceptable paradigm,[47] which he contrasts
in Reflections with "this new conquering empire of
light and reason" (171). The new "barbarous
philosophy" (171) is a "mechanic philosophy" (172),
which "in order to subvert antient institutions, has
destroyed antient principles" (172) and "banishes the
affections" (172). The reason, philosophy and
immorality of the Enlightenment progeny is adversely
contrasted with the medieval order (and its

47

successor), with its "moral imagination", "antient principles", sensibility, guardianship of learning (173) and development of civilization. For Burke, the State has a religious sanction because "Providence" (his fundamental principle) has ordained it and disposed the individuals within it.[48] He also holds in common with the Middle Ages a conception of states contributing to and partaking of the unity which is Christendom. This metaphysico-political concept of unity is important and recurrs in medievalist writings, an expression of the theme of reconciliation, and connected with the perceived need of a revival of an ancient spiritual outlook.

Similarly, Coleridge believed society's decay to be rooted in a loss of values and faith, rather than in a mere change of system, and suggested as a remedy for the divorce of philosophy and religion from politics, the closer alignment of Church, State and education, after the medieval way. In On the Constitution of the Church and State (1829) Coleridge proposes a national moral and spiritual reform, to be accomplished by a "National Church",[49] resembling the medieval Church in its relationship to the state and education, an idea possibly suggested to him, or given substance, by his reading of Aquinas and other scholastics of whom he approved.[50] Like the medieval Church as he understood it, the National Church was to be an estate of a paternalist realm, promoting a combination of culture, moral welfare and religious education. It would restore the medieval Church's functions of taking education into every parish and acting as a mediator between the classes of society. He thought the English Church had lost its chance at the Reformation, when it replaced its allegiance to Rome with allegiance to the monarchy, instead of making itself into a supra-party organization.[51] The notion of the National Church was balanced by his larger conception of Christianity as the universal church, not subject to any state. The Church was not to be simply an arm of the State. The Tractarians valued him as the formulator of the doctrines of the Church's spiritual independence, for he saw that Christianity had in the Middle Ages provided a guiding hand in religious and moral affairs, had stood against secular powers and that its witness was the embodiment of the spirit of God, which could not be subject to man's will.[52] He wanted a reformed understanding of the spiritual and moral powers of the soul: "the commercial spirit, and the ascendancy of the experimental philosophy which took place at the close of the fourteenth century ... combined to

48

foster [understanding's] corruption."[53] This statement implies that the medieval Church had in some
way a superior spiritual understanding. Indeed Basil
Willey speaks of his "reverence for the religion and
the religious philosophy of the Middle Ages".[54]
     By slight distortion and tailoring of facts to
suit his arguments, Coleridge mythifies the Middle
Ages, as can be seen in the miscellaneous criticism,
with its many bland, sweeping and unsupported
statements, frequently based on ignorance[55] and
hearsay (derived from A.W. Schlegel, himself a
polemicist, Catholic medievalist). For example, in
his search for an ideal he too readily adheres to
medieval race myths (borrowed from the historians),
such as the innate deference of the Gothic races to
woman finding expression in the cult of the Virgin,
with its "many beautiful associations".[56] He
supposes there was something innately and uniquely
transcendental about the "Gothic Mind" (itself a
mythification), its art expressing the infinite.[57]
This "tendency to the infinite" arose from the
"Northman's" intimacy with nature and his freedom[58]
(another myth).
     Like Burke, Robert Southey turned to the Catho-
lic age of faith for spiritual and moral reference.
He saw that the Middle Ages were an ideal battlefield
on which to test religious views. In Sir Thomas
More: or, Colloquies on the Progress and Prospects of
Society (1829) he expressed precisely Burke's view:
"the independence [of the majority] which has been
gained since the total decay of the feudal system,
has been dearly purchased by the loss of kindly
feelings and ennobling attachments";[59] these presumably dependant on medieval man's knowing the
"improvement of his moral and spiritual condition
ought to be the first concern of every intellectual
creature".[60] By contrast, he indicts modern materialism.[61] He has More says that "a patriarchal state
is better and happier than a commercial one" for
temporal, intellectual and spiritual reasons.[62] "The
connection," asserts Cobban, "in Southey's mind between the revived cult of feudalism and a religious
concept of society is obvious."[63] The connection is
that his social opinions are based on religion rather
than "liberal opinions", which are connected in his
mind with the "incentives to vice, impiety, and
rebellion" propagated by an over-zealous press.[64]
Again like Burke, he thought the Church profoundly
important in society[65] and stressed the connection
between State and Church.[66] So both are politically-
minded men whose touchstone and motive force

is religion; whose vision of heaven on earth is religious,[67] and whose attention is caught by medieval
values, morality and spirituality. Both see contemporary society's decay not simply in terms of a
change of system, but as a loss of bed-rock values,
and they look to the Middle Ages for correction. He
is sure that the replacement of religion by materialism has, or is, taking place: the majority "are less
religious than in the days of the Romish faith" says
More.[68] A final point of similarity is that both
warned against revolution and implicitly advocated as
a guard that the civil and religious structures
should co-operate in a paternalist hierarchy.[69] They
represent a brand of thought which had natural re-
course to the Middle Ages as the paradigm of Christian and benevolist hierarchical society. It is too
simple to say, like Chandler, that they were medievalists simply because they were Tories. They were
Tories because they thought Toryism Christian and,
looking to the Middle Ages, they thought they saw
something of their ideal. The restoration of social
order was a metaphysical imperative because it reflected the divine order, in the tradition of Richard
Hooker, and ultimately of Aquinas.

It is remarkable that Southey should choose as
the vehicle of his ideas a quasi-medieval Roman Catholic figure. Having selected an eminent Catholic
figure, one would have expected him to follow
Cobbett[70] on the Catholic question, and up to a point
he does. Like Cobbett, he deplores the spoliation of
Church property[71] and the Church's decline in influence,which has resulted not only in a lowered standard of devotion, but has also "prepared the way for
the uncontrolled dominion of that worldly spirit
which it is the tendency of the commercial system to
produce and foster".[72] Religious houses should be
revived,[73] though in a modified form, for charitable
work, and as outlets for zeal otherwise diverted to
Methodism. He especially recommends the Beguine
order,[74] which is bona fide because it is not bound
by vows, retains property, is not exceptionally ascetic, and had many enemies within the medieval
Church.[75] Disraeli followed his belief that "the
dissolution of the monastic houses ... was every way
injurious to the labouring classes".[76] And Burke
said of monasteries that in them was "a great power
for the mechanism of politic benevolence,what our
workmen call a purchase.... These institutions are
the products of enthusiasm; they are the instruments
of wisdom."[77]

Southey, though virulently anti-Catholic, had a

certain weakness for the enemy. Despite its harsh
criticism of the medieval Church, The Book of the
Church (1824) exhibits an advance of sympathy, as in
the eulogy of the missionary monks,[78] and praise for
the Papacy in its fight against Islam.[79] He even
believed that "the best interests of the country were
advanced by the clergy even during the darkest ages
of papal domination ...",[80] and expressed sympathy
with pilgrimaging.[81] As in The Book of the Church,
Southey betrays a slight Catholic sympathy in
Colloquies. With apparent approval of Catholic externalism, he has More say, "religion may be neglected in Roman Catholic countries, but it cannot be
forgotten; it is impressed upon the senses of the
people; travel where they will its symbols are perpetually presented to them".[82] Commenting on Catholicism in Portugal he says, "bad indeed must the
sinner be who will not be burnt white at last! Every
prayer at a crucifix helps him - and a Mass on purpose is a fine shove towards Paradise. It is a superstition of hope".[83] He could praise monks highly.[84]
In his poem "Written after Visiting the Convent of
Arrabida, Near Setubal" (c.1796), he praises monasticism lyrically, reminding one of Gray's favourable
comments on visiting the Great Charterhouse in 1739.
He even admits that the "better Papists ... worship
the Father in spirit and in truth".[85] So Southey was
truly in two minds about Catholicism, or at least
about its external manifestations, and did not simply
assume a disinterested stance in his medievalist
poetry for purely aesthetic reasons. The relationship of his poetry to his normal anti-Catholicism
represents the relationship of his imaginative and
emotional feeling for Catholicism to his Protestantism, nationalism, and rationalism. The rationalist-
romantic tension is epitomized when he says Catholicism is "a fine religion for an enthusiast - for one
who can let his feelings remain awake, and opiate his
reason. Never was goddess so calculated to win upon
the human heart as the Virgin Mary ...".[86]
    Southey's Roderick, The Last of the Goths (1814)
is more generally favourable to early medieval
Catholicism than his earlier Joan of Arc (1796),
which had displayed his interest in Catholic culture.
The quest - which is the central motif - is for
salvation through reconciliation. The eponymous hero
significantly dons the garb of a monk and vows to
"save" Spain. He achieves peace by renunciation of
wordly values[87] and by being instrumental in reconciliation, thus living out the vocation symbolized by,
and associated with, his monastic disguise. Roderick

continues the trend of sympathetic presentation of
the religious apparatus of the Middle Ages. For
example, Abbot Odoar and the monk Romano and his
hermitage are favourably depicted, while Marianism
and miracles are presented without denigratory
comment (pp.9, 146). Similarly, in Madoc (begun
1794) he places himself with much sympathy in the
hero's position, entering fully into the spirit of
twelfth-century Catholicism, as when celebrating his
conversion of the Hoamen tribe (Pt. II sec. 8).
Again, he describes the service ordered by Madoc on
returning home to the holy island of Bardsey with
relish (pp. 97-8).

His shorter medievalist poems are based on minor
legends and superstitions, and would have been
attractive to a quasi-religious department of the
imagination. He does not write with his own voice,
so that poems like "The Five Martyrs of Morocco"
(1803) and "Queen Mary's Christening" (1829) could be
mistaken for works of Catholic piety. In his Preface
to "St. Michael's Chair", he quotes Whitaker's
"Supplement to the First and Second Book of
Polywhele's 'History of Cornwall.'", which talks of
medieval Catholicism as "a religion, dealing more in
exteriors than our own, operating more than our own,
through the body, upon the soul; and so leaving,
perhaps, a more sensible impression upon the spirits"
(p.70). Southey exploited the rich vein of Catholic
"exteriority" or "externality" to make "a more
sensible impression upon the spirits". This poetic
tactic surely drew, inadvertently but very naturally,
something of religious consequence in its wake, for
both Southey and his audience; while the theme of
Roderick embodies the spiritual essence of religious
medievalism.

William Cobbett was an Anglican, and a propagator of medievel-based social ideas, though more
radical than Southey.[88] His medievalism also had a
neglected religious aspect. Both Chandler and
Raymond Williams interpret Cobbett's A History of
the Protestant Reformation in England and Ireland[89]
in social terms,[90] viewing the religious element as
a mere appendage of the social,[91] and their emphasis
is basically right. But the History is ostensibly
religious, and the work's subtitle - "... showing
how that event has impoverished and degraded the
main body of the People in those Countries" - would
suggest a dependence of the social effect on the
religious cause. He was particularly interested in
the communally-oriented monasteries, not so much for
their communism, but for their administration of a

vaguely benevolent society, a kind of welfare state.
So his emphasis is on the benevolent spirit rather
than social doctrine. Moreover, all his social
evidence of the benevolence of the monasteries is
used in the cause of Catholic rehabilitation, and
this because he was actively involved in the struggle
for Catholic Emancipation: indeed, the occasion for
the History was Daniel O'Connell's success with his
Catholic Association in 1823.

He tried to show that the Catholic Church was,
contrary to popular opinion, capable of goodness,
and, by speaking of past injustices, to remind the
Protestant world of present oppression of the Church
in England. The event was "not a reformation, but a
devastation",[92] and he vilifies Protestant historians
of the subject as "lying, hired, place-hunting,
pension-hunting, benefice-seeking, or romancing
historians".[93] His argument is that the Reformation
engendered not purification but pollution, and replaced "the ease ... and harmony and Christian
charity, enjoyed ... by our Catholic forefathers"
with "misery", "beggary" and "wrangling".[94] It
should be noted that good things were the result of
"Christian charity", not of any secular social consciousness. The benevolence of the medieval Church is
contrasted with the vulgar, commercial secularity of
present-day Norwich,[95] which has usurped the monks of
St. Andrew's Hall. He is so sympathetic to medieval
Catholicism - "the Church of our fathers"[96] - that he
can even express preference for Catholicism over
Anglicanism, as when he contrasts the founding of the
Oxford colleges by medieval Catholics with the fact
that no colleges had been founded there in the Protestant age.[97] He even defends celibacy of clergy.[98]

Williams emphasizes the importance of the
History: "this book had ... a huge circulation, and
there must for some time have been many thousands of
readers who came to these ideas through Cobbett rather than through contact with any of the more reliable
sources."[99] It made a lively contribution to the
debate on Catholic Emancipation and probably helped
the Catholic cause,[100] while helping to create an
atmosphere favourable to religious medievalism. The
ideas of the History are distilled in the Political
Register, where he says that in "Catholic times",
"there were no paupers in England. The Catholics
maintained the Poor, the Aged, the Widow, the Orphan,
the Stranger, and the Infirm, out of the Tithes and
other Revenues of the Church."[101] He may well have
emphasized the correct expenditure of ecclesiastical
wealth because this was an issue in his own day.

From the late 1820's-on, the Church of England was
ironically criticized from both within and without
for abuses such as misdirection of revenues, non-
residence, pluralities and inequalities of income,
for which the medieval Church had always been
criticized.[102] He continues: "the Catholics built
all our Cathedrals, founded and endowed all the great
Schools that are even now in England, and founded
every great Public Charity that now exists in
England."[103] This could be interpreted as social
propaganda; but he was writing at the height of the
Emancipation controversy, and was therefore specifically propagating the idea of Catholic worthiness,
and contrasting it with establishment injustice.
     Chandler tries to explain away Cobbett's
Catholic sympathies as merely "a dislike for something else".[104] But this only explains the vehemence
of his history, not its content, which is largely
based on Catholic Lingard's History of England.
Admittedly he exaggerates the facts, but at least he
uses facts. Consequently it is misleading to say he
was simply motivated by dislike: he clearly liked
what he saw of the medieval Church. He remained a
member of the established church, however, and wanted
religious conformity for the good of the country, but
he was ready to criticize it (to the point of calling
for its disestablishment)[105]when he felt it to be
slacking in its moral responsibility. His appeal to
the Middle Ages was pragmatic, yet, in his own terms,
religious, for he believed that "that which strengthens this natural propensity [in man to virtue], or
arrests the effects of corruption and perversion, and
does this through the means of reverence for God ...
is called RELIGION".[106] As Cobbett was not very
mystically or metaphysically inclined,[107] it is unlikely that his medievalism had anything to do with
ritual or theology: but for him a Christian is
essentially someone who loves his neighbour,[108] and
it is this principle which informs the History. In
his own terms, the History is religious as much as
social polemic.
     John Nicholson (1790-1843), the minor poet,
illustrates the ambiguity of the age by sharing the
attitudes of both Cobbett and Southey. In his best
known and very popular poem, "Airedale in Ancient
Times" (written about 1822 and published in 1825),
he speaks of medieval superstition, ignorance and
bigotry, but seems to locate these in the earlier,
rather than the later, Middle Ages, in contrast to
Southey. He gives an enthusiastic, idealized picture of medieval worship, with its pious zeal and

54

credal unity, which was, he suggests, such as to make
the modern worshipper ashamed. He has kind words for
Turgusius, the fourth abbot of Kirkstall Abbey,
praises the monastic function of protecting culture
and laments the Reformation attack on the monasteries. But when the Emancipation crisis came, he proclaimed his anti-popery, anti-Romanism, Erastianism
and even anti-monasticism, in "England's Lament for
the Loss of her Constitution".[109]

There are several reasons why William Wordsworth
did not exploit the religious aspect of the Middle
Ages more than he did: nature fulfilled most of his
requirements for spiritual source material, and he
was averse to mythology of the more recognizable
kind,[110] for he preferred personal experience of the
real world (a fact which persuaded him not to delve
into the distant, mythified past). He was averse to
speaking directly of Christianity, so Christian
medievalism was not a priority with him.[111] Also, he
disliked Roman Catholicism with its ritual : Ecclesiastical Sonnet XXX (Part II), "The Point at Issue"
(1826), says the soul should root in God, not in
forms. The Ecclesiastical Sonnets, written with the
Catholic question in mind,[112] are often antagonistic
to Catholic ritual, superstition and bigotry, and
often picture the Roman Church as an intruding foreign power. He once said that Catholicism was
"founded upon the overthrow of private judgement - it
is essentially at enmity with light and knowledge"
and that Catholics were necessarily persecutors.[113]
He also disliked "bigot zeal",[114] which was usually
attributed to Catholicism. Finally, there is his
tendency to create a man-centred or nature-centred,
rather than God-centred, universe. And yet he does
reflect preceding medievalist trends and anticipate
succeeding ones.

He strongly commended Percy's Reliques.[115] He
realized that his childhood reading in the romances
had been important to him,[116] and concluded that they
had a semi-mythical importance for others:

> ... something in the shape
> Of these will live till man shall be no more.
> Dumb yearnings, hidden appetites, are ours,
> And they must have their food.[117]

His anti-materialism and anti-rationalism, his love
of fancy and imagination, are natural concomitants
of, and incitements to, the use of an age steeped in
the supernatural and supra-rational. His fear of
ascendent materialism[118] was one reason for his

alliance with the High Church, since it seemed more
opposed to it than other groups. This alliance
doubtless led him to look with a kinder eye on the
medieval Church. His anti-rationalism finds
expression in the medievalist "Stanzas Suggested in
a Steamboat off Saint Bees' Heads, On the Coast of
Cumberland" (1833), in the concluding nine lines,
where he preferrs the "bold credulities" - the
miracles ascribed to the early monastic foundation -
to modern rationalism. The significance of Wordsworth's attitude is suggested by Frederick Faber, who
in 1844 quoted the poem (with the final stanza
modified by Wordsworth himself, to make the meaning
clearer) at the end of his "Life of St. Bega" in
Newman's Lives of the English Saints, as an example
of how his poems "did in divers places anticipate the
revival of Catholic doctrines among us",[119] and
points out that the sympathy of the poem is
particularly striking in view of his lack of sympathy
with Catholic doctrine and the "tone of sneering"
common in English authors at that time when speaking
of the Middle Ages.[120] He further suggestively
remarks how his "affectionate reverence for the
Catholic past, the humble consciousness of a loss
sustained by ourselves", and the readiness to "put
a good construction on what he cannot wholly conc-
eive" are in edifying contrast to Southey's writings
on similar matters.[121] In The Excursion (Book VII,
ll. 1008-1040), there is a knight who lived on into
the Elizabethan age and saw "his own bright order
fade,/ And its devotion gradually decline", as well
as

> That violent commotion, which o'erthrew,
>   . . . . .
> Altar, and cross, and church of solemn roof,
> And old religious house - pile after pile;
> And shook their tenants out into the fields,
> Like wild beasts without a home!

The brutality of change brings social brutalization
where there was once religion. The Middle Age was
an age of faith which succumbed to the "airy hopes,/
Dancing around [mutability]" (ll. 1034-5); hopes
grounded, one assumes, in the new rationalism and
materialism. His dislike of rationalism emerges in
"The Egyptian Maid", where Merlin is a type of
rationalism unaided by imagination, which leads to
destruction.
   Conversely, Wordsworth was attracted to the
"fanciful" or "imaginative" aspect of Catholicism.

In "Suggested on a Sabbath Morning in the Vale of
Chamouny" (1820), he watches a Catholic procession
with fascination, and looks

> upon the secret springs
> Of that licentious craving in the mind
> To act the God among external things
> (ll. 64-6)

but decides that it represents "Fable's dark abyss!"
- recalling Hurd's fascination with fable. As so
often with non-Catholic writers of the period, he
allows Catholicism to feed his "imaginative faculty"
(however we may understand that ambiguous concept),
but does not let it near his intellect or conscious
conviction. This religious schizophrenia is evident
throughout the Ecclesiastical Sonnets. Which part of
him was dominant, which the most significant?

The above rejection of externality cannot be
taken seriously. By "externality" I mean to connote
Catholic manifestations - forms, rituals, practices,
architecture and even stories of saints - which
express the invisible world of spirit and man's
response to it. I include also, since these manifestations unite the physical with the spiritual,
Catholic sacramentalism, the basis of externality,
which posits - broadly - the physical world as a way
of knowing and expressing God. Such externality
finds response in Wordsworth's imaginative faculty
because both recreate the intangible in visible form.
That he was attracted to religious externality and
understood its value is clear. In a note to "Laud"
he quotes his subject upon "the true and inward
worship of God, which while we live in the body,
needs external helps",[122] and expresses the same idea
in his own "Essay, Supplementary to the Preface" of
the second edition of Lyrical Ballads.[123] He sees
Catholicism as a poem, making a direct, forceful
appeal to the Imagination (especially understood, and
sometimes alternating in the poetry with "Fancy", in
spite of Coleridge's distinction). In accordance
with his sympathy for Catholic expression of the
spiritual, he criticizes the Reformation for the
destruction of spiritual manifestation in whatever
form. In "Regrets" he wishes that "our scrupulous
Sires had dared to leave / Less scanty measure of
those graceful rites", as he does also in "Devotional
Incitements". Similarly, he condemns the loss of
reverence for saints (in "Saints"), the destruction
of monastic architecture (in "Dissolution of the
Monasteries") and the overthrow of the cult of the

Virgin (in "The Virgin"). This attitude rests
uneasily with the anti-externality of "The Point at
Issue" and "Suggested On a Sabbath Morning In the
Vale of Chamouny". But whatever the intellectual
contradictions of Wordsworth's position,[124] while he
thought he ought to be entirely anti-Catholic, he was
strongly attracted by its externality.

Fairchild suggests the reason for medieval
Catholicism exercising such a spell over Wordsworth :
"Wordsworth," he says, "leans toward certain Catholic
doctrines and practices because he feels that,
precisely in being superstitious, they contain a
precious imaginative element which flouts that 'false
secondary power,' the lower reason."[125] The unspoken
implication is that Catholicism appealed to his
"higher reason", to his Imagination. Imagination,
not reason, is the important faculty where faith is
concerned : "Heaven rejects the lore / Of nicely-
calculated less or more."[126] "The Wishing-Gate"
(1828) expresses belief in the importance of superstition, and Wordsworth is reverent towards the gate
itself, which is the symbol of the world of superstition. (For "superstition" one may substitute
"Catholicism", since he often equated them.) Perhaps
a saint died there, he says, but something makes it
holy. "The Wishing-Gate Destroyed" (1841) associates
the gate with "old belief and dream" and tells of the

> spirit-stirring power it gained
> From faith which here was entertained,
> Though reason might say no.

With its destruction,

> the charm is fled;
> Indulgent centuries spun a thread,
> Which one harsh day has broken.

The gate spoke to the soul through the Imagination,
and had a positive effect, no matter what the facts
of its history. Similarly, in "Saint Bees' Heads",
stories of miracles - whether true or not is unimp-
ortant - are said to reap a spiritual harvest (ll.46-
8). Reason and empirical truth have no part to play
in the language of the soul, but Imagination does.
Since the gate is the focus of the Imagination he
reveres it, as a medieval Catholic might have
revered a relic. "Though reason might say no," he
"believes" in superstition, and his spirit is at home
"in days when faith was strong" : "O Fancy" (the oath
is noteworthy) "what an age was that for song!" when

> element and orb on <u>acts</u> did wait
> Of <u>Powers</u> endued with visible form, instinct
> With will, and to their work by passion
>   linked.[127]

If this is not the Middle Ages, it might as well be.
Song - Imagination made manifest - thrives, he seems
to say, in the age of faith, when Powers are themselves engaged in (creative) acts. It is admittedly
hard to see where all this leads : Wordsworth himself
would probably have been unable to articulate his
ideas on the Imagination-Catholicism-medievalism
nexus. But the problem has a bearing on all Protestant religious medievalists, and therefore demands a
solution. The problem resolves itself into the
question : did Wordsworth revere the age of faith
merely because it was poetic, or because it matched
his religious sensibility? The following speculation
suggests the second case is true, while not denying
that he regarded Catholic externality as poetic.

For Wordsworth, Imagination is a moral lever
(see "Crusades"), a faculty by which to recognize the
divine (see "The Cuckoo at Laverna", ll. 70-3), a
"sacred power" and the means of achieving faith (see
"Weak is the Will of Man, his judgement blind"), and
Fancy promotes the soul's interests (see "Apology",
sonnet XVIII, of Part I of <u>Ecclesiastical Sonnets</u>).
Imagination / Fancy seems to be a spiritual
faculty,[128] as it was for Coleridge. It is not faith
or the soul; it is the means by which faith is
achieved, sustained and expressed. When Imagination
expresses faith, the result is something like
Catholic externality, which focusses the divine, so
to speak, as art focusses the divinized romantic ego.
The unification of religion and poetry in the
missionary Imagination must have had great appeal to
a man who perceived the affinity between religion and
poetry in their relationship to reason and in their
transcendent and incarnational qualities.[129] Why
bother with the Middle Ages? Because traditionally
it was thought to be the high-point of Christian
anti-rationalism and superstition; because it was
the age of faith; because it saw the zenith of the
outward expression of Christianity, and was an
exponent of Imagination. An English Protestant
interested in Catholicism, yet patriotic, would tend
to reject contemporary Catholicism because it was
"foreign", in favour of medieval Catholicism, which
was "national".[130] His criticisms of medieval
Christianity should not be over-valued, since they
are the product of reason, and not Imagination, which

is, on his own principle, the proper tool of
appraisal; while medieval Catholic externality measured up to his poetical and religious yearnings.
Hence it is insufficient to say he found the medieval
Church merely poetic. The Church was indeed a poem,
an externalization of the internal, a vehicle for,
and propagator of, "tangible spirituality", but
Wordsworth, in finding it poetic - that is, in
finding that it answered to his Imagination - was in
fact finding it spiritually satisfying : his "dumb
yearnings" were articulated, his "hidden appetites"
fed. In him, the "subterranean" religious element in
Hurd's and Warton's response to the Imagination /
Fancy element of the Gothic, enters the light of day.
    English non-Catholic sympathy for St. Francis of
Assisi possibly began with Wordsworth's "The Cuckoo
at Laverna" (1837),[131] in which he eulogizes the
saint precisely because of his enthusiasm, because of
his "baptized imagination", which made him "rapt ...
above the power of sense" and gave him power over
nature. Perhaps the poet's approval was so entire
because he saw Francis as himself perfected. This is
suggested by the juxtaposition of his own appreciation of nature - introduced by the cuckoo and followed
up by his observations of plants - with Francis's
intimate relationship with nature. Such identification is historicist empathy taken to its logical
conclusion. Such was his affection for the saint
that in 1842 he was still trying to discover more
about his life, with a view to writing about him
again.[132]
    His ability to admire medieval saints, seen in
"The Cuckoo at Laverna", is matched by admiration
for monastic institutions and the conventual life.
In a letter to Henry Crabb Robinson, he makes an
illuminating comment on Samuel Roffey Maitland's
Dark Ages,[133] which "confirms, without alluding to
any thing of mine all that I had previously thrown
out upon the benefits conferred by monastic institutions, and exposing the ignorance of Robertson,
Milner, Mosheim and others upon this subject - repels
most successfully their calumnies".[134] "St. Bees'
Heads" epitomizes his respectful attitude, with its
praise of the piety and compassion of the founder of
the monastery, its admiration of the monastery's art
and culture, and its acknowledgement of the value of
the contemplative and socially useful life of the
monks. "Old Abbeys" gives his deepest feeling about
the monasteries :

        Once ye were holy, ye are holy still;

Your spirit freely let me drink, and live.

Wordsworth and Southey turned to the medieval
Church as patriots, seeking to defend the now-corrupt
Anglican establishment by reference to its past
record:

> the Anglican could only invoke an ideal of
> the Church of England as she had been, and
> as she ought to be : by painting her services
> in the past, as the embodiment of the nation's
> highest spiritual achievement; as the guardian
> of its civilisation and culture, and thereby
> the guarantor of its freedom.[135]

He held feudalist, benevolist views on the church-
state nexus. In Ecclesiastical Sonnets he traces the
history of what he believes to be the authentic
English Church, deeply involved with the state and
body politic.[136] These links are suggested in
sonnets XV-XVII of Part I, and symbolized by Arthur
in "Struggle of the Britons against the Barbarians"
and by Alfred in "Alfred". He seems to think that
the Church belongs to the State, yet wanted neither
Erastianism[137] nor hierocracy, but an alliance of
equals. The alliance is holy : in "Lowther" the
association of cathedral and castle is a "Union
significant of God adored"; and so the secular is
sanctified. He shared with Cobbett, Southey and
Coleridge the vision of a unified society, with the
individual in harmony with the State on the basis of
religious universalism - itself a medieval religious
vision.
　　Such, then, was the pre-Romantic and Romantic
development of religious medievalism; and development there was, despite the persistence of profound
ambiguities : towards being more considered, more
radical, more diverse and more widespread. All the
subjects of this chapter - with the exceptions of
Burke and Cobbett - were anti-Catholic; yet they
were not entirely anti-medievalist. To understand
why they were not, it is necessary - having begun the
story of medievalism, and before taking it further -
to turn to the nature of anti-medievalism.

NOTES

1. See Chap-Books of the Eighteenth Century ed. John Ashton (1882).

2. Yorkshire Chap-Books ed. Charles A. Federer (1889 - "First Series"), 43, 45, 68-9, 70, 140 respectively.

3. J.R. Hale England and the Italian Renaissance (1963) 58-60, 107.

4. Spacks The Insistence of Horror (Cambridge, Mass., 1962) 83.

5. Irene Bostram "The Novel and Catholic Emancipation" Studies in Romanticism II (1962-3) 158-63.

6. Sister Mary Muriel Tarr Catholicism in Gothic Fiction (Washington, 1946): summary in Dan. J. McNutt The Eighteenth-Century Gothic Novel: An Annotated Bibliography of Criticism and Selected Texts (Folkstone, 1975) 84.

7. Varma The Gothic Flame (New York, 1966) 211. Monasticism is mentioned 211, 219-20. Other refs. to Catholicism 171, 219. Related comments 15, 25, 26, 210.

8. Edmund Sheridan Purcell Life and Letters of Ambrose Phillipps de Lisle ed. and finished by Edwin de Lisle 2v. (1900) I, 25-6.

9. See Leah Dennis "Percy's Essay 'On the Ancient Metrical Romances'" PMLA XLIX (1934) 82.

10. Percy Reliques of Ancient English Poetry 2v. (Everyman, 1926) I, 289.

11. If Hurd had a precursor, it was William Collins's "An Ode on the Popular Superstitions of the Highlands of Scotland" (1749-50 ?).

12. Letters ed. Edith J. Morley (1911) 154. Refs. henceforth cited in text.

13. Dissertations Moral and Critical v. III of The Philosophical Works (1783) 505. (1970 facsimile reprint.)

14. Johnston Enchanted Ground (1964) 10.

15. Dissertations Moral and Critical 520.

16. "Ritson's Metrical Romances" ER VII (Jan. 1806) 412, 387 respectively.

17. Warton The History of English Poetry III, 286.

18. Ibid. III, 285.

19. Fairchild II, 346.

20. Observations (1762) II, 268.

21. Ibid. II, 101.

22. Ibid. II, 87.

23. History of English Poetry I, 125. Subsequent refs. cited in text.

24. History (1774) III, xvi; qu. Johnston

Enchanted Ground 111.
    25. Reason, Rule,and Revolt in English
Classicism (New York, 1965) 267; and see n.16.
    26. The Poetical Works [1777] ed. Richard Mant
5th. ed. (Oxford, 1802). Line refs. henceforth
cited in text.
    27. Cf. Raymond D. Havens "Thomas Warton and
the Eighteenth-Century Dilemma" Studies in Philology 25 (1928) 46, 46-8, 49-50.
    28. Fairchild II, 347.
    29. In Essay on Original Genius (1767) William
Duff said imagination "discloses truths that were
formerly unknown"; but this notion was not widespread. The word "fancy" was at that time standard
poetic usage for every aspect of imagination, so its
use here is not at all surprising. See John Bullitt
"Distinctions Between Fancy and Imagination in
Eighteenth-Century English Criticism" Modern
Language Notes LX (1945) 8-15.
    30. Neale Hierologus; or, The Church Tourists
(1843) 25-6.
    31. Fairchild II, 346.
    32. Ibid. II, 348.
    33. See James M. Osborn Dr. Johnson and the
Contrary Converts printed for the Johnsonians (Yale
U.P. 1954) especially 1-6.
    34. The Works of the English Poets, From
Chaucer to Cowper ed. Dr. Johnson and Alexander
Chalmers (1810) XVII, 482.
    35. Fairchild II, 283-4, 336-7.
    36. William Julius Mickle (1735-1788) was one
contemporary whom Chatterton led to look afresh at
medieval religion. See Works of the English Poets
XVII, 511, and the poem therein, "Almada Hill. An
Epistle from Lisbon" (1779 or 1780).
    37. Some of the following points are also made
in Frances Schouler Miller "The Historic Sense of
Thomas Chatterton" English Literary History II (1944)
117-134.
    38. "Elegy [II]". The Complete Works of Thomas
Chatterton ed. Donald S. Taylor (Oxford at the
Clarendon Press, 1971) I, 400-01. Henceforth cited
as Complete Works.
    39. "Elegy [III]" Complete Works I, 583-4.
    40. Qu. Fairchild II, 351.
    41. See "The Tournament. An Interlude" ll.
141-146, "Battle of Hastings [II]" 1.385, "The
Storie of Wyllyam Canynge" 1.308, in Complete Works.
    42. "The Parlyamente of Sprytes" Complete Works
I, 111, ll. 110-11.
    43. See Thomas Mahoney "Edmund Burke and Rome"

The Catholic Historical Review XLIII (Jan. 1958)
espec. 423-5; also Conor Cruise O'Brien's introduction to Reflections on the Revolution in France
(Harmondsworth, 1976) 27-40.
    44. See Cobban Edmund Burke and the Revolt
Against the Eighteenth Century 15, 85.
    45. Reflections on the Revolution in France
170. Refs. henceforth in text.
    46. Cf. A.R. Humphreys The Augustan World
(1964) 141. and Cobban Edmund Burke and the Revolt
Against the Eighteenth Century 88.
    47. Cf. Fairchild III, 224-5.
    48. Cf. Cobban Edmund Burke and the Revolt
Against the Eighteenth Century.93-4.
    49. Chandler mistakenly says the "Nationalty"
is a Coleridgean synonym for the "National Church"
(Chandler 96), whereas it was his name for the
portion of national wealth reserved for the support
of the "Clerisy", a fund existent in the Middle Ages,
but expropriated by Henry VIII. See On the Constitution of the Church and State R.J. White ed. in The
Collected Works of Samuel Taylor Coleridge X (1976)
35 and 117 n.4.
    50. An annotation on Tenneman Geschichte der
Philosophie IX; noted in Collected Works X, 134. n.I.
    51. See Table Talk Bohn's ed. (1873) 106, 187
and Cobban Edmund Burke and the Revolt Against the
Eighteenth Century 242.
    52. Eg. Richard W. Church The Oxford Movement
(1909) VIII 148-9.
    53. The Statesman's Manual (1st. pub. 1816),
The Collected Works VI (1972) 74.
    54. Willey Nineteenth-Century Studies (Harmond-
sworth,1969) 57.
    55. Thomas Raysor attests this: Coleridges'
Miscellaneous Criticism (1936) 12-13.
    56. Ibid. 7.
    57. Loc. cit.
    58. Ibid. 13.
    59. Colloquies 2v. (1829) v.I, 60. (Sir Thomas
More is generally referred to as Colloquies.)
    60. Ibid. v.I, 155.
    61. Ibid. v.II, 246-7.
    62. Ibid. II, 276.
    63. Cobban Edmund Burke and the Revolt Against
the Eighteenth Century 266.
    64. Colloquies I, 35.
    65. The Book of the Church 2v. (1824) I, 1.
    66. Colloquies I, 133.
    67. Ibid. I, 27-8.
    68. Ibid. I. 60.

69. Burke Reflections on the Revolution in France 172-3.
70. See below 52 et. seq.
71. Colloquies II, 35-6.
72. Ibid. I, 154.
73. Ibid. II, 36.
74. Ibid. II, 318.   Chandler says that in the Colloquies Southey criticized Protestant nunneries along with the national debt and the plague: Chandler 108.
75. Colloquies II, 327.
76. Ibid. I, 88.
77. Qu. R.W. Chambers Thomas More (1976) 258.
78. The Book of the Church I, 53-4.
79. Ibid. I, 284.
80. Ibid. I, 2.
81. Ibid. I, 289.
82. Colloquies I, 156.
83. Qu. Geoffrey Carnall Robert Southey (a British Council pamphlet, 1964) 9.
84. Robert Southey: Journals of a Residence in Portugal 1800-1801 and a Visit to France 1838 ed. Adolfo Cabral (Oxford at the Clarendon Press 1960) 99-100.
85. Colloquies I, 155.
86. The Life and Correspondence of the Late Robert Southey 6v. ed. Charles Cuthbert Southey (1850) v.II, 72; letter 23.5.1800.
87. The Poetical Works of Robert Southey (1838-40) 73. Further refs. to this ed. henceforth cited in the text.
88. On his conservatism and radicalism see John W. Osborne William Cobbett (New York, 1966) chs. II, III, and James Sambrook William Cobbett (1973) Chs. III, IX.
89. Cobbett's History in 2v. (1829) originally pub. in monthly parts, 1824-6.
90. Williams Culture and Society 1780-1950 (Harmondsworth, 1971) 37-8.
91. Chandler 123.
92. History II parag. 37. (No pagination.)
93. Ibid. II parag. 10.
94. Ibid. I parag. 4.
95. Ibid. II parag. 15; cf. ibid. I parag. 155.
96. Ibid. II parag. 12.
97. Ibid. II parags. 12-13.
98. Ibid. I parags. 121-3.
99. Culture and Society 37.
100. Cf. Osborne William Cobbett 209 and Sambrook William Cobbett 139.
101. Cobbett's Weekly Political Register 28.Feb.

1829 col. 257.
    102. See, eg., Brendon Hurrell Froude and the
Oxford Movement xv-xvi.
    103. Political Register 28. Feb. 1829 col.257.
    104. Chandler 64.
    105. Political Register 21 Sept. 1822 col. 342.
    106. Thirteen Sermons (1822) No.2, 26-7.
    107. Osborne William Cobbett 196.
    108. Political Register 15 Feb.1834 col. 386.
    109. See DNB, Airedale in ancient times ... and
other Poems (1825), Poems by John Nicholson ed.
John James 2nd. ed. (Bingley, 1876).
    110. Cf. Basil Willey The Seventeenth-Century
Background (1957) 298; and see 305-6.
    111. See Ernest de Selincourt ed. Letters of
William and Dorothy Wordsworth. The Later Years
(Oxford,1939) 1006-7; letter 21 Feb.1840.
    112. Thomas Hutchinson ed. (new ed. revised by
E. de Selincourt) Wordsworth : Poetical Works (1969)
721. Henceforth cited as Poetical Works.
    113. Letters of William and Dorothy Wordsworth.
The Later Years 209-210; 11.6.1825.
    114. Poetical Works, The Excursion VI, 1.34.
    115. "Essay, Supplementary to the Preface" of
2nd.ed. Lyrical Ballads, Poetical Works 749.
    116. Poetical Works, The Prelude Bk.V, 11.
448-455, 11. 496-507, Bk. VII, 1.455.
    117. Ibid. The Prelude Bk. V. 11. 504-507.
    118. Letters of William and Dorothy Wordsworth.
The Later Years 166.
    119. Lives of the English Saints (1901) IV,355.
    120. Ibid. 355-6.
    121. Loc. cit. 356.
    122. Cf. Southey quoting Whitaker: above 52.
    123. See n. 129 below.
    124. Apart from his genuine duality, his
characteristic inconsistency makes evaluation of his
real beliefs difficult: cf. Raymond Dexter Havens
The Mind of a Poet (Baltimore, 1941) I, 197.
    125. Fairchild III, 230.
    126. "Inside of King's College Chapel,
Cambridge".
    127. "At Sea Off the Isle of Man".
    128. M.H. Abrams points out that in The
Prelude imagination usurps the role of Christ as
redeemer : Natural Supernaturalism (New York,1971)119.
    129. "Essay, Supplementary to the Preface" of
the 2nd.ed.of Lyrical Ballads, Poetical Works 744.
    130. For Wordsworth, medieval English Cathol-
icism was inferior to seventeenth-century Anglicanism; yet he told Kenelm Digby that had he lived in

an earlier age he would have felt the need of and
obeyed "that scorned, most ancient creed" : see
Bernard Holland Memoir of Kenelm Henry Digby (1919)
83.

131. Cf. Edith C. Batho The Later Wordsworth
(New York, 1963) 296-7. According to Wallace K.
Ferguson, in The Renaissance in Historical Thought
(Cambridge Mass., 1948) 297-300, the continental
Romantic historians were the first to rediscover St.
Francis.

132. B.W. Martin "Wordsworth, Faber, and Keble"
RES n.s. XXVI (1975) 436-442.

133. Pub. in book form 1844.

134. The Correspondence of Henry Crabb
Robinson with the Wordsworth Circle ed. Edith J.
Morley (Oxford at the Clarendon Press, 1927) II,
579-80.

135. Sheridan Gilley "Charles Butler and
Robert Southey's Book of the Church"; an unpublished
paper, supplied by the author, and given at the 1976
meeting of the American Catholic Historical Association.

136. See also The Excursion Bk.VI,ll.6-16. He
notes that Southey has similar views: Poetical Works
721, n. to 329.

137. "Stanzas Suggested in a Steamboat Off
Saint Bees' Heads" ll. 145-8, and "Reflections" ll.
13-14.

Chapter III

ANTI-MEDIEVALISM: 1750-1900

> The superstition of science scoffs at the
> superstition of faith.
>
>   J.A. Froude "The Lives of the Saints"

Since the sixteenth century there was in Britain
an intense dislike of the Roman Catholic Church and
all its works, which was not based solely on an
objective review of that Church's activities. The
causes of anti-Catholicism were much the same as
those of anti-medievalism, by which term is meant
those who held up the medieval Church to special
ridicule and contempt. The nineteenth-century anti-
medievalists constructed a pseudo-historical view
every bit as partizan, rhetorical and mythical as
that of the medievalists; a view frequently designed
to glorify the modern age by blackening that which
preceded it, and often intended to counter the work
of Catholic sympathizers by showing how wicked Catholicism was when given full rein in its heyday.
Since anti-medievalism is the reverse of the medievalist dialectic, an understanding of its origins
and arguments clarifies religious medievalism by
contrast, and shows what a remarkable phenomenon
medievalism was by demonstrating the strength and
durability of that against which it rebelled.
Speaking in 1887 of the hatred of monasteries - which
was especially pronounced - Francis Gasquet said the
facts against them "are well known and have been
repeated, improved on and emphasized for three
centuries and a half, whilst that there is anything
to say on the other hand for the monks, has been
little recognized even by those who would be naturally predisposed in their favour".[1] Ignorance reinforced propaganda so powerfully that such attitudes
continued well into the twentieth century. Anti-

medievalism was part of the very fibre of the establishment, as is shown by the granting of university
chairs to such as Kingsley, Thomas Arnold and J.A.
Froude.

Enlightenment Foundations : Rationalism and Progressivism

Those who sought comfort, support and expression
for their assumptions and prejudices in this myth
included rationalists, humanists, naturalists,
utilitarians, Protestants, Whigs, progressivists,
classicists, nationalists, socialists and atheists -
and even the occasional Catholic. Even sex was an
operative factor. The anti-medievalists were
generally united in proclaiming the modern age as an
age of common sense, based on reason and Protestant
righteousness, an age which constantly progressed by
throwing off more and more completely the shackles
of the Middle Ages. Anti-medievalism had its fair
share of hypocrisy, on the national level, to match
the dichotomies of medievalism. That the medieval
Church - and Catholicism at large - was to some
extent a scapegoat is unprovable, but almost certainly true : the sins of the British nation were heaped
on alien Catholicism. A series of observable ironies
supports the scapegoat theory : the anti-medievalists
were complacent about the age, when they had no cause
to be, for an increasingly secular nation accused the
medieval Church of worldliness; Anglicans, whose
Church was decaying, accused it of gross corruption
and immorality; an increasingly materialist society
called its sacramentalism and externalism non-spirit-
ual,and so forth. The anti-medievalists were
presenting a close approximation of their own society
in their vision of the Middle Ages : perhaps they
were exorcizing themselves by attacking this
doppelgänger.
Progressivism was a child of the Enlightenment,
and a keystone in the anti-medievalist edifice.
Strengthened by historicism, with its belief in the
constructive flow of history, progressivism arose
from the Enlightenment faith in the transforming and
redemptive power of reason. Out of this developed a
Romantic progressivism, which would not allow
Romantics to regress to the Middle Ages,[2] a fact
which may help to account for the dearth of religious
medievalism in English Romanticism. Progressivism
was by its nature anti-medieval, and in the sense
that it laid stress on the virtues of man rather than
on the saving power of Christ, and was determinist,

69

it was also anti-Catholic. Progressivism was the
Whig view of history, and as such proclaimed the
present as the crowning of all past progressive
efforts, a present which was therefore superior to
any past age. The prognosis for man's welfare was
correspondingly optimistic, and it was so because of
the widespread romantic faith in man. (In one sense,
calling faith in man "romantic" is not entirely
satisfactory, since the classicists of the eighteenth
century also had such a faith; so when we say that
faith in man is romantic, we must mean that faith in
man from 1750-on became more pronounced and more
radical in its primitivism.) The resulting opposition between man and God was not a comfortable
phenomenon in a nominally Christian society. The
solution, however subconscious it may have been at
the time, was to tend to reconcile disparates, or at
least to blur distinctions, by identifying God more
and more directly with man and his world. Others
failed to build on this Enlightenment faith in man,
and embraced Catholicism or moved towards it, thereby splitting the romantic ranks, although both
parties were still attracted to transcendence, one
finding it primarily in man, the other primarily in
God. Walter Houghton makes kindred observations in
his essay on "The Issue Between Kingsley and Newman",
where he says that, due to the prestige of science,
the eighteenth-century "mechanical" view of nature
lived on into the nineteenth century, and that the
Victorian period saw not only the survival of faith
in human nature, but its flourishing; so that the
Victorians looked forward to a better future. The
liberals, he says, welcomed this secular progressivism, while clinging to the religious attitude : they
resolved the tension by sanctifying the natural
order.

> The old dichotomies of Christian thought -
> the natural and the supernatural, the human
> and the divine, the unconverted and the
> converted, the city of man and the city of
> God - all of them conveniently disappeared,
> merged together in what Carlyle called the
> natural-supernatural order.[3]

Progressivism was a type of natural supernaturalism
because it connoted the potential divinity of man. It
is interesting that Houghton should mention liberals,
for it was indeed the Whigs who believed in infinite
progress and interpreted history as evidence of this
notion. Herbert Butterfield described and criticized

this fallacy in The Whig Interpretation of History (1931), in which progressivists were judged to be determinist or Benthamite where they were not Protestant : they were also anti-Catholic (while supporting Emancipation), anti-medieval and inclined to regard themselves as moral law-givers. In every way they were enemies to religious medievalism, particularly in their perfectibilism, believing man could be perfected through social action (eg. education), government, natural development, science or other means.[4] Faith or lack of faith in man partly explains the political alignments of medievalists and anti-medievalists : since the medievalists distrusted man, they wanted to lay on him the constraints of authority and tradition, so they were almost always conservative. The Whigs assumed that since Protestants were always progressive, Catholics, in opposing them, were always reactionary, fighting for the past,[5] and doubtless this assumption hardened differences.

The eighteenth-century inheritance was a twofold contempt : for the Middle Ages, which originated in the Renaissance, and for Catholicism, which started with the Protestant histories of the sixteenth and seventeenth centuries.[6] Rationalism and Protestantism gave support to each other's assumptions about Catholicism. Medieval ignorance, barbarism and superstition became a byword, it being assumed that such qualities were the moral defects of a corrupt system; and precept was matched by the practice of history. The appeal of Voltaire, Hume, Robertson and Gibbon was primarily to taste and reason, which involved ideals of tolerance, public order, wealth and material comfort. By and large, they were anti-religious. They rejected all legends and miracles on the grounds that human nature and natural law were invariable, and detested Gothic art, scholastic philosophy, ecclesiasticism and the whole milieu of the medieval religion.[7] This position was typified by the German Lutheran rationalist John Lawrence Mosheim (1693 or 4-1755), whose Ecclesiastical History, translated into English in 1756 (and then regularly printed up to the 1840s),[8] was highly valued in England and plainly a part of the period's mental fabric; for its ideas were propagated or attacked by William Robertson, Joseph Berington, Charles Butler, Coleridge, Southey, Wordsworth, Newman, S.R, Maitland[9] and, most importantly, Gibbon. Mosheim was, in fact, highly significant as the fountain-head of articulated anti-medievalism as inherited by the nineteenth century.

Mosheim attacked every department of medieval
Christianity which strayed from Christianity's true
aim : "to render mankind truly and rationally FREE"[10]
St. Anselm was laudable because he "maintained that
most noble and natural connexion of FAITH with REAS-
ON,and of RELIGION with PHILOSOPHY"(321).But the age
was dark, ignorant and barbarous : even the learning
of the monks was useless (12); usually missionaries
were base (4-5, 360-1), the hierarchy ignorant and
indolent (13), the clergy ambitious, avaricious,
fraudulent, intolerably proud, supercilious and given
to "many other vices still more enormous" (17), the
monks the embodiment of "pharisaical affectation"
(18), the chief end of the papacy - the Pope is the
"Roman druid" - domination (63), and the crusades
were wholly evil (239-243), not least because they
augmented the authority of Rome and enriched churches
and monasteries. Catholic forms - images, relics,
pilgrimages, rituals - sinned against the classical,
rationalist, Protestant feel for simplicity (80). For
about 800 years, until the Reformation, "religion lay
expiring under a motley and enormous heap of superstitious inventions" (20). The very vocabulary is
witness to the revitalizing of the anti-Catholic
myth, that Catholicism was not Christian : "gross
ignorance", "odious frauds", "flagitious crimes",
"corruption", "scandalous" (405), "ludicrous pomp",
"gaudy worship", "vain ceremonies", "captious philosophy" (418-19). This kind of pabulum provided the
vast majority of the educated with their thought
categories and vocabulary - a vocabulary of moral
condemnation current throughout the nineteenth
century.
As R.G. Collingwood has commented, "the
historical outlook of the Enlightenment was not
genuinely historical; in its main motive it was
polemical and anti-historical".[11] The Enlightenment
historian wrote history on the basis of cultural,
political, and, sometimes, metaphysical assumptions.
William Robertson, for example, in 1769 condemned the
medieval notion of an intervening god, because,
according to his own mechanistic world-view, it
distracted the mind from contemplating the "regular
progress and execution of a general plan".[12] He
especially condemned papal authority and jurisdiction, which were always an interefering usurpation,
constructed on mass credulity and superstition.[13]
Edward Gibbon was, however, the chief exponent
of rationalist, polemicist history. Mosheim was his
chief authority for medieval ecclesiastical history[14]
and as his Decline and Fall of the Roman Empire

(1776-88) "became an active moral force in Victorian England",[15] so Mosheim's version of history came to be further disseminated and accepted. The Decline and Fall is profoundly significant both because it appeared to give definitive sanction to the received Protestant tradition of history - thus giving the establishment its view of things medieval in supposedly unassailable form - and because it was "the most total synthesis of the beliefs and attitudes of his age".[16] For Gibbon, the interregnum between classicism and its revival was a period of unrelieved gloom politically, culturally and spiritually, so that his real subject was the decline and fall of reason, his view of the fall of the Roman Empire being "the triumph of barbarism and Christianity", by which he meant "unreason and superstition". His nominal Low Church Protestantism made him anti-Catholic, while his rationalism made him essentially anti-religious![17] Opposed to religious enthusiasm, he particularly despised reverence for saints, relics and images, and crusades, marianism, ritualism and monasticism : his favourite word in this department being "fanaticism".

His most virulent and extended criticism is reserved for monastic institutions : "credulity and submission" destroyed mental freedom in them; the taste and appearance of monks was bad; they were responsible for the collapse of the empire; they were degenerate and greedy, yet, he says (having it both ways), the ascetics, because inspired by "the savage enthusiasm which represents man as a criminal, and God as a tyrant", committed the social crime of renouncing the "business and the pleasures of the age".[18] Monastic learning only darkened the cloud of superstition (XXXVII, 514), while monkish visions were but the "illusions of distempered fanaticism" (XXXVII, 516). Monks especially sinned against the eighteenth-century gospel of the social life (XXXVII, 508-16). The "worship of saints and relics" only corrupted the "pure and perfect simplicity of the Christian model" (XXVIII, 423) and "extinguished the light of history and of reason" (XXVIII, 423). Catholic externality was wrong because it reduced religion to the "standard of the imagination" to "affect the senses of the vulgar" (XXVIII, 425). His excellent rhetoric does not disguise the fact that he is writing polemics rather than history, a fact which is elucidated by his inconsistency : he is too unwilling to trust the "suspicious materials of ecclesiastical history" (XV, 143), while too willing to credit the equally, though contradictorily, partisan chronicles of historians like Zosimus and Eunapius.

73

And he argues that Christians were guilty of in-
activity and activity, servility and authoritarian-
ism, pusillanimity and valour, unmilitariness and
militariness.[19] His unfairness provoked a criticism[20] fired by the increasing devotion to sensibility, the Gothic and the numinous.
     Some eighteenth and nineteenth-century Catholics
were drawn to rationalism or classicism, and were
indifferent, or even antagonistic, to the medieval
Church. The Cisalpines (or Old Catholics) sought to
placate the English by emphasizing Catholic rationalism and loyalty. They were Whiggish, enthusiastic
and constitutionalists, self-consciously liberal in
religion, ecclesiastically democratic and anti-
medievalist. For example, the case of the Catholic
priest Joseph Berington (1746-1827) shows that a
rationalist outlook and Protestantism were not
exclusive partners, that anti-medievalism was
possible in a Catholic : and this would appear to
support the association between romanticism and
religious medievalism by showing that an association
between medievalism and Catholicism was not necessary. In works like Abeillard and Heloisa (1787), The
History of the Papal Power,[21] and A Literary History
of the Middle Ages (1814), he regurgitates Mosheim
and Gibbon, tracing the "progress of the human mind
through darkness into light",[22] and always looking to
"the lamp of science".[23] He even has to admit that
the Protestant Warton is more favourable to the monks
than he.[24] Even in more secure times, Catholics
were cool towards the Middle Ages, although the
balance of coolness shifted from the Cisalpines to
the Ultramontanes : Wiseman, for example, spoke in
1855 of "the mediaeval frostwork which late years
have deposited round English Catholic affections",
and which, he was glad to say, his novel Fabiola was
helping to undo.[25] Clearly one must view with reserve the assertion that later eighteenth-century
historians "overcame the opposition to the Middle
Ages and ... laid the foundation for the modern
appreciation of them".[26]

Romanticism: Enlightenment Survival

     This attitude has numerous literary examples
throughout the sensibilitarian and Romantic periods.
The dominant anti-medievalist tradition permeates
even medievalists such as Thomas Warton : "Written
at Vale-royal Abbey in Cheshire" (1777) gives the
stock image of the light of reason triumphing over
the dark spirit of the Middle Ages, an image which

recurs in the young Wordsworth's "Lines Written as a
School Exercise at Hawkeshead" (1784-5), where
"Science" banishes "Superstition".[27] Percy attacks
medieval religious culture, superstition and
prejudice,[28] while the nationalist objections emerge
in Hurd, who attacks the papacy,[29] and Warton, who
vilifies the "arbitrary encroachments of the court
of Rome" and the "intolerable bondage of papal
oppression".[30] The Whig version of history can be
seen in William Shenstone's "Ruined Abbey; or, The
Effects of Superstition",[31] which pictures the
English kings doing battle with the foreign power of
Rome, and displays Catholicism as a "dire disease"
which "seiz'd mankind", with "lawless" and
"murderous" priests, who were recognizable by their
paunches distended with the spoils of their flocks.
When the Reformation came, "Each angry friar/Crawl'd
from his bedded strumpet", and Henry VIII allied
himself with "reason, courage, learning", and put an
end to such wickedness. "Roman magic" was a foe to
British "Truth", "vows", "oaths" and the mutually
beneficial pact between sovereign and subject. Albion
is the pure victor over Roman darkness.

Thomas Love Peacock was aware of some of the
shortcomings of this type of view, but as a classicist, atheist and utilitarian he had no liking for the
medievalists. Nightmare Abbey (1818) mocks the
Gothic cult, caricaturing Coleridge as Mr. Flosky,
who believes that the

> overthrow of the feudal fortress of tyranny
> and superstition was the greatest calamity
> that had ever befallen mankind; and that
> their only hope now was to rake the rubbish
> together, and rebuild it without any of
> those loopholes by which the light had
> originally crept in.[32]

In Crotchet Castle (1831), Mr. Chainmail, the
medievalist, is the butt of Peacock's satire for his
romantic utopianism : "he is deep in monkish literature, and holds that the best state of society was
that of the twelfth century, when nothing was going
forward but fighting, feasting, and praying".[33]
When Mr. Chainmail expresses preference for the
religious spirit of the twelfth century over the
"commercial spirit", Mr. MacQuedy, the "political
economist" and antithesis of Mr. Chainmail, answers
that the "lazy monks and beggarly friars" were "more
occupied with taking than giving", made everybody
miserable "with fastings, and penances, and other

such trash" and "took very unbecoming liberties with
those [wives] of honester men".[34] The balance of
Peacock's sympathy was with MacQuedy, who certainly
represented the majority view. This also exemplifies
the almost universal assumption that Catholic celibates were sexually dishonest and utterly lascivious.
    Anti-medievalism was also promoted by the major
Romantics such as Southey and Coleridge.[35] What Sir
Walter Scott's readers thought he said about the
Middle Ages should not be allowed to obscure his
real position. It has long been recognized that he
was something of an Augustan,[36] and according to A.O.
J. Cockshut, he assumed Gibbon's general historical
view.[37] He rejected the attempt to renew the
"absurdities" of the medieval faith, and believed
that old monasteries, having gained by virtue of
antiquity the power of impressing awe and devotion,
were in fact originally monuments to superstitious
devotion and the pride of abbots.[38] He regarded
Catholicism as a "mean and depriving superstition",
hoped that, if unopposed, it would "sink into dust
with all its absurd ritual and solemnities", and expressed the desire to see "the old Lady of Babylon's
mouth stopd".[39]
    Chapter II of Ivanhoe (1820) depicts the Prior
of the Cistercian Abbey of Jorvaulx not as a
paradigm of self-denying piety, but as a proud and
epicurean voluptuary, covering his multitude of sins
with charity and impressing the ignorant with little
learning. So low are ecclesiastical standards that
the Prior's character is well-regarded. Scott's
description is ironically Gibbonian, the tone neither
sentimental nor reverential, but witty and judicious.
Archbishop Baldwin in The Betrothed (1825) and Prior
Anselm in The Fair Maid of Perth (1828) are similar
characters, and their similarity argues that Scott's
attitude to the medieval Church, especially as an
institution, was hostile.[40] Their virtues are not
spiritual but worldly, and as such, they are emblems
of what was believed to have been a basically secular
institution masquerading as a religious one.
    Other anti-medievalists of the early nineteenth
century include John Sterling, Mill and Macaulay.
Sterling judged that chivalry had been corrupted by
Catholicism, and, interestingly, supposed that
Kenelm Henry Digby's chivalric enthusiasm was then,
in 1829, unique because discredited.[41] His essay on
Wycliffe (1829)[42] rejects Lingard's "disgraceful"
and "pitiable" account of the fourteenth-century
reformers, and takes the pro-Waldensian line established by Mosheim, developed by Milner and celebrated

76

by the religious Independent Robert Vaughan in his
Life of Wycliffe (1828), which last Sterling regards
as the best account. Sterling likes Wycliffe's
Erastianism, emphasis on conscience and his reason-
ableness, which are opposed to Catholic "worldly
ambition". The attacks of Sterling and Southey on
Lingard illustrate the difficulties then involved in
challenging the general faith in the received
historical tradition: the high quality of Lingard's
History was not a factor to be seriously considered.
The rationalist and utilitarian John Stuart Mill also
did not wish to see the majority placed under the
despotism of the aristocracy or hierarchy as in the
Middle Ages.[43] Macaulay represents the Whig progressivist, with his dictum that "the history of England
is emphatically the history of progress".[44] For him,
twelfth-century society was utterly "miserable", the
"most debasing and cruel superstition exercising
boundless dominion over the most elevated and
benevolent minds", and he insists that "nothing is
so interesting and delightful as to contemplate the
steps by which ... the England of crusaders, monks,
schoolmen ... became ... the classic ground of
liberty and philosophy, the school of all knowledge,
the mart of all trade".[45] In 1830 he further
insisted that, in contrast to the Middle Ages, his
own was "the most enlightened generation of the most
enlightened people that ever existed".[46] His
complacency is largely predicated on his faith in the
"natural tendency of the human intellect to truth,
and ... the natural tendency of society to improvement".[47] This faith was, of course, denied by the
medievalists.
      The holders of this type of view were satirized
by Neale and Disraeli. Neale's character Practicus,
who believed "you cannot stop the onward progress of
rational improvement", was concerned with financial
wastage in the Middle Ages : in the "dark ages"
money was wasted on cathedrals, whereas now its use
leads to a "more public spirit" and rapid and grand
"improvements",such as "railroads"; and charity is
now given to hospitals, whereas it used to be given
to "a pack of idle monks". Neale thinks that such
is the opinion of "most of the so-called philosophers
of the day".[48] Disraeli puts into the mouth of Mme.
Carolina an ironic echo of Burke :

      the age of chivalry is past; and very
      fortunate that it is. What resources
      could they have had in the age of chivalry?
      an age without either moral or experimental

philosophy; an age in which they were
equally ignorant of the doctrine of
association of ideas, and of the doctrine
of electricity; and when they were as
devoid of a knowledge of the incalculable
powers of the human mind as of the incalculable powers of steam![49]

It would seem that the medievalists regarded the
anti-medievalists as materialists, and Macaulay's
descriptions of the qualities of progress would seem
to bear this out.

Victorians : Enlightenment Revival

The 1840s saw a significant strengthening of the
position of English Catholics; but this did not
imply any greater love for them on behalf of non-
Catholics. Growth in the Catholic body happened in
spite of the establishment, rather than because of
it : Emancipation had been almost as restricting as
it had been emancipating; and the result of this
growth was "a social antagonism to Catholicism far
greater than had existed in penal days".[50] Anti-
Catholic literature,a mixture of "biblical fundamen-
talism,apocalyptic prophecy and offensive apologetic,
manifesting attitudes of incredulity and fear ...
with occasional suggestions of pornography",[51]
became more popular at this time.
Underlying Protestant rhetoric was the notion
that Catholics - and this includes Tractarians -
were not Christians, a point which could forcibly be
made by pointing to the heathenism of medieval
Catholicism. The Catholic response was undercut by
another myth, that of Catholic Jesuitical sophistry
and lying hypocrisy : if Catholics argued their case,
they were seen as casuistical deceivers; and when
they remained silent, in accordance with the doctrine
of reserve, they were accused of plotting in secret,
and their discretion was called lying. It was also
supposed that a full-scale Romish attack on Britain
was underway. It is surprising that any Catholic
progress was made, in the face of the generally
accepted view, described by Newman, that the Catholic
Church was "too absurd to be inquired into, and too
corrupt to be defended, and too dangerous to be
treated with equity and fair dealing".[52] For all
this, the Middle Ages provided ample evidence. It
was feared, moreover, that Catholics - quintessentially represented by Jesuits - were good, as

Macaulay expressed it, at "stealing away the hearts
of the young".[53] Heine believed that Jesuits were
behind a plot to lure German youth to their ruin
through medievalism.[54] In England, Charles Kingsley
also thought medievalism was tempting the young.[55]
Robert Montgomery's poetry was highly respected and
very popular,[56] and Luther (1842) typifies the
nationalist anti-Catholicism, anti-medievalism and
anti-Tractarianism of the period. He believed that
"swarms of unsuspected emissaries of Popery" were
insinuating themselves into families and "every
social circle", and "working indefatigably" against
the "RELIGION, LIBERTIES, AND PROPERTY OF ENGLAND" by
means of "historical perversions, and romantic tales,
and by decoying the thoughtless and inexperienced to
attend the imposing formalities of Popish worship".[57]
He was an Erastian, believing with Southey that co-
operation of Church and State was vital for the
kingdom's health, and a providentialist, believing
that England, as the new Jerusalem - her Constitution
the Ark of the Covenant - had been made mighty by God
in return for faithful and truly Catholic service.
Rome was, by contrast, a mere alien sect, intent on
destroying England's happy unity.[58] One may suppose
this was a common view.
     Another writer who substantially anticipated
Kingsley was Henry Rogers (1806-77), a Christian
apologist and Nonconformist man of letters, with an
eighteenth-century turn of mind,[59] who expressed his
anti-medievalism in an article called "Recent Developments of Puseyism". He thought Mosheim "candid",
and relied on Gibbon, while condemning Newman's
defence of medieval miracles and advocacy of the
medieval religious system, with its monasticism,
pilgrimages and superstitions.[60] While conceding
the "poetical and picturesque" aspects of the Middle
Ages, he condemns their utilization as propaganda as
an attempt to sway the minds of "thousands of the
young, the imaginative, and the ardent". It would
seem from this that medievalism was having some
proselytizing success. He singles out The Lives of
the Saints, edited by Newman, as particularly
responsible,[61] and condemns all those medieval things
over which romantics and Catholics have diffused "the
awe of a 'Divine presence'" : "Gothic arches", chant,
monasticism, hermits, bells, pilgrimages. He quotes
the Camden Society editor on the "depravation of the
Christian religion by the means of saint worship"
found in The Chronicle of Jocelin of Brakelond, and
regards the religious system therein illustrated as
a "sham" and "effete". He also attacks "the more

dangerous nonsense of a widely diffused popular
literature" - by which he seems to mean John Mason
Neale's ballads - for it perverts historical truth,
is uncharitable and bigoted. The alternative facing
the public is a return to the "darkness and superstitions of the Middle Ages", or a strengthening of
Protestant principles of which he sees signs.[62]
     One can hardly disagree with Lord Acton's asse-
ssment of Charles Kingsley as "a focus of various
views and doctrines that pervade society";[63] or with
Martin's view, that"in his answers to the questions
which exercised the Victorians, we hear the tones and
see the reactions of a mass of educated upper-middle-
class men living a century ago".[64] Kingsley imbibed
the spirit of the age and regurgitated it in highly
desirable, concentrated form, thereby reinforcing the
assumptions of a society which needed reassurance.
Since he embodied the essentially materialist version
of Christianity espoused by the bourgeoisie, his
religious views are extremely significant. In
essence, he was a modernist and a materialist, and
as such hated the Middle Ages and the spirituality of
medieval religion : "we must," he said,

> make friends of the Mammon of unrighteous-
> ness. It is the new commercial aristocracy;
> it is the scientific go-a-head-ism of the day
> which must save us, and which we must save.
> We have licked the feet of the feudal arist-
> ocrats for centuries, and see whither they
> have brought us, or let us bring ourselves.[65]

"My whole heart is set," he emphasized, "not on
retrogression ... but on progression", and "progression" means democracy (LM I, 141); and though he
could sympathize with "the ecclesiologists, and the
young Englanders", their truth was dead, and he would
"gently withdraw the corpse from the mourners, and
present to them the same spirit of their creed,
clothed in a fresh form to suit the present exigencies of the time" (LM I, 142), that form being
humanistic, science-based, middle-class democracy.
The Church had to attach itself to modernism to
Christianize it (LM I, 141), for otherwise "religion,
like a rootless plant, may be brushed away" in the
threatening crisis (LM I, 142). Compromise with
modernism was his solution, and religious medievalism
was anything but such a compromise. But Kingsley
does not surrender to the compromise - he embraces
it, for the ending of the present order is the will
of God, just as was the ending of the medieval

Catholic order (LM I, 143). So he sets himself to
abolish, on behalf of the Whig spirit, the distinction between natural and supernatural, to promote
naturalism (the identification of the divine will
with natural law and all its consequences),[66] and to
preach the gospel of natural supernaturalism, thereby
opposing Christian orthodoxy epitomized by Newman.[67]
He also illustrates the Fairchildean thesis of
Evangelicalism decayed into "the religion of the
heart", tainted by pantheism and having - for a
Christian - overmuch faith in man and an undiscrim-
inating acceptance of the world.
    Kingsley admires chivalry on the grounds that it
concurs with the "human Christianity" of the Bible
(LM II, 213), and the belief that the only feasible
foundation is "Jesus Christ - THE MAN";[68] and he
says, what is "most human" is "most divine" (LM I,
431), that the "essential idea of Protestantism is
the dignity and divinity of man as God made him!"[69]
Such is Kingsley's homocentricity, which encourages
in him a delight in modern endeavour. A visit to the
Great Exhibition led him to comment that if medievals
could see nineteenth-century progress, they would
have "proofs of the kingdom of god, realizations of
the gifts which Christ received for men" greater
than those miracles which they mistook as proofs (LM
I, 280-1). In Yeast he says, through Lancelot Smith,
writing to his Catholic cousin, "take you the
[Romish] Sanctity, and give me the [English] Civilization!"; for he prefers "the political economist,
the sanitary reformer, the engineer" to "saints and
virgins, relics and miracles".[70] Another striking
phrase from Yeast is, "a truly consistent and logical
Protestant - and therefore a Materialist".[71] He was
a meliorist according to Howard R. Murphy's
definition of the word :

        'meliorism' refers to the notion ... that
        the life of man on this earth both can and
        should be progressively improved through a
        sustained application of human effort and
        intelligence. Because it served as a sub-
        stitute for the otherworldly - salvation
        motif that has so dominated the history of
        Christianity, it tended to bring Christian-
        ity itself into question, and to put all
        forms of orthodoxy on trial.[72]

It is most pertinent that Murphy sees the meliorist
bias of the early Victorian period as the prime
specific instigator of the attack on orthodoxy,

giving Francis Newman, George Eliot and J.A. Froude
(significantly of Kingsley's circle) as evidence of
his thesis.
      Against this, Kingsley set the attitude of St.
Francis of Assisi, which he identified with the whole
medieval outlook. He thought the saint "unmanly,
superstitious" and generally theologically defective
from his allegedly incorrect view of man (LM I, 257),
which was that

> man is not a spirit necessarily embodied in,
> and expressed by an animal; but a spirit
> accidentally connected with, and burdened by
> an animal. ... The ideal of man, therefore,
> is to deny, not himself, but the animal part
> which is not himself, and to strive after a
> non-human or angelic state.

This view leads to "aristocratic exclusiveness; to
absolute hatred of anything which looked like a
gospel for the merely human masses", to worship of
intellect, to polytheism, image worship, theurgy,
miracle-working and finally "utter scepticism".
This syndrome is evident in "the mediaeval Church,
between the eleventh and sixteenth century", the
fault being the theory "which made an angel the ideal
of man, and therefore celibacy his highest state" (LM
I, 256-7). Celibacy was anti-human, and therefore
anti-Christian, as well as being anti-democratic:when
the medieval clergy were not wickedly lascivious,
they were wickedly celibate. In the Introduction to
his unpublished Life of St. Elizabeth, he says he
rejected medieval beliefs because their Manichaeism
(ie. their rejection of the physical world) struck
at marriage; and his study of medieval theology told
him "the battle was for life or death to Love".[73]
The Introduction shows that the alternative in his
mind before marriage was between Popery, celibacy
and monasticism, and marriage, so that in accepting
marriage he necessarily rejected the others as life-
denying (or sex-denying) things. Also on the sexual
theme, he castigated Catholicism as effeminate,
believing that Christianity should be manly. Indeed,
sex was such an all-embracing thing for him that even
his nationalism and racism, which also stimulated his
anti-Catholicism, were sexually inspired : since the
Anglo-Saxons, "a female race", had been impregnated
by "the great male race, - the Norse" (LM I, 201),
the English had had the correct proportions of male
and female, and could not, therefore,tolerate the
intrusion of an effeminate Latin Church. Medieval

monasticism typified this effeminacy, for it was
"essentially a feminine life", wherein men resorted
to "the weapons of crafty, ambitious, and unprincip-
led women" (LM II, 212-13).

Kingsley was not alone in regarding St. Francis
as a malign influence. Enlightenment writers did not
understand him, and what they did not understand they
ridiculed. For example, John Langhorne (1735-79) saw
St. Francis's "enthusiasm" as an offence against
"pure religion" and reason.[74] Anyone who was thought
to especially embody Catholicism, such as this saint,
was presumed to be fit for scorn; so when Southey
visited the Franciscan establishment in Lisbon in
1795-6, he was repelled by the saint's life, and was
always convinced that he was either a "madman or
imposter".[75] The Whig historian Henry Hallam decided
that he was mad, though a "harmless enthusiast, pious
and sincere".[76] This view was upheld in the Victorian period : Charles Reade described him as having
"the folly without the poetry" of Diogenes,[77] while
the lawyer and bureaucrat James Stephen gave a
standard, patronizing, sardonic account of him in a
review article, chiding him for hallucinating and
lacking filial obedience, and ridiculing the recorded
miracles, although conceding that the Franciscans
protected the weak from tyranny.[78] Kingsley, with
his pronounced duality, disliked Stephen's effort but
hated Alban Butler's account, despized Francis's
asceticism, which he believed infected the medieval
Church with unmanliness and superstition,[79] yet in
1845 confessed, "I sometimes long for a St. Francis
... to lay hold of one's will, soul, and body, and
coax ... one along some definite path of doctrine
and labour".[80] Indeed, he revered him.[81]

It is worth emphasizing, since it represents a
general truth, that even the most hardened anti-
medievalists, like Kingsley, harboured a "soft spot"
for their beleaguered enemy. In Kingsley's later
writings, including his book on The Hermits (1868),
there is a hint of penitence about his earlier
attitude to the medieval Church - at least, the early
medieval Church, for he realized that the preceding
generation's contempt for it had been "unjust", that
"in this age, as in every other age of materialism
and practical atheism, a revulsion in favour of
superstition [in this case Catholicism] is at hand".[82]
He would not embrace "superstition", but he was
deeply attracted by its language, its symbols, its
embodiments, [83] and by 1864 he even managed to look
favourably on legends of saints, because they were
morally instructive,[84] legends which he valued more

than theology because they speak of an unseen world
with "visible things, with passion manifested in
action".[85] He valued the medieval religion for its
ability to communicate with the "religious
imagination" : early-medieval celibacy was good
because it communicated something of the gospel
message to the heathen, in the shape of a living
symbol.[86] In this field, as in others, he both
summed up his age and encouraged it to be more like
itself.

Kingsley, aware of the widespread fear that
Popery threatened to become the popular religion of
England,[87] decided to fight with every means available "all superstitions about 'the good old times,'
and fancies that they belonged to God, while this age
belongs only to man, blind chance, and the Evil
One".[88] Two of the results of this decision were
The Saint's Tragedy (1848) and Hereward the Wake
(1866), the first of which had the required propag-
andistic effect in Oxford, which was the heart of
High Church controversy following Newman's secess-
ion.[89] There is no doubt that The Saint's Tragedy
was a polemical work, designed to damp down the rife
contemporary "spiritual 'Werterism'"[90] manifested in
the reading of Catholic devotional literature and
lives of the saints.[91] F.D. Maurice notes correctly
in his Preface that Kingsley "has meditated upon the
past in its connection with the present" (P xix), an
assertion born out by Kingsley's ambiguous reference
to the "reigning madness in religion" (P 142), namely
the medieval Inquisition and the making of a saint,
and the Oxford Movement and Catholic Revival of the
nineteenth century; and by another parallel : between the emergent Protestantism of the play, the
"dawning manhood of Europe" (P 7), and the nineteenth
-century "dawn of an age of faith", which he thought
he detected (P 159).

This play is an attack on asceticism, and on
celibacy in particular. Its heroine, St.Elizabeth
of Hungary, whom he judged to be "the only ...
healthy popish saint" (LM I, 97), is depicted, not-
withstanding his admiration, as a mean neurotic, made
so by thwarted sexuality, who is occasionally granted
the grace of perceiving the selfishness of her self-
sacrifice.[92] When he advised his fiancée that "matter
is holy ... Our animal enjoyments must be religious
ceremonies",[93] he was not indulging in epistolary
exaggeration, but stating a manifesto by which he
stood in this play. God's image and glory are to be
found in "woman's beauty" (P 25); while I.ii is a
lesson in the error of transferring reverence for

such beauty to the Virgin, who is called - by
analogy - a sham (P 27), the implication being that
sexual relations are the best way to know God and
that Marianism is a neurotic sex-substitute for
celibates. The saint's real tragedy is not that
Lewis goes on crusade, putting an end to Elizabeth's
sex life (though that is operative), but that she is
a saint, the implication of the play being that in
revering female saints such as herself - pale
imitations of the Virgin - and particularly if such
saints are celibate or forced to celibacy, Romanists
are indulging the sexual perversion hinted at in
I.ii.
    The play contains further evidence of Kingsley's
tendency to secularize Christianity, and thence to
distrust medieval piety. Even in Elizabeth's time,
he says, "a noble lay-religion, founded on faith in
the divine and universal symbolism of humanity and
nature, was gradually arising", to issue finally in
Luther (P 6); and this emphasis leads him to regard
piety as worse than useless : miraculous legends are
"worthless to the student of human character" (P 3),
relics and images are sordid (P 137) and church
offerings distasteful (P 139). Conversely, the
secular becomes the religious, for marriage is a
holier state than celibacy, while the religious is
irreligious, as when the inquisitor Conrad chants a
psalm, and a proto-Protestant says "Psalm us no
psalms; bless us no devil's blessings" (P 153).
When Elizabeth says she must go "to him I love",
Conrad thinks she means Christ (for she is dying),
but she insists she means her husband (P 138), as if
to suggest the earthly is more important than the
heavenly spouse. Walter, who represents the "healthy
animalism" of the Teutonic mind (P 6), is the scale
against which the pietistic Conrad and Elizabeth are
measured and found wanting. This inversion of the
religious and the secular is intimately connected
with his belief that Catholicism is anti-Christian :
Rome, he said, is "Manicheeism (Atheism as I should
call it)".[94]
    Kingsley vilifies the Church in the person of
Conrad, who may be a representation of Newman : he is
said to have "a noble nature warped and blinded by
unnatural exclusions from ... family ties" (P 5), and
to be effeminate, which was also his judgement on
Newman.[95] Also like Newman, Conrad has "heavenly
craft" (P 24), and is fascinated by "a ghost of fixed
purposes ... from which neither reason nor pity will
turn him" (P 48). This "ghost" is not God but
"Catholic system" (P 5), for Catholics worship

doctrine, not God (P 75), and the Virgin "is a
doctrine, and a picture:- / I cannot live on dreams"
(P 25), disposing of Marianism and doctrine in one
blow. Thus Kingsley banishes the evident, miracle-
working god of the Middle Ages, replacing Him with
the God-man who performs the miracle of telegraphy.
The increasing emphasis on God's immanence was a
reaction to the anxiety that God was dead : the
propulsion towards the immanentist position was faith
in man, love of the material world and the idea that
God could be conjured to life by seeing Him in railroads and Cunard's liners.[96] The result is faith in
a future heaven-on-earth, achieved through man's
promethean gifts : a faith wholly in accord with the
Whig interpretation of history.
     Hereward the Wake concentrates on other aspects
of Kingsley's anti-medievalism, such as anti-cleric-
alism[97] and nationalism, for Hereward is the nationalist hero fighting the foreign foe, which includes
Rome: the clergy are blamed for the decay of the
Anglo-Saxon race and for subjecting the Danes by the
force of superstition (H Prelude 4,9, ch.I, 21). The
conflict is also associated with the principle of
Erastianism, as the episode of Crowland Minster
shows. He allows the Crowland monks some credit (H
XX, 184), and the reason for this is that the Minster
was in the special service of the kings and run by
the "Common Council of the kingdom" - that is, it was
dominated by the secular power. He can afford to
praise it because it was unique : Crowland was the
exception that proves the rule of monastic awfulness
(a theme previously developed in The Roman and the
Teuton of 1864). Later, when the national interest
demands it, Hereward supports its destruction (H
XXIII, 213); so the Church must give way to nationalism, especially since it was through the patronage
of the secular body that it had acquired its point
of excellence.
     The evil of the Norman Conquest lies in its
infecting England with Romanism, which injures the
political and cultural integrity of England (H
Prelude 7) by being international. Nationalism is
exhibited in the objection to placing French monks
in English monasteries (H XIX, 179), and in Hereward
preferring the English St. Guthlac to St. Peter (H
XIX,179). The Conquest is seen primarily as the
agency whereby "the Church's darlings" (the French
clergy) destroyed "the liberties of England" on behalf of Rome (H XLI, 369). Finally, the monks of
Crowland degenerate into "that lying brotherhood"
(H XLII, 372) after being infected with internation-

alism. His anti-internationalism doubtless appealed
to his contemporaries, fed, as they were, on the myth
of early English liberties having been eroded by the
medieval Church, to be regained only at the Reformation,[98] when national identity was re-affirmed. It
also fed on the fear that nineteenth-century Catholicism was a world-wide subverter of national
integrity.

To summarize, Kingsley's starting point is an
ideal of what it is to be fully and properly human,
which consists in the syndrome of manliness, sexual
and social activity, nationalism and antagonism to
piety and the "purely" religious: "family and national life" are the "divine roots of the Church".[99] He
is consequently antagonistic to the syndrome of
effeminacy, Marianism, theology, piety and celibacy.
His Weltanschauung is based on the masculine-feminine
dichotomy : effeminacy is wrong because it is
passive, weak, accepting, whereas the ideal is
active, strong and reformative, an ideal embodied in
"muscular" Christianity, which is this-wordly and
socially involved. So he attacks Catholicism, and
especially medieval Catholicism, because it represents Catholicism in its unadulterated, unmanly,pious,
dogmatic, traditionalist, internationalist, Latin
(rather than Teutonic) and ultimately anti-Christian
form. He is prompted to propaganda by fear of
Catholic resurgence : as late as 1868 he was
expressing the belief that contemporary atheism and
materialism, coupled with deeper knowledge of the
medieval Church, were driving people to "superstition", by which he meant Catholic medievalism.[100]
The evils of contemporary popery are best told by
reference to the "high-relief" Catholicism of the
Middle Ages; and medieval Catholicism is especially
useful because there is a reservoir of anti-medievalist Protestant sentiment, originating in the
Reformation, to build on : its evils are well known -
better known than modern Catholic corruptions. The
historical mode is admirably suited to the purpose
because a reputed scholar like Kingsley can slip in
the prejudice amongst the facts, almost unnoticed.

Charles Reade (1814-84) was like a clone of
Kingsley's anti-medievalism : he hated Puseyism,[101]
and had a Whig faith in progress and reason, seeing
it as his duty to warn society of the dangers of
religious medievalism.[102] Like Kingsley, he scorns
those who decry the present and admire the past, and
claims greater wisdom for the present over the Middle
Ages.[103] Modern youth is tricked into medievalism by
Grub Street hacks, who promote it with "painted

glass, gilt rags, and fancy" rather than "fact"[104] :
such fraud - he calls it turning "Mr. Burke into
poetry"[105] - is easy to perpetrate where there is
ignorance.[106] His position is summed up accurately
by Rance, who says Reade was careful in his research
for his immensely popular novel The Cloister and the
Hearth (1861) to work "from those sources most out of
sympathy with their own age, and his version of the
past was no more than the Whiggish, anti-Catholic
propaganda of the Enlightenment historians".[107]

Reade shared Kingsley's notion that whatever was
good in the Middle Ages was proto-Protestant, and
this idea is evident in The Cloister and the Hearth
in the hero Gerard. While the Church was corrupt -
"the papal inkstands were all glorious externally;
but within the ink was vile" - Gerard "carried ever
good ink, home-made, in a dirty little inkhorn"[108] :
Gerard is not taken in by Catholic externals, and
his proto-Protestantism, his ability to use reason in
thinking for himself, reflects Reade's own individualism; for both his Evangelicalism and Benthamism
pointed in the direction of individualism.[109] The
Dominican Fra Colonna represents something of his
Gibbonian self : sceptical, rationalist, preferring
the classical to the Christian age, and asserting
that medieval Christianity is no better than paganism.[110] He also shares Kingsley's hatred of clerical
celibacy:[111] in monasteries there are no women, and
"nobody is a man";[112] and the conflict between
cloister and hearth, between celibacy and married
life, emerges in chapter III. Celibacy, the reader
is instructed, is "a vile heresy", and "an invention
truly fiendish".[113] Celibacy is unnatural, and what
is unnatural is unreasonable : his priorities are
"brains first, virility next".[114] Finally, he is
like Kingsley in that he detests monasticism : Denys,
the soldier of Kingsleyan virility (representing
another aspect of Reade's mind), hates monasteries,
for they are "great dungeons", gloomy, cold and
silent, where "nobody is a man ... but all are
slaves",[115] recalling Gibbon's dislike of monastic
obedience. Both Reade and Kingsley profess adherence
to truth, assuming the liberal, rationalist mantle;
yet they are dominated by Protestant individualism,
sexual concerns and residual Enlightenment anti-
medievalist bias.

Kingsley's brother-in-law J.A. Froude shared his
keen anti-Catholicism and anti-medievalism, which
were synonymous for Froude, since in his essay "The
Oxford Counter-Reformation" he refers to the Catholic
Revival as "mediaevalism". In this essay he condemns

medieval sacramentalism, while monasticism is
condemned in "Annals of an English Abbey", and
saints are scorned, their cults derided as behind
the times, and asceticism is judged to be mere
Manichaeism. The Kingsleyan frame of mind was fired
by the restoration of the Roman hierarchy, which was
attacked as presumptuous and usurpatious even by
liberals. This event made John-Bullish, Evangelical
Punch "the most violent champion of English Protestantism",[116] and it duly attacked the monastic
revival[117] and Catholic historical revisionism in a
ballad called "The Historical Hoaxes of Heretics",
wherein Protestant belief in History, with the consequent rejection of Catholicism, is affirmed.[118]
And in 1851 George Borrow declared that medieval
Catholicism "was more prolific of debasement and
crime than all other causes united" and made England
into "a pestilent marsh where swine-like ignorance
wallowed".[119] He too believed that medievalism was
a powerful seducer : he believed that "gentility"
(which he despized) was evident in Catholic phenomena
like "Templars, Hospitalers, mitred abbots, Gothic
abbeys, long-drawn aisles, golden censers, incense",
and seduced people who liked gentility away from a
simpler faith.[120]
        In 1851 Newman reviewed the state of anti-
Catholic prejudice in Lectures on the Present
Position of Catholics in England, noting anti-monasticism, and accusations of lying, profligacy,
tyranny, superstition, corruption, blasphemy,
idolatry and sorcery. He describes the belief of
"most people" that "Christianity was very pure in its
beginning, very corrupt in the middle age, and very
pure in England now ... that in the middle age, a
tyrannical institution, called the Church, arose and
swallowed up Christianity". The Church's defence
was prevented from being heard by "reasons of state,
political and national": she is "the victim of a
prejudice which perpetuates itself, and gives birth
to what it feeds upon".[121] This prejudice is
enforced by the pressure of "tradition, immemorial
unauthenticated tradition", which is itself strengthened by being rooted in the Establishment, which
ensures that

> no one can take part in the business of
> the great world ... no one can write a
> book, without the necessity of professing
> that Protestant ideas are self-evident,
> and that the religion of Alfred, St. Edward,
> Stephen Langton and Friar Bacon, is a

bygone dream.

And the force of this tradition made people like
Pope, Johnson, Scott and Wordsworth suppress their
Catholic instincts.[122] This power is corroborated
by reference to the striking fact that even Catholic,
medievalist Digby was totally convinced by the
tradition in his youth, when he wrote of

> that dark empire when Priests held a
> dominion over the minds and bodies of
> men, which kept all Europe in ignorance
> and misery, which was the disgrace of
> Christianity, and the scourge of human
> kind.[123]

Throughout the 1830s Newman himself supported the
tradition until he became so informed that he
realized it was invalid, whereupon he published a
formal retraction of his accusations against Rome.
There he describes the personal feelings which made
him accept the tradition, feelings which must have
been very common :

> If you ask me how an individual could
> venture ... to publish such views of a
> communion so ancient, so widespreading,
> so fruitful in Saints, I answer that I
> said to myself, "I am not speaking my
> own words, I am but following almost a
> consensus of the divines of my own Church.
> ... I wish to throw myself into their
> system. While I say what they say, I am
> safe. Such views, too, are necessary for
> our position." ... such language is to be
> ascribed, in no small measure, to ... a
> hope of approving myself to persons I
> respect, and a wish to repel the charge
> of Romanism.[124]

This description of the operation of the herd
mentality is especially striking, since it comes from
such an intellectual, well-informed, involved and
responsible individual : how much stronger must have
been the operation of this mentality in less able
men! Newman himself describes the operation of the
tradition amongst capable men in a specific, anti-
medievalist example, where a point made by Mosheim
was propagated by Robertson, White, Maclaine, Jortin
and Hallam; which, being shown to be false by
Waddington and Maitland, was still uncorrected in the

1841 edition of Mosheim.[125]
There were, of course, anti-medievalists
affiliated to ideologies other than the Protestant,
usually of a rationalist type. George Eliot, a
meliorist, Comteian positivist, showed in Romola
(1863) that she believed medieval Catholicism
belonged strictly in the past,[126] and should not be
allowed to interfere with the onward march of
progress. Anti-medievalist though she was, in The
Mill on the Floss (1860) she shows that she understands - and to some degree sympathizes with -
religious medievalism. Book IV Chapter I contrasts
the sordidness and ideological deadness of the Mill-
St. Oggs milieu with the life-enhancing vitality of
the romantic age of castles and cathedrals : "that
was a time," she says in the authorial voice,

> of colour, ... of living, religious art
> and religious enthusiasm; for were not
> cathedrals built in those days, and did
> not great emperors leave their Western
> palaces, to die before the infidel strong-
> holds in the sacred East?

She ponders that even a superstition of suffering is
more appropriate to the mystery of the human lot than
the outlook of the "emmet-like Dodsons and Tullivers."
In Book IV Chapter III, "A Voice from the Past",
Maggie Tulliver is shown turning away from the dream-
world of Scott and Byron to something with more
substance to help her cope with the pain of living;
that something being the medieval piety of Thomas à
Kempis's The Imitation of Christ, which instructs her
in self-renunciation. There is a suggestion that
such self-renunciation is a possible means of estab-
lishing responsible social relations; although, of
course, Eliot was not literally sympathetic to
medieval Catholicism.
Matthew Arnold and Walter Pater believed that
irrational medieval spirituality had denigrated human
life, while the classical spirit had emancipated
it.[127] Arnold, blinkered to the stimulus given to
medievalism by the French Revolution, praised the
Revolution for emancipating Europe from the Middle
Ages, thereby allowing it to progress.[128] Pater said
that the medieval religion had restricted "the heart
and the imagination",[129] and that the excellent
sculptor at Notre Dame D'Amiens was "an unconscious
Greek", because he was a humanist : Pater used the
Middle Ages as a lens by which to see the Hellenic
virtues more clearly.[130] By contrast, he gives the

abbey church of Vézelay as a typification of the
monastic spirit, which he thought was anti-human, a
view shared by Robert Louis Stevenson in "Our Lady
of the Snows", where he describes monks as "volunt-
eers of death". Ruskin remarked on such "fierceness
of steady enmity to the monkish character and
principle", which he attributed to religious ambition
and the "avarice ... of the modern laic mind".[131]
Medieval asceticism was also attacked at the end of
the century by the Nietzschean John Davidson in "A
New Ballad of Tannhaüser" and other poems. Such
views had their Continental equivalents : Heine
opposed the anti-sensual asceticism of the Middle
Ages, with his Saint-Simonian faith in the fundamental harmony of flesh and spirit, and looked forward
to their reconciliation in a future utopia. His
ideals were those of the French Revolution :
humanism, liberty, egalitarianism, democracy - all
founded on reason;[132] and his correlative anti-
medievalism was but the reflection of a general
"reaction against the reintroduction of that catholic, feudal mode of thought".[133] Similarly, the
French historian Michelet thought medievalism was
opposed to progress :

> the past, that is the enemy - the barbaric
> Middle Ages - and its representative Spain
> ... the Spain that burnt the books of
> Voltaire and Montesquieu. The future,that
> is the friend; progress and the new spirit,
> 1789 distantly appearing above the horizon.[134]

Retrospect

The anti-medievalist syndrome lived on into the
twentieth century : medievalism failed to change
long-held attitudes. In 1906 a well known History
of English Rationalism in the Nineteenth Century by
Alfred W. Benn was published, and its verdict on the
Middle Ages completed the circle : "the Middle Ages,"
Benn said, "so far from offering a picture of ideal
justice and romantic spirituality, were really what
Voltaire had shown them to be, a period of barbarism,
delusion, profligacy, and oppression".[135] In the
same year, an anti-medievalist fantasy by the eminent
historian of the Middle Ages G.G. Coulton, called
Friar's Lantern,was published, and its purpose was
to nail down the coffin-lid on medieval Catholicism's
reputation. Coulton had several opponents, like
Chesterton, Belloc and Gasquet, but perhaps only
David Knowles was in a position to prove Coulton was,

as he said, biassed![136] His bias was Protestant, and
in favour of the modern age, for he believed that
"homo sapiens is ... an improving animal, and History
has seemed to confirm this probability more and more,"
and had faith in "the final victory of reason".[137]
    Friar's Lantern dramatizes the belief that
medievalists - especially Anglo-Catholics - were
people who so disliked the sordid realities of modern
life that they escaped into the writings of medieval
ascetics, who were themselves escapists,[138] and read
into history what they wanted to find, thereby
constructing an utopia with which to criticize the
present (16,17). Such men, Coulton says, ignore
"modern toleration, modern justice, and the enormous
decrease of crime" (16), in favour of religious
aestheticism, the "picturesque side of medieval
religion" (19), the "small matters" of Catholic
ritual (20). The Catholic priest, Fr. Duvet, has no
more sense than the Anglicans, having learnt his
medievalism from the Anglican John Mason Neale, whom
he quotes, saying he would like to return to the
Middle Ages, "Ere, in her evil day, / From their
holy faith and their ancient rites the people fell
away" (31). He magically gets his wish, whereupon
the medievalists find out how terrible the medieval
Church was, how out of sympathy with Anglo-Catholicism (37,46,77,80-83,89-91,116-117), how quite like
Protestantism. The nightmare makes them yearn to see
a "common modern railway train" (109). They return
to the modern age, where men have become so amiable
through Protestantism, rationalism, commonsense and
the general "spiritual power of a higher civilization" (208). While the Protestant rebellion
resulted in outward disunity, this does not trouble
Coulton as it had the romantics; for spiritual unity
may demand obedience to conscience (213-14). While
the monastic principle had been empty and egotistical
(217-18), and the Middle Ages generally were sunk in
"spiritual and moral bankruptcy"(220) and corruption,
of which the clergy were especially guilty (221),
Protestantism made for greater prosperity than
Catholicism and for freedom (231) (as Macaulay had
argued); and by contrast with the Catholic Middle
Ages, Protestant modernity wars much less frequently
and cruelly, is superior in learning, religiously
free, peaceful and pure (232). Catholics in England
live in "profound" peace and have a voice in
Parliament "far beyond their numbers or deserts"
(232). His lesson is that "the so-called Ages of
Faith were in fact too often ages of doubt and
despair" (248), and that moderns should be content,

for the present is best served not by hankering after
the ideals of a dead past, but by looking forwards
(249). He criticizes the Middle Ages by comparing
them with the present, just as the medievalists had
criticized the modern age by reference to the Middle
Ages, so raising modernity to an utopian paradigm to
replace that of the medievalists. It was an old
message : fifty years earlier, William Bell Scott had
delivered it in the reverse way, by having Wiseman
resuscitate Bede, in a poem called "Bede in the
Nineteenth Century". Bede is full of wonder at the
material and spiritual advantages of the nineteenth
century over his own age. "The past," he says,
returns "like a dark cold sea,/ Drowning my new brave
Life."139
　　To the nineteenth century it seemed that the
spirit of the Middle Ages was only recently dead, and
that its corpse still haunted society : Digby
believed that its body was still warm and might be
revived. "In this country," he wrote in 1831,
"several old Catholic customs of the middle ages have
been transmitted down to us," and "every thing solid
and valuable is ... a remnant or a revival of
Catholic thinking or institution".140 "Until quite
recently," wrote Baldwin Brown in 1869, "our modes
of thought and speech, our habits of action, our
forms of procedure in things social and political,
were still feudal."141 This feeling of the past
haunting the present was epitomized by Thackeray
when he wrote, "we are of the time of chivalry....
We are of the age of steam".142 In his essay on
"Heinrich Heine", Matthew Arnold made the comment -
relevant, although concerning Germany - that

　　the process of liberation, as Goethe worked
　　it, though sure, is undoubtedly slow; he
　　came, as Heine says, to be eighty years old
　　in thus working it, and at the end of that
　　time the old Middle-Age machine was still
　　creaking on, ... and the visible triumph
　　of the modern spirit over prescription and
　　routine seemed as far off as ever.

In 1828 Heine himself wrote that

　　England is still congealed in a mediaeval
　　condition, or rather in the condition of
　　a fashionable Middle Age. The concessions
　　which have there been made to liberal ideas,
　　have been with difficulty wrested from this
　　mediaeval rigidity.... The religious

94

> reformation in England is consequently
> but half completed....[143]

The anti-medievalists, like Kingsley, felt that the
threads of the medieval shroud were still fouling the
works of society, that the medievalists had to be
prevented from embalming society in the shroud they
were busy re-weaving, and that the remains should be
cast on the fire of post-Reformation thought, from
which, phoenix-like, society would be reborn. The
constituent elements of this fire were Protestantism
and rationalism, which produced the heat of the
religion of the heart, nationalism, ideological
individualism, progressivism, liberalism and
materialism. The anti-medievalists felt that a new
society, perhaps an utopia, was struggling to be
born, and they searched for a mid-wife : they could
look anywhere but to medievalism, for both Protestantism and rationalism had been its fatal poison.
The inquisition which conducted this auto-da-fé was,
in its fervent self-righteousness, not always fair :
typically, while Coulton teazed the medievalist
ritualists with the alleged poverty of medieval
ritual,[144] Walter Walsh taunted them with the
allegation that the English Sarum Rite (which they
wanted to revive) was "far more elaborate, superstitious, and puerile than that termed 'Roman'";[145]
and medieval Catholics were condemned for trivial and
materialist externalism when their spirituality and
asceticism were not under attack, their intellectual-
ism was condemned when not their ignorance, their
lasciviousness when not their celibacy, their
political and social activity when not their
idleness. While the Protestants condemned the
medieval Church for being Catholic - and therefore
not Christian - the rationalists condemned it for
being too Christian.
　　It may be that the works of Max Weber, R.H.
Tawney and Christopher Hill on the relationship
between Protestantism and capitalism throw some light
on this auto-da-fé;[146] one cannot be more decisive,
since the scholars of the subject have yet to agree
on their conclusions. They posit that the religion
of the heart, namely Protestantism, held that anything could be sanctified by having the right
attitude towards it; and this included capitalism,
which was rejected in the Middle Ages. And religious
liberty, which Protestantism professed, was a basis
for, and correlative to, individualistic capitalism :
medieval religious structures had had to be over-
thrown to enable capitalist development. Since the

anti-medievalists certainly defended modern society,
they would also have defended capitalism, as one of
the chief structures of their society; and some of
the anti-medievalist themes can be viewed as corrob-
orating this approach. For example, it may be that
the alleged élitism of medieval ascetic ideals was
felt to interfere with bourgeois, capitalist
democracy and offended the idea that capitalist
enterprize could be as spiritual as the monastic
vocation; monastic society is essentially communist,
and this may have been viewed as an affront to a
supremely capitalist society; the alleged idleness
of monks may have offended the Protestant ethic of
hard (capitalist) work; and rationalism may have
been favoured to the exclusion of medieval other-
worldliness,since it facilitated capitalist
operations.

The anti-medievalists were united in the belief
that there was an anti-medievalist battle to be
fought. What one may broadly call the establishment
milieu and mentality doggedly stood its ground,
attaching its hopes to ideals born in the Enlightenment and the new world of science and technology.
History came to be used as propaganda, and part of
the foundation on which the propagandist edifice was
built was the fact of resurgent Catholicism, which
fed medievalism, the growth of which helped to
stimulate anti-medievalism and anti-Catholicism.
Kenelm Henry Digby stood for everything which the
anti-medievalists feared and detested; so the next
chapter is an account of Digby - in himself the
zenith of English religious medievalism - and some
of his followers.

NOTES
1. Henry VIII and the English Monasteries 2v.
5th. ed. (1893) I, xi.
2. Cf. Collingwood The Idea of History 87-8.
3. In Victorian Literature : Selected Essays
ed. Robert O. Preyer (New York, 1967) 17; reprinted
from Theology Today (Apr. 1947) 80-101.
4. See John Passmore The Perfectibility of Man
(1970) especially chs. I,VIII-XI.
5. Butterfield The Whig Interpretation of
History 27.
6. Ferguson The Renaisaance in Historical
Thought ch. II.
7. Cf. Peter Gay The Enlightenment : An
Interpretation (1967) 209-12.

8. See National Union Catalogue for details.

9. Maitland interestingly criticized Robertson's use of Mosheim : see rev. article of Maitland's "The Dark Ages" in DR XVII (Sept. 1844) 159 ff. 18th-c. evaluation may be gleaned from John Nichols Literary Anecdotes (1812) II, 452, VIII, 258, 426.

10. Mosheim An Ecclesiastical History ed. Archibald Maclaine (1774) v.II,5. Subsequent refs. to this v. in text.

11. The Idea of History 77.

12. The History of the Reign of the Emperor Charles V in Works III (1840) 48.

13. Ibid. 60, 116-17, 163-4.

14. Joseph Ward Swain Edward Gibbon the Historian (1966) 122.

15. Ibid. 144 and see 145. His influence has survived in the second half of the twentieth century : a good example of modern, anti-medievalist Gibbonianism is Charles Seltman's Women in Antiquity (1956) especially ch. XII.

16. James W. Johnson The Formation of English Neo-classical Thought (1967) 194.

17. See Harold L. Bond The Literary Art of Edward Gibbon (1960) 36 for Gibbon's religious standing.

18. The Decline and Fall of the Roman Empire (Harmondsworth, 1966) abridged by Low ch. XXXVII, 512, loc. cit., XXXVII, 507 and 511, XXXII, 463, XXXVII, 507 respectively. (This text used because, while retaining relevant chs., is less corrupt than earlier ones.) Subsequent refs. in text.

19. Compare XXXVIII, 525-6 with XV, 180, XVI, 238, LXI, 792.

20. See NCBEL II, 1724-1727 and Cambridge History of English Literature ed. A.W. Ward, A.R. Waller (1913) X, 307-10.

21. 1797 but never pub. : qu. Berington A Literary History of the Middle Ages (1814) 150-6.

22. A Literary History of the Middle Ages 276.

23. The History of the Papal Power qu. ibid. 151.

24. A Literary History of the Middle Ages 193.

25. Ward Life and Times of Cardinal Wiseman II, 191.

26. H. Weisinger "The Middle Ages and the Late Eighteenth-Century Historians" PQ XXVII (1948) 63.

27. The Poetical Works of William Wordsworth ed. E. de Selincourt (1940) I, 259-60.

28. Reliques I,88, 112, 345, and "Essay on the

Origin of the English Stage", Reliques II, 170.
    29. An Introduction to the Prophecies
Concerning the Christian Church, The Works (1811)
V, Sermon VII 172-3, 193.
    30. History of English Poetry II, 144.
    31. The Works of the English Poets Chalmers
and Johnson XIII, 321-24.
    32. Nightmare Abbey, Crotchet Castle ed. R.
Wright (Harmondsworth, 1969) I,44.
    33. Ibid. V, 163.
    34. Ibid. X, 205-6.
    35. Eg. Coleridge's Miscellaneous Criticism
147, Collected Works I, 209, 210, 211, X, 136.
    36. Eg. Patrick Crutwell "Walter Scott" The
Pelican Guide to English Lit. v.5., J.E. Duncan "The
Anti-Romantic in Ivanhoe" in Walter Scott: Modern
Judgements ed. D.D. Devlin (1968) 142-7.
    37. The Achievement of Walter Scott (1969)
100-1.
    38. See P.D. Garside "Scott, the Romantic Past
and the Nineteenth Century" RES XXIII (1972) 147-161,
espec. 155.
    39. The Journal of Sir Walter Scott ed. W.E.K.
Anderson (Oxford, Clarendon Press, 1972) 28.Feb.1829,
525-6.
    40. Cf. Andrew L. Drummond The Churches in
English Fiction (Leicester, 1950) 106.
    41. Rev. of Digby's Broad Stone of Honour in
Athenaeum 1829, given in Essays and Tales, by John
Sterling ed. Julius C. Hare 2v. (1848) I, 116.
    42. Ibid. I, 30-46.
    43. See Chandler 114.
    44. Rev. of Mackintosh's History of the
Revolution (1835) in Lord Macaulay's Essays and Lays
of Ancient Rome (1893) 325.
    45. Loc. cit.
    46. Complete Works of Lord Macaulay 12v. (1898)
VII, 451.
    47. Lord Macaulay's Essays 121 : rev. of
Southey's Colloquies (1830).
    48. John Mason Neale Hierologus(1843) ch. IX,
190-1.
    49. Vivian Grey(1826), Hughenden ed. (1882) Bk.
VII, ch. ix, 437.
    50. M.D.R. Leys Catholics in England 1559-1829
Catholic Book Club ed. (n.d.) 152.
    51. J. Derek Holmes More Roman than Rome :
English Catholicism in the Nineteenth Century (1978)
44.
    52. Present Position of Catholics in England
5th.ed. (n.d.) Lecture I, 11.

53. Lord Macaulay's Essays 557.
54. The Romantic School in Prose Writings 93.
55. Rev. Anna Jameson's Sacred and Legendary Art (1848) in Literary and General Lectures and Essays.
56. See Macaulay's rev. of Montgomery's poetry.
57. Luther : or the Spirit of the Reformation (1843) vii.
58. Ibid. "A Poet's Retrospect, and Patriot's Conclusion".
59. See DNB on Rogers.
60. ER LXXX (Oct. 1844) 350, 314, 343 respectively.
61. Ibid. 365.
62. Ibid. 365-70, 374 respectively.
63. The Correspondence of Lord Acton and Richard Simpson 3v. ed. Josef L. Altholz etc.(C.U.P., 1975) III, 262, Letter 17 Dec. 1868.
64. Robert B. Martin The Dust of Combat. A Life of Charles Kingsley (1959) 15.
65. Charles Kingsley : His Letters and Memories of His Life ed. Fanny Kingsley 2v. (1878) I, 143. Henceforth cited in text as LM.
66. Cf. rev. of Southey's Colloquies, Lord Macaulay's Essays 121.
67. Some of the ideas in this account of Kingsley are supported in Houghton "The Issue Between Kingsley and Newman" Victorian Literature 13-36. where further evidence is adduced on Kingsley's secularization of Christianity.
68. Yeast 9th.ed. (1878) XVII, 309. Yeast was first written in 1848 for Frazer's Magazine, it was reprinted with corrections and additions in 1851.
69. Ibid. III, 48.
70. Ibid, V. 82.
71. Ibid. X, 157.
72. "The Ethical Revolt Against Christian Orthodoxy in Early Victorian England" The American Historical Rev. LX (Jul. 1955) 801 n.2.
73. Charles Kingsley : His Letters and Memories of His Life ed. Fanny Kingsley (1885) 23.
74. Letters on Religious Retirment and Melancholy (1762) 16; qu. Knox Enthusiasm 426.
75. The Book of the Church I, 323.
76. View of the State of Europe in the Middle Ages (1818); qu. John R. Moorman The Franciscans in England (1974) 111.
77. The Cloister and the Hearth (1939) 496. Numbering of chapters is not consistent in all editions.
78. ER no. 173, reprinted in Essays in

Ecclesiastical Biography.
    79. LM I, 257.
    80. LM I, 138.
    81. LM I, 257.
    82. The Hermits (1878) 197.
    83. See below pp. 207-8.
    84. The Roman and the Teuton (1864) 203-4.
    85. "On English Literature" Literary and
General Lectures and Essays (1890) 253.
    86. "The Clergy and the Heathen" in The Roman
and the Teuton.
    87. Eg. "Why Should We Fear the Romish
Priests?" FM XXXVII (Apr. 1848) 467.
    88. Literary and General Lectures and Essays
254. This comment is strongly reminiscent of Macaulay's condemnation of the contemporary placing of
the "golden age of England" in the Middle Ages :
History of England from the Accession of James the
Second (1858) v.I, III, 442-3.
    89. Una Pope-Hennessy Canon Charles Kingsley
(1948) 58.
    90. Carlyle's phrase, signifying morbid,
ineffectual,romantic longing.
    91. Poems (1902) 159. Henceforth cited in
text as P.
    92. Kingsley also remarks on the selfishness
of pietistic self-sacrifice in LM I, 190, 431.
    93. Letter 2 Oct. 1843 qu. Susan Chitty The
Beast and the Monk. A Life of Charles Kingsley (1974)
80.
    94. LM I,252.
    95. Cf. Chitty The Beast and the Monk 236.
    96. Yeast V, 82.
    97. Hereward the Wake (1900) ch.I, 28, 29,
XXXIII, 290-1. Henceforth cited in text as H.
    98. See LM I, 253, Literary and General
Lectures and Essays 189.
    99. Preface to Hypatia.
    100. The Hermits (1878) 197.
    101. Wayne Burns Charles Reade (New York, 1961)
53.
    102. Cf. Andrew Sanders The Victorian Histori-
cal Novel 1840-1880 (1978) 28.
    103. Christie Johnstone (1853) in Peg
Woffington and Christie Johnstone (1927) IX, 192-3.
    104. Ibid. II, 153.
    105. Ibid. IX, 189.
    106. This illustrated ibid. II, 157-8.
    107. Nicholas Rance The Historical Novel and
Popular Politics in Nineteenth-Century England
(Plymouth 1975) 59.

108. The Cloister and the Hearth
LXI, 425.
109. Burns points out that Evangelicalism and
Benthamism were almost identical in many respects,
because they shared individualism: Charles Reade 60.
110. The Cloister and the Hearth LXXIV,491-4.
111. Malcolm Elwin suggests that the strength
of Reade's feelings about celibacy was due to his
own enforced celibacy : Charles Reade (1931) 44-5;
cf. Burns Charles Reade 317-19.
112. Cloister and the Hearth XXXI, 169.
113. Ibid. CI, 663.
114. Compton L. Reade "Charles Reade A Memoir"
Contemporary Rev. XLV (1884) 707.
115. Cloister and the Hearth XXXI, 169.
116. Charles L. Graves Mr. Punch's History of
Modern England (1921) v.I 1841-1857; cf. D.Wallace
Duthie The Church in the Pages of "Punch" (1912)
chs. IV, V.
117. Punch XIX (July-Dec.1850) 189, 199, 213,
215.
118. Punch XIX, 242.
119. Lavengro Preface to 1st. ed. (1851)
Everyman ed. (1909) 2-3.
120. The Romany Rye (1914) Appendix ch.V.
332-3; 1st. ed. 1857.
121. Lectures on the Present Position of
Catholics in England (1851) 11-16, 19.
122. Ibid. 42-4, 48, 54-5, 63, 68-9.
123. Holland Memoir of Kenelm Henry Digby 39.
124. Qu. Newman Apologia Pro Vita Sua ed.
Martin J. Svaglic (1967) ch. IV, 182.
125. Lectures on the Present Position of
Catholics in England 93 ff.
126. And see Martin J. Svaglic "Religion in
the Novels of George Eliot" Journal of English and
Germanic Philology 53 (1954) 152.
127. See Arnold "Dante and Beatrice" (1863)
Complete Prose Works III, 3-11; Pater "Coleridge";
DeLaura Hebrew and Hellene 199-201.
128. Schools and Universities on the Continent
in Complete Prose Works of Matthew Arnold IV ed.
R.H. Super (Michigan U.P., 1964) 147.
129. The Renaissance (1963) Preface xv.
130. Cf. Jerome Bump "Hopkins, Pater, and
Medievalism" VNL L (Fall, 1976) 13-15.
131. CW XXXIII 206.
132. "The Liberation" in Prose Writings 61.
133. The Romantic School in Prose Writings 92.
134. Qu. Chadwick The Secularization of the
European Mind in the Nineteenth Century 155.

135. The History of English Rationalism in the Nineteenth Century (1906) II, 185.
136. The Religious Orders in England (C.U.P., 1959) III, 294.
137. Coulton Fourscore Years : An Autobiography (C.U.P., 1944) 329.
138. Friar's Lantern (1906) 13-14. Henceforth cited in text.
139. W.B. Scott Poems (1854) 90.
140. Mores Catholici v.I (1831) 27.
141. First Principles of Ecclesiastical Truth qu. Houghton Victorian Frame of Mind 2-3.
142. "De Juventute" (1860), qu. Houghton Victorian Frame of Mind 3.
143. "The Liberation" Prose Writings 59-60.
144. Friar's Lantern 37, 46, 77.
145. The Secret History of the Oxford Movement (1899) 241.
146. See Capitalism and the Reformation ed. M.J. Kitch (1969) especially xiv-xx, 3-8.

Chapter IV

KENELM HENRY DIGBY AND YOUNG ENGLAND

> The thing that haunts the historical
> imagination most, I think, is not ...
> the Golden Age or the New Jerusalem,
> not the Good Old Days or the Good Time
> Coming, but the gold that man missed or
> rejected and the good time that might
> have come.
>
> G.K. Chesterton "What Might Have Been"

Digby

Kenelm Henry Digby (1796 or 97-1880) was the
chief British religious medievalist of the nineteenth
century. His whole medievalist work was an enthusiastic metaphor of the medieval Church, and he vener-
ated the Middle Ages because he believed them holy
and Catholic, valuing them as a corrective lesson
for the present. His work was a bridge between eighteenth and early nineteenth-century romantic religious medievalism and the truer "religious medievalism" of Victorian Catholicism, and between Continental religious medievalism and English medievalism.
If not one of the seminal minds of the age, his
position in literary and religious history is unique
and symbolic. Before his conversion to Catholicism
in 1825 - years before the Oxford Movement began -
he was first anti-Catholic, then becoming interested
in the Middle Ages through Sir Walter Scott's poetry,
visits to the Continent, reading medieval literature
and familiarity with Catholic and anti-Catholic polemical writings. While it is generally supposed that
he was little known by his contemporaries, he was
known by many who mattered. A.G.Hill judges that "his
message... did something to set the tone and direction of early Victorian culture",[1] while James

Merriman calls Digby's Broad Stone of Honour "the
most influential" of the flood of books on chivalry
which poured on to the market between 1815 and 1830,
and a "crucial formative influence" on the Young
England movement.[2] His influence was also noted by
contemporaries: Lord Acton testified to his influence
on Catholics,[3] while a writer in the Dublin Review
suggested that the writings of Digby had helped to
remove anti-medieval prejudice and promote piety in
opposition to utilitarianism.[4] When Charles Kingsley
lamented in 1849 that the young were rebelling
against the anti-medieval teachings of their parents,
due to reading histories of the Middle Ages and re-
tellings of old legends,[5] he may well have had
Digby's writings in mind. Eminent contemporaries who
were connected with him, and therefore possibly influenced by him, include Newman, Acton, Wiseman,
Frederick Faber, Wordsworth, Sara Hutchinson,
Coventry Patmore, Aubrey de Vere, Pugin, Ambrose
Phillipps de Lisle, J.R. Bloxam, Gladstone, Disraeli,
Charles Butler, Julius Hare, Edward FitzGerald, John
Sterling, Charles Reade, William Morris, Edward
Burne-Jones, Ruskin, George Saintsbury, Richard
Monkton Milnes the third Marquess of Bute and Charles
Kingsley: and he knew such Continentals as Montalembert and Chateaubriand.
    Digby's most widely known work was The Broad
Stone of Honour,first published in 1822, with enlarged editions following in 1823,1826-9,1844-8,1876-7
and 1883. The first two editions, written before his
conversion to Roman Catholicism, evince a sympathy
with Catholicism which forshadows the Oxford Movement
and anticipates the Catholic Revival. For example,
he specifies "the Catholic faith [as] the very basis
of the character which belonged to the knight",[6] and
though the work is ostensibly about chivalry, it is
really about the Catholic foundation of chivalry.
Like all his work, it is marked by naivety, an elevated moral sense and a deep love of the Christian
Church. There is also a pugnacious, polemical,
crusading intent : he says he has written a book of

> ensamples and doctrines, which I call The
> Broad Stone of Honour; seeing that it will
> be a fortress like that rock upon the Rhine
> [the Ehrenbreitstein] where coward or traitor
> never stood ... where all may stand who love
> honour and true nobility....[7]

He wants to be free of the world's baseness, and the
rock which gives him that freedom is medieval

Christianity; and he wants to teach, to propagate
an alternative view of the medieval faith to that
which had hitherto prevailed : it was a view he had
learnt at first hand from medieval documents, thus
bypassing the anti-Catholic histories. He thinks of
the chivalric tales as true myths which are spiritually edifying;[8] and perhaps he saw all his medievalism in this light. His work was certainly a type of
mythification, and not history, although also not a
lie.
      Chivalry was for Digby essentially Christianity
in action, and was "altogether a religious doctrine"
(BS II. xxiii, BS V. II, 8-9). This point has been
overlooked in the past. His interest was not
secular.[9] Later, he stated that chivalry was only
valid when "drawing all its excellence from the faith
and influence of the Catholic Church", and outside of
that it was "only one of the many forms in which
pride and sin ensnare the hearts of men".[10] He
associates all positive things with the chivalric
tales : "Christian faith, virtue and honour ... love,
courtesy, humanity, friendship, generosity and
heroism ..." (BS II. xlvi), as well as hope, gratit-
ude, joy, fidelity, mercy and duty (BS II. 46).
Particularly valued is generosity, which must be
understood as the Christian virtue of self-sacrifice,
a virtue he opposes to the meanness, small-mindedness
and selfishness of the modern age. In praising
chivalry he is ever conscious of the modern attitude
towards the things nearest to his heart, and he deals
with such criticism : "let it not be said that their
faith [ie. of the chivalric order] was superstition :
it was not the creed of the human philosopher, but it
was the doctrine of Christ and his Apostles" (BS II.
93-4). He even defends the chivalric adventure of
the crusades - he is the first English writer
seriously to do so - as a response to "the call of
piety and honour", and wonders, "is it for them to
blush and to be troubled at the scorn of a world
which is destitute of both?" (BS II. 95-6).
      The aim of Mores Catholici was similar : to let
the Middle Ages speak for themselves through liberal
quotation and the retelling of medieval stories.
Here he exchanges the rock of the Ehrenbreitstein for
the mount of the eight Beatitudes, which are the
irritants provoking his discourse; and the mount is
the vantage-point from which he surveys the medieval
ground, "so as to mark how far the form and acts of
that life, in ages past ... agreed, not with this or
that modern standard of political and social happiness and grandeur", but with divine standards (MC 1,

6-7). His plan is to show the great extent to which the spirit of each Beatitude was understood and acted upon in the Middle Ages and the high degree to which the promised beatitude was received. He supports this unlikely proposition with amazing erudition, which is, however, weakened by total lack of analytical method. He also intends to show that the great Christian ideals then propagated by the Catholic Church, and all-pervasive, were disrupted by the Reformation. He says he is writing for Catholics in countries separated from the faith (MC.I,21), the implication being that the faith of such Catholics is endangered by anti-Catholic indoctrination. But he also seeks to fight fire with fire, hoping that if he can level the scales of propaganda, his own religious community will be seen to be at least as worthy, intelligent, creative and sincere as those of the prevailing religious sects. Moreover, he expresses his faith in the potential of England to return to the pre-Reformation religion : "thy solemn woods would give shelter to the lonely eremite" (MC.I,26). In thus preaching the good news, his function is very specifically prophetical, and there is evidence that he consciously regarded himself as a prophet. The following address to England could be taken as an epigraph to all his medievalist works :

> Thou art still a noble instrument, though now mute or discordant. Ignorant and un-skilful hands have played upon thee till they broke thee into a thousand parts; but, though thus broken and disarranged, let but the master arise who can revive the Catholic chord, and thou wilt again send forth the sweetest music.
>
> (MC.I,27.)

Perhaps he saw himself as the "master", and even if he did not, he assumed the prophetic tone often. This quotation clearly exemplifies the medievalist anxiety about the disintegration of society, and the belief in a metaphysical solution.

The Catholic response to these works was very favourable, but even a friendly Protestant like Julius C. Hare took increasing exception to Digby's position as it became more firmly Catholic. The controversy between the two is worth a brief survey because it clarifies Digby's polemical approach and because Hare doubtless - as Digby himself said (MC. XI, 460) - represented a faction. In 1826 Hare greatly admired the 1823 edition of The Broad Stone,

written in Hare's own spirit of Catholic sympathy
restrained by Protestant good sense. In 1837 he
continued to express admiration for the idealism and
beauty of the expanded version of The Broad Stone,
but thought it, and Mores Catholici, disfigured by
polemicism : he disliked the prejudice in favour of
Rome and the strong dislike of Protestantism. He
judged Digby to be deluded rather than sophistical,
and yet accused him of selecting for discussion only
"the purest and sublimest morsels of the great
religious writers between the time of the Apostles
and the Reformation", while neglecting the bad and
atttributing only baseness and worldliness to modern,
post-Reformation Europe.[11] In 1842, Hare wrote to
him, accusing him of "virulent bigotry", expressing
offence at his treatment of Protestant heroes and
advocating a balanced, liberal view of the past.[12]
In 1847 (approximately) he repeated this advocacy and
hostilely protested against his "misrepresentations
of the whole of modern history ... the apotheosis of
the Middle Ages, and the apodiabolosis of the
Reformation and its effects". He condemned Digby's
polemic as an unconvincing failure : "the theological
and ecclesiastical controversies of the nineteenth
century are not to be decided by any selection of
the anecdotes or apophthegms of the twelfth and
thirteenth".[13] Hare's position is, at first sight,
very fair; but his call for balance on Digby's part
is easily interpreted as anger that Catholics should
do anything but meekly accept the constant ridicule
to which they were subject. It was not for Digby -
outraged as he was by such treatment - to write
kindly of Protestant Reformers : that had been done
in England amply in the past. His mission was to
present the other case, which had been so resolutely
obscured over the centuries.
    Although he did not mention him by name, Digby
intended the last chapter of the last volume of
Mores Catholici (1842) as an answer to Hare's
criticisms. Here he admits that he has presented
history "in a Catholic character" to afford testimony
to "general truths of the highest importance to
mankind", yet he protests he has not made "the truth
of history subordinate to its moral use"; nor has he
described a mere dream; and he insists that the
impression of medieval greatness does not derive
"from their being past and distant ages" (MC.XI,456).
He would deny that his work is "romantic" history.
He freely admits that that his work is apologistic : "the
chief object was to defend the middle ages from the
charges of those who attack religion through them"

(MC.XI, 456); although it was not his intention to claim that the Middle Ages were without fault (MC. XI, 457-8). His work is also evangelistic, since he wants to improve his fellow-countrymen's lot by introducing them to Catholicism; and, indeed, he has observed their plight : "to mourn ... over the condition of the majority of the people now is to utter but a just complaint" (MC. XI, 462). He recommends imitation of the medieval religious order as the antidote to modern anxieties, and he advertises the Middle Ages as the spiritual home for which all romantics quested : indeed, he uses the archetypal romantic quest - Odysseus's voyage - as an image of the return to Catholicism, which, he says, "can sweeten and compose to order the uncertain wanderings of the human existence" (MC.XI, 477). "Fly," he advises all English men, "from that benighted region, from that horrid servitude, to the assemblies of your native clime", escape "all the wastes of human speculation" and the land where souls are offered up "on the shrine of a cold and barbarous misbelief" (MC. XI, 488).

He challenges Hare's position thus : if he regards Digby's witnesses as pure, sublime and worthy, why is he not a Catholic? How does he accommodate this judgement with his profession as an Anglican clergyman, by which he is bound to consider such characters as "idolaters and enemies of truth"? (MC. XI, 460). Then he criticizes all of Hare's faction : those Anglicans who flirt with Catholicism, who sentimentally hope for reunion : "from early times," he comments wryly, "there have been men without the Church, who seemed to think that they were within; that all might be well again without a palinode" (MC. XI, 481). Such men occasionally "look back on the Catholic unity which their fathers had broken ... like fallen angels turning back their face to Paradise. Yet their habitual disposition with regard to it was indifference ..." (MC. XI, 481). (It is significant that Digby knew Johann Adam Möhler's Symbolics of 1832, a classical nineteenth-century Catholic statement of the dogmatic gap between Catholicism and Protestantism, which provided him with invaluable insight into the fundamental obstacles to church unity.) His attitude to the non-Catholic romantic medievalists is a rebuke to those historians[14] who without qualification classify Digby as a romanticist. Hare's type, he continues,

> procured copies of pinnacles and crosses,
> and even of the iron hinges of the old doors

of churches; while the spiritual hinge,
on which the whole system of religion turns,
they were content to suppress for ever, forgetting that poetic delineations are not
necessarily religious faith; that "faith
itself must first be there, and then that
these will gather round it, as the fit
body round its soul".

(<u>MC</u>. XI, 482)

He is clear on the folly of pseudo-Catholicism, or
"romantic" Catholicism, which finds expression in
romantic medievalism; clear that all religious
externals have value only if they match the
"internal" doctrine.

Compitum; or, The Meeting of the Ways at the
Catholic Church (1848-54)[15] is not specifically
medievalist, although it is incidentally. It is
designed to show that all roads of human experience
lead to the unifying and reconciling centre of Rome,
that there is a close affinity between the Church and
man in his ingenuous and unperverted state, and that
the Church is ideally suited to train such a nature.
Compitum also shows how the Church, because of its
universal quality, is relevant to all departments of
life, and how every part of life indicates the truth
of the Church's teaching. The central image, for
which he quotes medieval sources (C. v.I, 7-10), is
a French ex-Augustinian monastery (with its association of medieval wisdom), set in the midst of a
wood, with many paths leading to it : "for so in the
centre of the vast wilderness through which our
spirits wander the Catholic church stands alone, with
all ways concentrating and meeting in it" (C.I, 7).
It is too match - almost to embody - this theme of
the all-encompassing universality and plenitude of
the Church that Digby wrote at such great length.[16]
And this universality was most fittingly illustrated
by reference to the Middle Ages, when the Church was
truly universal. He constructed his ideal of unity
and reconciliation and plenitude in the very fibre
of his works : he demonstrates unity by grouping
hundreds of apparently disparate quotations and
anecdotes - classical and modern,as well as medieval,
from French, Italian, Spanish and German literature,
as well as from Latin and Greek - under one theme,
and by attaching at every turn disparate elements to
the service of one idea. He emphasizes the message
simply and effectively by means of rhetorical lists.
The following example contradicts the popular notion
of universal ignorance cultivated by the medieval

109

Church:

> Who that has had any acquaintance with
> letters can ever pass near Tours or Lyons,
> Fontanelle or Fulda, Osnabury or Metz,
> Auxerre or Laon, either Corby, Hirschau
> or St. Gall, Prum or Mayence, Reims or
> Hildesheim, [etc.] ... without being
> moved to a consideration of that zeal for
> instruction emanating from the Catholic
> faith, which induced so many bishops and
> abbots, and believing emperors and kings,
> at the demand of councils, to found and
> favour schools of learning for all classes....

(C.II,322)

The generosity of reference, with its cumulative
impact, reflects the Church's cosmopolitanism, as
well as the strength of its egalitarian educational
concern. This type of rhetoric characterizes his
method : analysis was not his mode because disput-
ation was not congenial to his nature, for he was a
praise-singer, not a controversialist. Possibly he
felt that logical argument would never be enough to
convince Protestants and unbelievers of his cause, so
his appeal was directed to the cognitive imagination.
He saw the Middle Ages as a space wider than the
present reality, in which the imagination could
wander (MC. I, 8) and be convinced - thereby convincing the whole person - of the attractiveness and
viability of an alternative world. His works were
therefore as highly coloured as fiction, with little
regard to scientific history. The monastery of
Compitum is symbolically "that point towards which ..
the human spirit tends ... the last end, referable
itself to nothing else, but to which all other things
are to be referred ..." (C. I, 7-8) : a person can
argue from faith, but not to it, and it is this
conviction which leads Digby to try to "infect" his
audience with the faith, rather than try to prove it
to them. It would therefore be unfair to attribute
his method, which is lack of method, to mere romantic
vagueness.

Digby's mode matches his feeling for the greatness of the medieval Church. He converts romantic
feeling for the vastness and transcendent sublime of
landscape into feeling for the universality, plenit-
de and transcendence of the medieval Church. "There
is nothing," he says, "narrow, nothing of slavery,
nothing confined in religion; it is the immense, the

110

infinite, the eternal" (BS II. 149). The following
eulogy, which is his classic statement of the greatness of medieval religion, exemplifies this concept
of the Church :

> The middle ages ... were ages of highest
> grace to men; ages of faith; ages when
> all Europe was Catholic; when vast temples
> were seen to rise in every place ... when
> houses of holy peace and order were found
> amidst woods and desolate mountains ...
> ages of sanctity which witnessed a Bede,
> an Alcuin, a Bernard, a Francis, and crowds
> who followed them as they did Christ : ages
> of vast and beneficent intelligence, ...
> ages of the highest civil virtue ... ages
> of the noblest art, ... ages of more than
> mortal heroism, ... ages of majesty which
> knew a Charlemagne, an Alfred, and the
> sainted youth who bore the lily : ages too
> of England's glory, when ... heroes flock
> to her courts to behold the models of
> reproachless chivalry, and Emperors leave
> their thrones to adore God at the tombs of
> her martyrs! as Dante says,
> > No tongue
> > So vast a theme could equal, speech
> > and thought
> > Both impotent alike.

(MC. I, 2-3)

Here he stresses medieval European unity while
emphasizing patriotism, proclaims the scale of
collective endeavour while highlighting individual
achievement, and expresses the belief that religion
suffused all walks of life, sanctifying the secular.
Later, he quotes Michelet to the effect that almost
everyone was embraced by religion (MC. V, 293), and
claims that, especially in the early Middle Ages,
Christian doctrine was "adopted universally as the
basis of civil government, and of their whole
domestic customs and manners" (MC. I, 14). He speaks
of the "Catholic Church expanding its immense
branches" (C. I, 319), and the pivotal image of
Compitum, of pathways through the forest leading to
the monastery, is a symbol of this inclusivity and
universality : for all paths do not only lead to the
Church, they also spread out from it, to every corner
of the forest, which is the forest of human life
(C I, 413).

Digby's view of the Church as sanctifier of the material world was an answer to those Romantics and Victorians who were searching for an antidote to contemporary materialism. This anxiety led to a widespread delight in Catholic externalism, which symbolized the sanctification of the material, and Digby shared this appreciation. But his view was not, as has already been suggested, that of the ecclesiological or ritualist dilettante : this possibly reflects Möhler's Symbolics, with its thesis that a basic religious idea "was reflected in every detail and permeated the whole as well as its parts".[17] Hence Catholic externals were imbued with Catholic spiritual essence. His defence of externals was also part of his apologetic, since Protestants and unbelievers attacked them as evidence of trivial- ity and materialism. He spoke in favour of externals even before he became a Romanist (BS II. lxi-lxii), because he believed the manifold beauties of the Middle Ages were evidences of the truth of Catholic- ism. Everywhere there were "images of quiet wisdom, sanctity, and innocence; symbols of infinite love" (MC. I, 102), and this love of ceremonies and worship "undoubtedly originated in a thirst for justice, a thirst for order, a thirst for the invisible supreme good" which transmutes earthly forms of beauty into spiritually valid symbol (MC V, 16). (This view must also have appealed inadvertently to those with the converging but opposite view, that beauty, or culture, was a part of the new "supernatural natural- ism".)

This vision of the medieval Church was a solution to, and implicit criticism of, the poverty of modern society and its ideology: Catholicism was for him the absolute opposite of what he felt was the constricting, base, mean small-mindedness of his own day. The fact that he described Catholicism "three- dimensionally", by embodying it in a past society, is evidence that he was not discussing it as an abstra- ct,but that he wished it to be applied to present so- ciety. If his hortatory mode was rather oblique, his rôle was as much that of prophet as Carlyle's. Some of his critical passages ante-date Signs of the Times (1829), Carlyle's first work of social criticism. In a sense, Digby - who was well acquainted with Carlyle's works - and Carlyle are the obverse and reverse of the same coin, which was a vision of the eternal. But while Carlyle's divinity was ultimately secular, Fichteian (or perhaps Feuerbachian) and profoundly romantic, Digby's God was transcendent, orthodox and Catholic. Whether heterodoxy or

orthodoxy is to be preferred, both were radicals in
proposing enormous change in the fabric of society.
Digby's argument is that the modern age is
unhappy and modern society threatening to collapse
because of its irreligiousness, in which it contrasts
with the medieval world : the "new philosophy"
falsely "teaches the young that there may be
happiness without the exercise of virtue" (BS V. I,
178), and since faith is effaced, the "present good"
is lost, and "the earth is infected by its inhabit-
ants and its joy is passed away" (MC. III,210). This
age of sadness was ushered in by the French Revolution which "so fearfully developed" the principle of
hatred : "hatred of God, ... hatred of priests, ...
hatred of kings, of nobles, of all established
institutions; hatred of all authority, of all order,
and of freedom ..." (BS V. IV, v. II,334). This
disease had been latent in the world since the
Reformation, but philosophical rationalism had lifted
the lid of Pandora's box.[18] By contrast, "the spirit
of the church was universal love" (loc.cit.),as can
be seen by regarding the age of chivalry and faith,
which was "free from the infection of a base world"
(BS II. xiv). The modern age condemns itself in
condemning the humility (MC. I, 101, 113), zeal and
piety (MC. V, 357) of the Middle Ages, for they are
to be identified with the working-out of the Beatitudes (MC. I, 13): the calumniators of the Age of
Faith are worthy of hell (MC. II, 250-1). Like
Cobbett, he condemns the Reformation for having been
a secularizing revolution rather than a religious
reformation, symbolically replacing monasteries with
palaces (BS V. III, 58-9). He does not condemn
free-thinkers because they are free-thinking, but
because they presume to destroy in one generation the
wisdom of ages, because they "set up the private
judgement of every individual ... against the general
judgement of the Church" (BS V. III, 58). This is an
attack on romantic individualism. The right
alternative to private judgement is the accumulated
wisdom of the Church (BS V. I, 177).
He holds no brief for the "modern philosophic
writers on history", who malign the Catholic past.[19]
Hence his own practice of quoting medieval sources at
length, so that the Middle Ages can be seen at first-
hand, instead of through the usual distorting lens,
like those of "infidels" and "Scotch Presbyterian
preachers" (BS II.99). One interesting example of
modernist criticism of medieval Catholicism is their
censure of monasticism. Yet moderns - which is to
say sentimentalists - favoured the cult of rural

retirment and contemplation on secular grounds. Why,
then,should they censure retirement and contemplation
on worthier, religious grounds, he ways, quoting the
first volume of Milner's History of Winchester to
this effect (BS V. II, 211). Similarly, he criticizes "political sophists" who preach the Enlightenment notion of the "perfectibility of human society".
Almost alone amongst nineteenth-century social
critics, he holds that utopia is truly nowhere
(undermining to some extent his medievalist myth),[20]
due to original sin : "we must not expect any future
state on earth, in which men will possess more perfectly than hitherto, the grace of the Holy Spirit"
(MC.XI, 478). If man progresses in one direction he
relapses in another : "sins and miseries will always
be found in the earthly city" (MC.II, 220-2). The
present is insupportable; "progress" is an empty
promise, so where to look but backwards? He deals
ironically with those "fatalists" who give specious
body to progressivism by insisting that civilization
"follows an invariable and irresistible law", and who
attack real principle by referring

> the whole character of the Ages of Faith to
> the necessary consequences of such external
> causes as were connected with the stage in
> which society then existed. The men whom
> we have seen, say they, were the creatures
> of the time; the time called them forth;
> the time did everything.
>
> (MC.XI,470)

The corollary of this statement is not necessarily a
plea for individualism, which would be unlike Digby,
but for responsibility and free will: and he insists
on the transcendence of the faith, as well as its
eternal importance,.regardless of social conditions
(MC.XI,470-71). Since the faith is not relativistic,
medievalism is justified; since it is absolute and
transcendent, it is worth revivifying. So medieval
faith is set against the "fond and sottish dotage
upon corporeal sense" of materialists and rationalists (BS II. xx, xxi-xxiii, and lvi; BS V. I, 44),
and looks especially attractive when compared with it
(MC.V, 362-3). With Carlyle, he believes the
resurgence of Mammon marks society's final stage of
spiritual decadence (BS V.I, 44), while his condemnation of modern pragmatism (BS II. lii-liii) typifies his association of all modernisms with selfishness, which he constantly opposes to the generosity
of medieval Christendom.

114

Not only does Digby castigate modernism in the
light of medievalism, and defend the Middle Ages
against the moderns, he also goes on to rebuke the
results of modernism. Hope and courage are destroyed
by the rejection of faith :

> you mourn; you fear sickness; and, above
> all, you shrink in terror from the thought
> of death; at least, you cannot pretend that
> men in these days die with as much tranqui-
> llity, and with as bright and stedfast a
> hope as the men whose dissolution we have
> been witnessing in the ages which you
> designate as those of monastic darkness.
> You mourn, and your mourning is avowedly
> without hope, without a blessing.

(<u>MC</u>. IV, 257)

The remedy is to turn away from secular materialism
to the medieval faith (<u>MC</u>. IV, 258). Materialism
also breeds dishonour and the divinization of exped-
iency (<u>C</u>. I, 281), preaching "avarice and ambition"
(ie. the pursuit of wealth and rank), instead of love
and duty (<u>BS V</u>. I, 178). Political currents are also
adversely affected by irreligious modern attitudes,
placing man "perpetually between slavery and rebellion" (<u>MC</u>. II, 102). Even the medieval serf was
better off than the modern workman because of the
Church's influence in favour of social interrelated-
ness (<u>MC</u>. I, 65),and this unity was a function of the
unique and pervasive spiritual and intellectual
authority of the Catholic Church (<u>BS V</u>. I, 177) :
when spiritual unity collapsed, social disunity was
the natural result. The solution was universal
submission to Catholicism, and only such a radical
cure would do :

> The writers who neglect [the Church] in
> endeavouring to correct men are, as
> Friedrich Schlegel says of the modern
> writers of England, only physicians who
> make use of palliatives, but who are
> incapable or unambitious of effecting
> a radical cure.

(<u>BS V</u>. I,72)

In view of the status of the physicians, only a
pessimistic prognosis was possible : "how far do the
men of religious and chivalrous spirit, differ from

115

these modern sophists? ... - as much as the living from the dead" (BS II. lix).

Like many others of the Romantic period, Digby was deeply interested in the notion of unity and community, and order, which was a part of it. What was to be the agent of reconciliation on the individual, community and national levels? Everything, he decided, could be harmonized in Catholicism : its practices were "capable of conducing to inspire the soul with happiness and peace, and of being united with the occupations and innocent diversions of life, in a countless variety of instances, so as to make these harmonize with religion".[21] Because of the Church's tendency to unify, he believes that medieval Europe was essentially united (BS II.185), and thinks the medieval idea of community was based on a vision of the universe united in God and centring, through His Church, on His goodness (C.I,10). Also, unity of faith results in the community of people (BS VI,177). Even before his conversion, he stresses the prime importance of a Christian's affiliation to a supranational Church (BS II.63-4), and correspondingly claims that "Christian gentlemen" are members of the "common country" of Europe because of their spiritual association with the medieval nobility, who were patrons of an international Church and defenders of the poor, irrespective of their nationality (BS II. xi). The principle extends to the family, for the medieval Church promoted family unity by its teaching of responsibility, mutual forbearance and filial obedience (C.I,118,121). As generosity is the "oil" which makes community work, and the sacred virtue of mutual loyalty (BS V. IV,v.I,193,203) its bond, so pride is the agent of modern isolationism and the disrupter of medieval Catholic associations. Like Carlyle, he hates the capitalist bougeoisie as a group of materialist, grasping individualists (BS V. IV,v.II,107) who, in the pursuit of profit, are aiding social collapse. With romantic theoreticians before him, such as the Catholic anti-capitalist Adam Müller,[22] he saw liberalism and democracy as the vehicles of alienating bourgeois individualism, classifying them with the anarchy of the Revolution. Individualism (he calls it "independence") is "the last extravagance of human error", for "the spirit of sect favours the development of mental alienation" (MC. II,50). When "the modern philosophy" - whose soul is pride - triumphs, "the state becomes only a nation of individuals, of wretched men" (MC. II,286); for then

> each man has his own motives, his own rule
> of right and wrong, his own end in view;
> perhaps he thinks virtues what you regard as
> sins, and sins against his type of perfection
> what you regard as the highest virtue : in the
> Catholic states there was only one standard
> even admist desertions, only one morality
> understood even by those who departed from it,
> as there was but one faith : what an increase
> of public and social happiness resulted from
> such unity!
>
> (MC. II, 176-7)

The teaching authority of the church promotes and
seals the happy community mentality (MC.II,50), and
this contrasts with the "present distracted state of
the religious and social mind in Europe", a phenomenon ultimately caused by the abandonment of "those
principles of Christian unity" at the Reformation
(BS V. III,3). The unifying fountain-head of these
benefits was, and could be again, the Papacy.[23]

It is generally assumed that Digby was an important influence on Disraeli's Young England movement,[24]
and to estimate the worth of this notion it is necessary to look closer at his politics. He is usually
identified as a paternalistic, monarchistic feudalist; but this is an over-simplification. His politics
were based entirely on religion, and he was unquest-
ionably heavily influenced by the right-wing Catholic
history and politics of Chateaubriand, Count Louis de
Bonald and Count Joseph de Maistre, representing the
"throne and altar" school of authoritarian Ultramon-
tanists, who wished to see the episcopacy deeply
involved in national politics. Paradoxically, Digby
was more in favour of this view before his conversion
than after; although there is a difficulty in judging, because he never gave complete, coherent expression to his political views. He was, however, consistently opposed to the spirit of the French Revolution, for its rationalism had led to pragmatism, and
pragmatism had led to the terror. But he was also
influenced by the Catholic liberals Lacordaire,
Montalembert and Lamennais, who were his friends. By
sentiment he was a monarchist and traditionalist, for
- unlike Lamennais - he could see no Christian alternative; but by conviction he was a Papalist and benevolist, who - unlike De Maistre - did not wish to see
the Church servile to the State or involved in
politics as such, on the grounds that this would infect the purity of the Church with national foibles.[25]
In fact, he was sui generis, envisaging a society

based on the family, with a paternalist aristocracy.
But his appeal to the aristocracy had little to do
with their wealth (BS V.IV,v.I, 5-6, BS V. IV,v.II,
137), social position or blood (C. I,259) : it was to
do with their traditional link with medieval chivalry,
which had been a class of men inspired by the Church
to dedicate themselves to spiritualizing secular
aspects of society (BS V. I, 178,303, C. I, 269,281).
The key to his vision was of a society whose nature
would facilitate the operation of Catholic principles, and this he saw in the Middle Ages. In an
extraordinary passage he indicates that he does not
mind what name is applied to the structure of a
society, so long as it is truly Catholic : he approv-
ingly quotes de Haller's Restoration of Political
Science to the effect that republicanism has much in
common with the principles of Catholicism, and that
it is viable if governed by such principles.[26] It is
striking that Digby talks as much of freedom as of
authority.

Digby's central social concern is the welfare
of the poor, not the rich, and there are hints of
egalitarianism in his work. For him, the aristocrat
is the man of spiritual maturity and accomplishment
(BS V. I, 302), exactly as the medieval knight was a
knight because Catholicism was the very basis of his
character (BS II. 42-3, BS V. II, 76), and such
nobility could be found in any rank of society (BS V.
I, 251). Aristocrats were - and should be again -
by definition the best people to govern. An aristocracy was necessary to rule what he called the
"churls" : ie. the majority of ordinary men. By
"churl" he connoted not a class, but "the corruption
and depravity of that class of mankind, which is not
radically corrected by religion" (BS II. 14). The
churl is the "enemy of your religion" (BS II. 27),
and the aristocrat must correct such men and lead
them to God. This concept of aristocracy is not
unlike Coleridge's of what he called the "clerisy",
which had been in the Middle Ages that part of the
Church which looked to the education of the people,
a function which, he believed, had preserved the
State and promoted civilization and the cause of
liberty : but Coleridge's was essentially a secular
concern, although he acknowledged that then theology
had been the "root and trunk" of the knowledge
disseminated by the clerisy.[27]

Despite his knowledge of the Christian doctrine
of the equality of men before God, social hierarchy
is considered right because authority is considered
so, and because it is, in the Thomist fashion, in the
natural order of things (BS V. I, 177-8)[28] : the

"democratic" alternative would entail moral, social and spiritual anarchy (BS II. 133, BS V. I, 301, 315-16). The Church sanctified hierarchy : "according to the ... philosophy of the Catholic Church, every man had his post and his honourable employment" (BS V.I, 302). Hierarchy and true equality were compatible because honour and sanctity could be equally achieved by any member of society. The modern age, by contrast, has lost the Christian perspective, so that the poor are hateful in the eyes of the bourgeoisie, and spend their lives in irritated aspiration after the bourgeois state. Traditional class distinctions and snobbery are vain because true nobility was to do with religion, not class (C. I, 282), and because of the revelation that was the supposed catalyst of medieval social unity : "that all men are equal before God" (BS V. I, 7). He firmly believes in the "equality of master and servant" and the "human fraternity which constituted Christian equality" (C. I, 149,247), and delights in medieval educational egalitarianism, promoted by the monasteries (BS V. II, 249). Indeed, there is "nothing more vain or futile than pride of birth. ... Human nature is one and simple, equal in all" (C, I, 269). His ideal society is where there are no lords and only servants (MC.I, 62). He quotes St.Augustine saying that the Christian in command governs because it is his duty and is good to provide for others. "This," he adds, "is the lesson pressed upon the great all through the middle ages ..." (C.I, 149). It should also be remembered that Augustine, whose writings Digby loved above all others, taught the equality of men, community of property and brotherly love. One may deduce from his "egalitarianism", from his doctrines that true nobility was not defined by class, and that each man had his responsibility in society, and from the respect paid to the individual, that, along with Aquinas, he supported the involvement of all right-minded men in government. So while such a statement as that Digby was dependent on "the reactionary romanticism of the continent" 29 is partly true, it needs serious qualification, since he was also an independent thinker.

Young England : Lord John Manners and Disraeli

Digby, claimed Charles Whibley, "found in the champions of Young England his most willing pupils", because they believed in the ability of religion to reform society, and in the notion of a natural alliance between the aristocracy and the people.30

How true is this? "If one book," wrote Whibley,
"were chosen as the breviary of Young England, that
book would be Kenelm Digby's ... 'The Broad Stone of
Honour'",[31] and they were certainly attracted to the
reactionary aspect of Digby, as expressed in the
first two editions of The Broad Stone,[32] and particularly to the message that there were obligations
attached to high position (BS II.2). They were also
influenced by Scott and Southey - George Smythe named
Southey as a founder of their movement[33] - and by
Carlyle's anti-Mammonism and feudalism,[34] so the
force of Digby's particular influence can only be
surmised, and then only from parallels. (Of course,
Pugin and De Lisle were even more willing pupils
than Young England, if only because they were Catholics.) Both Smythe and Lord John Manners were
personally influenced by F.W. Faber in lamenting the
passing of chivalry and in identifying themselves with
Anglo-Catholicism.[35] Their politics were strongly
flavoured with religion, though in private Manners'
feudalism got the better of his Christianity, as
when he supports the owning of one man by another,[36]
itself a total distortion of Digby's teaching, having
more in common with Carlyle's position. Perhaps
surprisingly, Digby never explicitly promoted feudalism : feudalism had been good because it was a
milieu in which leaders could thrive, and because
its leaders had been influenced by Christianity
(BS V. IV, v.I, 78). On the contrary, his ideals
were in the direction rather of a meritocracy (BS V.
IV, v.I, 102) than a land-based oligarchy.

Taking his lessons from Southey's Colloquies and
probably from Mores Catholici, Manners - who at
Trinity College, Cambridge had been an active member
of the Gothic-revivalist Camden Society - sought the
restoration of monastic life to England. In 1840 he
said that "nothing but monastic institutions can
christianise Manchester"; and in 1845, after the
launching of a relative circular of appeal bearing an
epigraph from Southey's Colloquies, the Sisterhood of
Mercy was founded.[37] The circular, called The Monastic and Manufacturing Systems (1843), said that
"great and deeply-seated evils ... exist throughout
the whole of our manufacturing society", and that
"through the Church alone" can "we look for a
permanent amelioration of those evils".[38] The answer
was the establishment of Protestant monastic orders.
He regarded England as a Christian nation unchrist-
ianised : when the process was reversed, social
benefits would follow. "To him ... the religious
aspect of the [Young England] movement was all-

important."[39] Like Digby, Manners looked to the
medieval Church as the prime example of the Christ-
ianizing of society and the alleviation of social
distress. But like Coleridge, he especially wished
to see the revitalization of the national Church to
this end. (His fellow Anglo-Catholic, the Reverend
John Mason Neale, foresaw and worked for the restoration of the monasteries, particularly for their
social benefits.)[40] Another pamphlet, A Plea for
National Holidays, shows his idealization of the role
of the medieval Church in society, with its Digbeian
view of the Church as champion of the poor :

> It was the Church that, in ruder but more
> humble times than these, arrested the
> sword of war by her blessed truce of God -
> it was the Church that then was the defence
> of the poor and the weak against the rich
> and the strong....[41]

Such idealization may also be witnessed in his
volume of poetry England's Trust, and Other Poems
(1841). The title poem has often been criticized
for its mindless Toryism, especially the lines

> Let wealth and commerce, laws and learning
>   die,
> But leave us still our old Nobility! (p.24)

Reginald Lucas wrote of these lines that they did not
represent his real aspirations, for he "entertained
no selfish claims to privilege of caste, and was
ambitious, before all things, of helping to improve
the condition of the poor".[42] This sounds very like
Digby. Whibley defends these lines by interpreting
"Nobility" as "Nobility of Man, the Nobility of
Character",[43] rather than as "mere titled nobodies".
If this is correct - and in the light of Digby's
understanding of aristocracy it would appear to be
so - Manners shared Digby's desire for the rule of
England by good "Catholic" men. Moreover, these
lines show a bitter contempt for modern utilitarianism, pragmatism and rationalism, very like Digby's.
In the same poem (pp. 16-17) he takes it for granted
that the medieval structure of society was divinely
sanctioned because it resulted in mutual responsibility and a spirit of humane "generous feeling", a
virtue of special importance to Digby. By contrast,
the "Independence" which the cash-nexus brings in the
nineteenth century is the independence to suffer
without aid. The Digbeian notion of social unity

based on a sense of mutual responsibility and
obedience to the Church here emerges.[44] This poem's
message is basically religious, for the ruins of St.
Alban's Abbey symbolize the holy voice of salvation
calling from the Middle Ages, and give a glimpse of
utopian times,

> When Mother-Church her richest stores
>   displayed,
> And Sister-State on her behalf arrayed
> The tempered majesty of sacred law,
>   . . . . . .
> When kings were taught to feel the
>   dreadful weight
> Of power derived from One than kings
>   more great ....
>   (pp. 3-4)

That is to say, politics is a function of religion;
and social degree and order are good for man, so long
as they are informed by Catholic teaching,[45] as in
the Middle Ages. (Digby would have jibbed at the
phrase "Sister-State".) The interdependent unity
was broken up at the Reformation, and, as in Digby,
the result was metaphysically and socially
catastrophic (pp. 5-6). The one ray of hope is

> that our sons may from experience know
> What bitter streams from modern fountains
>   flow;
> And turn their steps, e'er 'tis too late
>   to turn,
> To ancient Faith's yet unforgotten urn.

The job of "counter-reformation"lies with the Church,
not the State, for the State can only be the executor
of the people's spirit, which is itself ordained and
matured by the Church : "through the CHURCH must come
the healing power,/ To bind our wounds in this
tumultuous hour" (p. 26).
    The note of Digbeian prophecy and eulogy is
evident in other poems, like "Hope" and "Christmas";
while "Vallambrosa" is interesting because it betrays
hesitancy about identification with the medieval
faith and because it repeats Digby's defensive
awareness of modern rationalist contempt for medieval
religion. Towards the end of the poem, he seems to
commit himself to the religion of the past by leaping
backwards in time to sympathetically observe "a meek
unworldly band" offering intercessory prayers. He
makes an open challenge to deny the validity of these

prayers, and perhaps he is challenging himself as an
Anglican watching Roman worship. This divorce is why
he gives the sign of hesitancy near the beginning of
"Vallambrosa", and it is what finally distinguishes
him from the Catholic Digby : though he was friendly
to Catholics, he did not become one. "Rome"
indicates why he will not become a Roman Catholic.
Here he sees Rome as having ruthlessly sent Anglicans
into exile (thereby contradicting "England's Trust",
which blames the Reformation for splits in the
Church), and pursued "wordly pomp and rule", Manners,
like Wordsworth, is in two minds about medieval
religion : he gives his sanction to medieval Catholicism in England because this was Anglo-Catholicism,
subject (as Coleridge would say) to the State and
profoundly connected with, and specially adapted to,
England; while Continental Catholicism was another
matter. It may be that there is a conflict between
Manners' notion of the State as handmaid of the
Church, and that of the Church as constitutionally
subject to the State and adapted to the nation :
Digby would have thought so.[46]
     When Disraeli, the ostensible leader of Young
England, wrote in (part IV, chapter VIII of) Sybil
(1845) that the "Privileged and the People formed Two
Nations", he could have had Digby's principle of
community in mind. He may even have been recalling
Digby's comment that "the moderns practically divide
the human race into two classes", depending on
country, political party, philosophy, society or
family, while the medievals divided men according to
the only meaningful distinction : whether or not they
were for Christ (MC. II, 58). Young England
philosophy seems to have been influenced by Digby's
ideas, and appears to have assumed something of his
religious medievalist orientation. But Disraeli was
a shrewd politician with a purely romantic admiration
for Catholicism, who used Digby to bolster his own
ideas of a society governed by an élite class and
stabilised by the support and divine sanction of a
national Church : in short, his religious medievalist
interest was secular rather than religious. Nevertheless, there were strands of nostalgic and
aesthetic empathy in his attitude to Roman Catholicism (or at least, to English Catholicism).[47] In 1824
he was deeply moved by High Mass in Ghent Cathedral[48]
and this taste became nostalgia when applied to the
Middle Ages, as in Coningsby (1844) and Sybil.
He also appreciated the dedicated traditionalism of
the old, aristocratic, recusant families. He was
always devoted to his Jewish background, and this

emerged in his faint pro-Romanism : believing that
Christianity is either fulfilled Judaism or nothing[49]
he respected Rome as "the only Hebraeo-christian
church extant".[50] Yet since it is the rooting of
Catholic practice in the Old Testament which is of
supreme importance, he attaches no special value to
the Church as localized either in the Middle Ages
(when it held an "exaggerated position") or at Rome[51]
Looking back on the 1840s, he regretted that the
religious initiative had passed from the Anglican
"rock of truth" to "monks and schoolmen" and the
Newmanite seceders who "sought refuge in mediaeval
superstitions".[52] Moreover, since he could distance
himself from Young England passions and be ironic
about them,[53] his religious medievalist enthusiasm
was clearly not heartfelt; nor, if we are to believe
George Smythe, was his Tractarianism.[54]

Disraeli sided with Coleridge and Southey in
their radical traditionalism, with its strongly held
belief in a firm link between Church and State, and
their antagonism to utilitarian Whiggery and
bourgeois individualism : "views ... long prevalent
in England".[55] He said the Young England trilogy
(Coningsby, Sybil, Tancred) "recognized imagination
in the government of nations as a quality not less
important than reason", was anti-egalitarian and
proposed that social durability could only be built
upon principles of "loyalty and religious reverence".[56] His appeal to the medieval Church in
England ("in England" because his concern - as with
all Anglicans - was with a national Church) was as a
buttress against Whiggery; and he wished the Church
to be the second Estate of the realm, probably not
because he wished primarily to see religion elevated,
but because he wished to see the restoration of the
wider medieval political structure. The medieval
Church had been the "spiritual and intellectual
trainer of the people", a principle social remedial
agency, the principle bastion against "the demon
tyranny of Capital", a provider of "succour, counsel,
and protection", especially for the poor.[57] The key
to such praise is, as with Manners, the monastic
economy. The thesis expounded in Sybil is that,
until the Reformation destroyed it, there was a
proper human relationship between labourer and
employer, a sense of community, instead of the modern
polarization of master and slave. The monastic land-
holders were responsible for this relationship,
especially since they were deathless landlords
(thereby avoiding all the problems of the poor
consequent on a change of ownership) and never

absentee. Unlike modern landlords, they fulfilled
Carlyle's maxim of a fair day's pay for a fair day's
work, encouraged patriotism by beautifying the
country and displayed a Christian generosity of
spirit (so important to Digby) by planning for the
well-being of posterity. Finally, because of the
community between monks and labourers, property
indirectly worked for the latter.[58] This view of a
secular Disraeli does not ignore the fact that
utilitarianism and the Whig spirit are usually
opposed to Coleridgean spirituality : he opposed
"custom" - not any kind of spirituality - to "the
Spirit of Utility"; so when Eustace Lyle, an anti-
Whig, anti-sectarian, transplanted medieval (based
on Ambrose Phillipps de Lisle), says he has "revived
the monastic customs",[59] one feels that the emphasis
is on "customs" rather than "monastic", and that the
almsgiving, which is one of the customs, is important
not because it is a religious activity, but because
it embodies the spirit of generosity which Disraeli
opposes to utilitarianism.

     Disraeli said that "how an oligarchy had been
substituted for a kingdom" was a dominant problem
for him in the 1840s,[60] as was the question of how
the process could be reversed.. Modernism began,
according to Disraeli, with the Reformation, which
introduced the Whig spirit and gave monastic property
to a new, upstart "factitious aristocracy", whose
ethic was opportunistic and selfish. Truth, freedom,
happiness and religion were largely ousted at the
Reformation by crime, slavery, suffering and spiritual poverty.[61] In his account of the rise of the
post-Reformation Whig oligarchy, he says "it is in
the plunder of the Church that we must seek for the
primary cause of our political exclusion, and our
commercial restraint".[62] The "excluders" were the
Whigs, and by "exclusion" he meant "exclusion from
power of all other interests or institutions : the
Crown, the Church, the 'People'".[63] While the
Reformation is termed "unhallowed" and "sacrilegious",
that the central concern is the revolutionary re-
distribution of property is barely disguised. The
real sacrilege is the endowing of the "factitious
aristocracy", the creation of a new political order,
and it is never made clear why this argument revolves
around the Church and not the late-medieval aristocracy, the sphere where, in his own terms, it more
truly belongs. It seems he believes the Reformation
was engineered by the oligarchy to promote their own
power at the expense of the monarch, whereas it had
more to do with the monarch strengthening his own

125

position. This sleight-of-hand results from
Disraeli's riding the High-Church boom for political
ends. And the thesis that the Low Church sects were
invented by the Whigs and then harnessed to protect
their prosperity emerges as the real reason why he
supports the High Church : and correlatively, the
revitalized High Church is seen as a potential bridge
to a monarchical and aristocratic past. His stated
reason for seeking the restoration of medieval Crown
and Church rights was, indeed, to fortify "the
popular estate" and to ameliorate the lives of the
lower classes, which had been damaged and degraded by
"oligarchic" self-interest.[64]

Whatever the subtleties of Disraeli's position,
the ordinary reader of the 1840s would probably have
extracted from the novels a High Church, if not
Anglo-Catholic, pro-monastic message. Yet some, like
Richard Monckton Milnes, were suspicious, and he
pointed out that the religious attitudes expressed in
the trilogy are undermined by racism, hero-worship
and the desire for a new aristocracy.[65] In using
religion politically, Disraeli is guilty of the Whig
manipulation he castigates: religion - at least, in
its High Church form - is for him a means rather than
an end.[66] So Disraeli is further from Digby than
Manners or Smythe. Like Digby, however, he is something of a romantic, idealizes the past, is concerned
for the poor, believes in the possibility of a special
relationship between aristocracy and working class,
supports the alliance of Church, monarch, landed
interest and people against the despized, Whig,
utilitarian middle class, believes in the social
efficacy of the Church and the need for creative
leaders,[67] and promotes an extraordinary mixture of
conservatism and radicalism. On the other hand,
Young England was more politically-oriented than
Digby, more exclusively pro-aristocracy, and in
favour of a national Church rather than an universal
one. They clearly drew inspiration from their
"breviary", but did not take Digby's mature position
into account. They were, so to speak, Southey and
Coleridge tempered by Digby.

The movement collapsed in 1845 after only a few
active years and lacked large practical issue,
although Saintsbury witnesses to its "extraordinary
influence on the Universities",[68] while Blake asserts
that the influence of Disraeli's theory of history
stretched as far as Belloc and Chesterton,[69] both of
whom were religious medievalists. Their failure is
not surprising, since the great weight of progressivist, materialist, Protestant society was against

126

them: the bourgeoisie would never have tolerated a
"Catholic" view of society which did not take them
into full account. One or two tepidly applauded, but
for the most part the reaction was scorn. George
Francis rightly judged that Manners' protest was a
romantic one against the "tyrannical ascendancy of
reason in human affairs", and in favour of restoring
the "feelings and sympathies" of men to their legitimate place.[70] Such romanticism was not in the ascendancy in socio-political spheres, and Catholics like
Faber and Digby realized such a thing could not be
legislated for. Nevertheless, in 1859 Kingsley aver-
red that "Neo-Anglicanism" had had an improving
effect on the aristocracy; and he may well have had
Digby - or at least the Digbeian frame of mind - in
view, since by 1857 he certainly was aware of The
Broad Stone of Honour, having named a chapter in Two
Years Ago (1857) with that title. Neo-Anglicanism
had left a legacy of "grand old authors disinterred,
of art, of music; of churches too, schools, cottages,
and charitable institutions", and had sowed the seed
in the hearts of gentlemen of a

> virtue more stately and reverent, more
> chivalrous and self-sacrificing, more
> genial and human, than can be learnt from
> the religion of the Stock Exchange, which
> reigned triumphant - for a year and a day
> - in the popular pulpits.[71]

The same reasons for basic failure apply to
Digby himself. Hill suggests he failed because in
the second half of the century social unrest died
away and with it the stimulus to radical solutions,
and because in the 1820s his romantic medievalism was
acceptable, while his earnestness was not; while by
his death the cause of his lack of persuasiveness
was reversed.[72] Utilitarian liberals ignored him,
Low Church Protestants denounced him, Puseyites
stoutly defended their conviction that the modern
Church of England was one and the same as the medieval Church in England, leading Catholics were tepid
in their admiration for the medieval Church and ordinary Catholics were mostly too poor and ill-educated
to purchase or understand his books. Digby also cut
his own throat : he never satisfactorily accounted
for the decline of the Church at the end of the
Middle Ages (a decline he acknowledged),for the
partial victory of Protestantism, or for the Church's
loss of influence in the modern world. Had he done
this,he would have clarified his position,thereby

achieving far greater impact and cogency; and he
would certainly have been more popular had he adjus-
ted his tone to the surrounding religious controversy
and made his books more sharply relevant to his
contemporaries.

NOTES
    1.   "A Medieval Victorian" TLS 5 Sept.1958,504
paragraph I.
    2.   The Flower of Kings 174, 124 respectively.
Cf. Margaret R. Grennan William Morris : Medievalist
and Revolutionary (New York, 1945) 28.
    3.   The Correspondence of Lord Acton and
Richard Simpson III, 22, letter 1 Oct.1862.
    4.   Charles William Russell DR XIV(Feb.1843)99.
    5.   Kingsley Literary and General Lectures and
Essays (1890) 192.
    6.   Broad Stone of Honour 2nd.ed. (1823) 42-3.
Henceforth cited as BS II.
    7.   BS II. xiii. Henceforth cited in text.
    8.   Broad Stone of Honour 5th. ed. (1876-77) I,
179-94. Henceforth cited in text as BS V. 5v.ed.
    9.   His interest may have been secular at first
(c.1820), this leading him to Catholicism. Moore
Smith speculates in this way : MLR (Oct.1919) XIV
431; cf. Hill TLS 5 Sept. 1958 504 parag. 2.
    10.   Digby Mores Catholici : or, Ages of Faith
II v. (1831-42) I, 118,119. Henceforth cited in
text as MC.
    11.   J.C. Hare and A.W.Hare Guesses at Truth by
Two Brothers 1st. ser. 2v., 3rd.ed. (1847) 230-34.
Note that the comments on Digby were supplemented
with each successive ed.
    12.   Bernard Holland Memoir of Kenelm Henry
Digby (1919) 63-4. Henceforth cited as Memoir.
    13.   Guesses at Truth 234-37.
    14.   Eg. Chandler, Friedrich Heyer, Mark
Girouard and E.I. Watkin.
    15.   "Compitum" is a "Latin word for a point at
which roads meet, or to which roads converge" :
Memoir 122. Cited in text as C.
    16.   As Henry Bagshawe noted, Digby never sought
to batter his opponents into submission with logic;
rather he sought to seduce by charm and enchantment,
to convince by the accumulation of detail and example
(DR XXV [Dec.1848] 464-5). His resulting prolixity,
which in turn led to his practice of issuing volumes
of a work in consecutive years, made it difficult for
the public to follow him.
    17.   Qu. Heyer The Catholic Church From 1648 to
1870 129-30.

18. Cf. Heyer The Catholic Church from 1648 to 1870 131, Houghton The Victorian Frame of Mind 2.

19. BS II. xl, 96-100, where he singles out Gibbon, Hume and Robertson; BS V.II, 45, where Warton is mentioned; BS V. III, 322-3, where the naivety and stupidity of Hurd's Letters are noted.

20. Digby is capable of stepping outside his myth, while still preferring the medieval to the modern, admitting that it was imperfect : BS V. III 45, 47, 58.

21. Broad Stone of Honour, Morus (1848) 163.

22. Heyer The Catholic Church from 1648 to 1870 169-70; John Weiss Conservatism in Europe 1770-1945 (1977) 41-3.

23. Broad Stone of Honour, Tancredus (1846) 298.

24. Eg. Hill TLS 5 Sept. 1958 504 parag. 9, Amy Cruse The Victorians and Their Books (1962) 141, Houghton The Victorian Frame of Mind 325-6, Chandler 160.

25. Broad Stone of Honour, Tancredus (1846)295.

26. Broad Stone of Honour, Tancredus (1846) 299-300.

27. On the Constitution of the Church and State (1830) 49.

28. Digby's political views may have been influenced by Thomas Aquinas, who thought that authority and inequality were rooted in natural law and thereby in divine law; that government - the common ruling power - should care primarily for the common good, in resistance to men's preoccupation with self; that superior men should lead inferior men to God. He advocated universal participation in government and the mixing of the best from the best forms of constitution to make a well-balanced state. He believed that when state affairs impinge on the supernatural life, the state - normally autonomous - should subordinate itself to the Church. See Aquinas De Regimine Principum, F.C. Copleston Aquinas (Harmondsworth, 1963) ch.V, Walter Ullman A History of Political Thought : The Middle Ages (Harmondsworth 1968) ch.VII, F.C. Copleston A History of Philosophy (New York, 1962) v.II, pt.II, ch.XL, Etienne Gilson The Elements of Christian Philosophy (London, 1963) ch.XII.

29. Yngve Brilioth The Anglican Revival (1933) 57.

30. Whibley Lord John Manners and His Friends 2v. (1925) I, 135. Henceforth cited as 'Whibley'.

31. Ibid. I, 133.

32. Whibley notes that The Broad Stone was "twenty years old" before they used it, and if he

was being accurate, this means that they used the
first or second edition, which were less Catholic
and more prescriptive - with their subtitle "Rules
for the Gentlemen of England" - than later editions.

33. Whibley I, 131, 260.

34. Charles H. Kegel "Lord John Manners and the
Young England Movement : Romanticism in Politics"
Western Political Quarterly XIV (1961) 691-2.

35. Whibley I, 66, 131, 153, Kegel Western
Political Quarterly XIV 692-3.

36. Whibley I, 106.

37. Ibid. I, 107, 260-1, Grennan William Morris
12.

38. Qu. Kegel Western Political Quarterly XIV,
695.

39. Whibley I, 185.

40. Hierologus; or, The Church Tourists (1843)
27-8.

41. A Plea for National Holy Days 2nd. ed.
(1843) 31.

42. DNB on Manners.

43. Whibley I, 114, and see 113, 115-16.

44. See Chandler 161-2 on Manners and social
unity based on the Church's activity and teaching.

45. Cf. Fairchild IV, 279 and Chandler 161 on
Manners and his view of the relationship between
Church and State.

46. George Smythe - who had a mutual acquaintance with Digby in Julius Hare - wrote a volume
similar to Manners' England's Trust called Historic
Fancies (1844). He also wanted to escape the modern
world, symbolized by the French Revolution, and to
return to the beauties of the age of faith. For
example, he describes revolutionary Paris,

Where Fraud, and Crime, and Marat reign, and
     the Triple Colours wave
O'er the Churches of Our Lady, and the Blessed
     Geneviève;
Where Agnus, Pix, and Crucifix, are made the
     wanton's spoil,
And the bells which called to vespers, now
     call to blood and broil.

(Historic Fancies 2nd.ed. [1844] "The Loyalist of the
Vendée" st.V,173.) He was probably more Catholic
than Manners, writing in a letter to him that he
would like to go over to Rome, "pull down this rotten
citadel of heresy - the Protestant Establishment -
and bear a hand in raising upon its ruins a hierarchy
- strong and stable" (Whibley I, 136, 74).

47. Cf. Nils Clausson "English Catholics and
Roman Catholicism in Disraeli's Novels" NCF XXXIII

(Mar. 1979) 454-6.
    48. Qu. Bernard McCabe "Disraeli and the 'Baronial Principle'" VNL XXXIV (1968) 8, n.4.
    49. Sybil (1882) Bk.II, ch.XII, 130. Hughenden ed. used throughout.
    50. Ibid. II, XII, 129.
    51. Ibid. II, XII, 130, 131 respectively.
    52. Disraeli "General Preface" Lothair xv, written 1870.
    53. Cf. McCabe "Disraeli and the 'Baronial Principle'" VNL XXXIV 8-12.
    54. Whibley I, 153, Clausson NCF XXXIII 461.
    55. Lothair xiv.
    56. Loc. cit.
    57. Lothair x, xii, Sybil V, VIII, 375,II,V,72.
    58. Sybil II, V, 71, 73-5. His respect for monasteries was probably learnt from Cobbett : Chandler 177-80.
    59. Coningsby III, III, 134, 135 respectively.
    60. Lothair ix.
    61. Sybil I, III, 12, II, XIV, 143.
    62. This exposition in Coningsby II, I, 75.
    63. Robert Blake Disraeli (1966) 194.
    64. Lothair x.
    65. ER LXXXVI (Jul. 1847) 138-55.
    66. Richard A. Levine says that in Tancred Disraeli saw politics as dependent on religion : "Disraeli's Tancred and 'The Great Asian Mystery'" NCF XXII (1967-8), 81-2, 85. But Tancred deals not with the medieval Church, but with Disraeli's deeper Hebraeo-Christian concern.
    67. See Houghton The Victorian Frame of Mind 313, 332-3.
    68. The Collected Essays and Papers of George Saintsbury 1875-1920 3v. (1923) v. III 267.
    69. Disraeli 209.
    70. FM XXXV (Mar. 1847) 321-9.
    71. Preface to 4th. ed. of Yeast, Yeast 9th.ed. (1878) x.
    72. TLS 5 Sept. 1958 parags. 12, 13; cf. Moore Smith MLR XIV 434.

Chapter V

CATHOLICS AND ANGLO-CATHOLICS

Catholicism is not medievalism.
                G.K. Chesterton Chaucer

The attraction of the Catholic Faith for
the artistic temperament ... is one of
the facts of psychology.
                A.J.A. Symons The Quest for Corvo

Scott, the Tractarians and their Influence

If Digby was the heart of English Catholic
religious medievalism, there were many other parts
to the body. Despite the fact that no religious
medievalist "school", no firm and unambiguous trend,
developed in the Victorian period, there was a more
varied and frequent resort to it. Even anti-medievalists were encouraged to express a narrow regard for
the medieval Church : Macaulay, believing in the
gospel of progress, and seeing that the medieval
Church had something of a monopoly in the Middle
Ages,decided that it must have played its part in the
pattern of progress. If it did nothing for religion,
medieval Roman rule was "generally favourable to
science, to civilisation, and to good government,"[1]
although it held no lessons for today. And J.A.
Froude's "The Lives of the Saints" betrayed a
lingering admiration for medieval ascetics, while
Kingsley, also in two minds, took much from Macaulay,
and shared his approval of the material benefits
bestowed by medieval Catholicism, a fact which for
him had a religious inflection independent of the
agent.[2]
        Anglo-Catholics and Catholics were naturally
more sympathetic, but the occasional kind words of
the anti-medievalists give point to the paradoxical
nature of their not being completely united in their

acclamation. The paradoxicality of the Anglo-Catholic position is heightened by the notion that they were medievalistically invigorated by Sir Walter Scott,[3] whose works were, however, overtly anti-Catholic.[4] So is this influence assumed or real; and if it is real, what - since Scott is usually taken to be in some sense a romantic writer - does that say about the relationship of Tractarianism to romanticism and the nature of Tractarian medievalism?

Victorians certainly believed that Scott's influence had been far-reaching in reducing anti-Catholic feeling and in promoting Catholicism, among them George Borrow, Fraser's Magazine, Gladstone and Edmund Purcell.[5] Hazlitt perceived him as the supremely popular writer of the age, who preferred the past to the present and "dotes on all well-authenticated superstitions"; as one whose pen "levels our bristling prejudices ... and sees fair play between Roundheads and Cavaliers, between Protestant and Papist".[6] Scott certainly prompted Digby to look at medieval Catholicism.[7]

The High Church believed that Scott's writings were empathetic with their cause: in 1841 The Ecclesiologist (the organ of the Cambridge Camden Society) welcomed his medievalism;[8] and in 1868 a High Churchman called J. Hicks Smith told how Scott led him to desire more ritual, and how The Abbot made him want respect for confession re-established.[9] The Tractarians were definitely interested in Scott. Froude first learnt his enthusiasm for the Middle Ages from him,[10] and doubtless his medievalism encouraged his doctrinal stance. Keble saw in Scott someone receptive to the Catholic spirit,[11] while Newman thought he had prepared men for "some closer and more practical approximation to Catholic truth" by laying a subconscious bate to catch those who needed "something deeper and more attractive than what had offered itself elsewhere".[12] This point must have had considerable significance for him, because he reproduced the passage 25 years later in the Apologia. It continues :

> by means of his popularity he re-acted on his readers, stimulating their mental thirst, feeding their hopes, setting before them visions, which, when once seen, are not easily forgotten, and silently indoctrinating them with nobler ideas, which might afterwards be appealed to as first principles.[13]

He believed Scott to have had Catholic tendencies
which he had suppressed in the face of "tyrant
tradition".[14] Andrew Sanders thinks it was Scott's
supposedly inspiring respect for conservatism and
tradition which gained Newman's and Keble's favour,[15]
a suggestion born out (so far as it goes) by Rev.
Henry Parry Liddon (1829-1890), who, considering the
horrors of the French Revolution and its fearsome
shadows in the 1830s, said that Pusey "often dwelt"
on Scott's medievalism and his "indirect" relation
to the Oxford Movement. But while the stimulus was
political, the essential concern was noted as having
been religious : religion was thought to be the
answer to political barbarism.[16] The Tractarians
were not mere traditionalists in their view of
Scott : they saw in him an agitator of medieval
spirituality.
        Scott's presentation showed that the medieval
faith was dramatic and colourful, a part of the
superstitions, the supernatural and wild imaginings
which the public had long found irresistible. And
perhaps his not unsympathetic presentation of
"Catholic" Cavaliers and Jacobites came to be
confused with his medievalism, thereby benefitting
the medieval Church in the popular view. The
uncertainties surrounding his attitude allowed
people to interpret him as a Romanizer, an
interpretation doubtless encouraged by contemporary
sensitivities, which would naturally seize on the
sensational novelty rather than the conventions of
anti-Catholicism. Ruskin's response reflects the
importance of Scott's ambiguity. He often read his
medievalist works, and believed Scott to be
prejudiced against Catholicism. He thought
Protestants misunderstood him because of his
"imaginative enjoyment of the outer paraphernalia
of Catholicism", believing that for Scott the only
use of imagination was to amuse. Yet he himself
felt "aided and inspired by Scott" in his own
"romantic expeditions" in castle and cloister,[17]
and he could single out the introduction to The
Monastery as being positively favourable to
Catholicism.[18]
        The Monastery (1820) is the locus classicus of
Scott's apparently deliberate socially and psycholog-
ically self-protective ambiguity. The 1830 introduction evinces reverence for Melrose Abbey, but he
immediately distances himself from medievalist supernaturalism. The "Introductory Epistle" by "Captain
Clutterbuck", presents a Benedictine monk who vaguely
defends monks, then admits he has altered his text,

134

on which The Monastery is said to be based, to
accommodate his Protestant audience. The "Answer"
by "The Author of Waverley" says he will further
adjust it to suit "this critical age", excising
whatever appears too favourable to Rome, which he
abominates, he says, "were it but for her fasts and
penances". Again, he says on the first page of the
introduction that he has selected two pure, dedicated
and sincere characters, one Catholic, one Protestant,
to give - it is implied - a fair account of the
effects of the Reformation in Scotland. The ambiguity
continues in the novel. When Henry Warden, the
evangelical preacher, and the sub-prior, Fr.Eustace,
confront each other they are evenly matched, Scott
saying they are more like each other than they
recognize. But he disapproves of the Reformation for
it is destructive and strengthens English hegemony,
and, as Lord Murray says in the last chapter (ch.
XXXVII), "times of action make princes into peasants,
and boors into barons".
      The Abbot (1820), the sequel to The Monastery is
also ambiguous. He says in his "Introductory Epistle
... To Captain Clutterbuck" that "we do not feel deep
sympathy at this period with what was once the most
powerful and animating principle in Europe";[19] yet
there are signs of sympathy in the book. There is
the suggestion that Catholicism can be patriotic (eg.
II, 22, VIII, 79, 82, XXIV, 270), especially on
account of Queen Mary; Henry Warden is again presented as a self-righteous prig; he suggests there
are evils on both sides (VI, 64, XV, 146); there is
implicit condemnation of the destructive spirit of
the Reformation (VIII, 74, 76, 77, XIII, 118, 119,
XX, 210); and there is admiration for Abbot Ambrose
(XIII, 122-3). He appreciates Catholic ritual : he
refers to "those beautiful old Latin hymns" (X,91),
and describes how

        the new Abbot appeared ... his hoary
        standard-bearers, and his juvenile
        dispensers of incense preceding him,
        and the venerable train of monks behind
        him ... his appearance was a signal for
        the magnificent Jubilate ... (XIII,121).

For Scott, monasticism was a valued source of order
and alms, and its Catholic authority matched his Bur-
kean, conservative notion that civilized man in orderly society must divest himself of "the first fund-
mental right of uncovenanted man ... to judge for
himself and to assert his own cause".[20] Perhaps it

is, then, yet another ironic ambiguity which makes
the young Catholic hero Roland Graeme protest against
religious authority (IX, 87-8, XII, 109) and finally
leave the Church.

The Lay of the Last Minstrel (1805), Marmion
(1808), The Lady of the Lake (1810) and The Bridal of
Triermain (1813) all attractively mix legend, the
supernatural and Catholic elements. The ballad
"March of the Monks of Bangor" (1817) gives a romantically amiable picture of medieval clergy, and its
refrain "O misere, Domine!" calls to mind the fact
that on his death-bed he said the Dies Irae and
Stabat Mater,[21] which may indicate his real attitude.
And perhaps the ambiguous Scott meant these poems to
have a religious significance, for he said, "the
original purpose of poetry is either religious or
historical, or, as must frequently happen, a mixture
of both".[22] Whatever his real views, his propaganda
value for Catholicism was proportionate to his
immense popularity. Rightly or wrongly, people found
in his works sustenance and encouragement for their
own spiritual needs.

It seems that Scott's medievalism influenced the
Tractarians, and Tractarianism does indeed bear
traces of religious medievalism.[23] It is well known
that they were not primarily or strongly medievalist,
being more concerned with the primitive Church; but
this did not exempt them from the accusation of
medievalism, particularly in the case of Newman.[24]
Tractarians valued the medieval Church in England as
a testimony of their Catholicity, while preserving
the emphasis on nationalism, and saw it as an
integral part of Anglicanism's ancient heritage[25] -
the principle of antiquity being important in
Tractarian polemics. It was generally felt by the
Anglican right that the medieval English Church had
been providentially preserved from Roman corruptions.[26] They praised the medieval English Church to
fortify their Anglo-Catholic polemic. Yet it is too
much to say that medievalism was the "wellspring of
the Oxford Movement".[27]

In Newman's view, Keble loved "authority and
old times so far, as to be more than gentle towards
the Catholic Religion",[28] while Froude was "powerfully drawn to the Medieval Church",[29] and especially
willing to credit large-scale miraculous intervention
in the Middle Ages,[30] while desiring the restoration
of English monasticism.[31] It has been wrongly
supposed that Newman himself was indifferent to the
medieval Church;[32] but as a young man his imagination was strongly swayed by the medievalist or quasi-

medievalist writings of Scott, Coleridge and Southey, and then by the medievalist Froude.[33] In his youth, he said, "my imagination ran on unknown influences, on magical powers, and talismans",[34] so that he was susceptible to the vocabulary of contemporary metaphysical explorations. As early as 15 July 1830 he was prepared to admit in a letter that "we certainly have lost something by old Luther"; and six months earlier he had written the poem "Monks", which was most favourable to its subject. Towards the end of his Anglican period he undertook the rather medievalist project of compiling the lives of the English saints, and in the "Advertisement" to The Family of St. Richard, the Saxon (1844) he shocked Anglicans by professing belief in the story of St. Walburga. The project was designed to give his followers factual food for thought and "to promote the spread of right views".[35] As with many others, his "imagination", as he called it, led him to empathize with Catholicism before his intellect led him to identify with it[36] : imagination was the horse which pulled the cart of reason.

The Tractarians were attracted to medieval Catholicism primarily as part of the history of the Apostolical Church, though they spoke of it little; but since medievalism was not essential for their argument, it is striking that they contemplated it at all : it does seem to have appealed to the Tractarian imagination. Yet neither medievalism nor romanticism were mainsprings of Tractarianism,[37] though there was an overlap of interests with medievalism, and strength was drawn unawares from aspects of romanticism. Tractarianism had to do with the non-romantic, Catholic spirit, with such things as asceticism, self-denial, belief in authority, dogmatic discipline and logic, "objective ritualistic technique"[38] (its ritualism being not aesthetic but dogmatic), precision of truth; nor was it naturalistic, or anti-reason, or sentimentally deistic, as romanticism so often was. This means that their medievalism was not romantic, or that it was only marginally romantic. While the connection between medievalism and romanticism and Tractarianism is not overt or substantive, it is there in shared concerns not exclusively or necessarily medievalist or romantic. Tractarianism did have some things in common with romanticism,[39] such as the sacramental outlook, the historical enthusiasm, the willingness to consider alien perspectives and emphasis on hierarchy. Scott and the romantics prepared the way for the Tractarians; but, as Chadwick says, "theology

137

did not move because literature moved", though they
went pari passu because "the human spirit yearned for
new depth", and the Tractarians "expressed their
divinity with the aid of romantic images and attitudes common to their day".[40] The Tractarians were
essentially trying to discover a more profound model
for a reconciled, healed world, a model which would
help to effect that which it symbolized, as a sacrament in the Catholic view effects that which it symbolizes : medievalism was a tiny fragment of their
quest. Their quest was not aesthetic but realist,
not "romantic" but "Catholic", their ritual and
imagery being not matters of pleasure or egocentric
satisfaction, but of communicating the theme of reconciliation and effecting that reconciliation in the
real world, amongst the community. Admiring the
Middle Ages was a matter of reconciling the past with
the present and the even-more-distant past, while the
adoption of the Catholic grammar of spirituality was
a means of ecclesial reconciliation and a realization
of the reconciliatory sacramental view in the English
Church. In a sense, this was the medieval view.
According to Beek, John Keble,"like medieval man, ...
conceived the universe as one whole of which God is
the centre";[41] and, correspondingly (and again in the
medieval way), he saw in the material universe an
allegorical system reflecting God, which gave it
meaning. In "Septuagesima Sunday" he begs God to

> Give me a heart to find out Thee,
> And read Thee every where.[42]

The Tractarians influenced a large number of
Anglicans, who, in accord with their Catholic
sympathies, expressed high regard for the Catholic
Middle Ages.[43] Charlotte Yonge's Tractarian-
inspired and phenomenally popular novel The Heir of
Redclyffe (1853) was "the best example of Victorian
life Medievalized";[44] Richard Monckton Milnes, a
friend of Digby and one of the first to call himself
an "English Catholic",[45] wrote occasional religious
medievalist poems, such as "Charlemagne, and the
Hymn of Christ";[46] historians were also sympathetic :
S.R. Maitland's The Dark Ages attacked the anti-
Catholic histories of Mosheim, Robertson and Hume;
Aubrey De Vere thought Archbishop Richard Chenevix
Trench "evinced a higher sympathy with the devotional
mind of the Middle Ages than is to be found in the
Oxford poets";[47] and even J.A. Froude expressed
respect for medieval Catholicism, believing that
modern historians had been wrong to set at nought the

spirituality of medieval Christians : "mankind have
not been so long on this planet altogether, that we
can allow so large a chasm to be scooped out of their
spiritual existence".[48] Richard Watson Dixon planned
in his youth at Oxford to restore with his friends
the age of chivalry and to establish a quasi-monastic
community. A number of poems issued from his medieval frame of mind. James Sambrook believes his "very
ideas are medieval".[49] His History of the Church of
England from the Abolition of the Roman Jurisdiction
expresses the belief that the late-medieval clergy
in England - "the purest in the world" - had been
abused by modern historians, for England prior to the
Reformation Parliament had "resembled one of those
great edifices dedicated to religion, with which she
abounded then".[50]
      John Mason Neale represented the more romantic
side of "English Catholicism", and through his novels
of the 1840s and 1850s, his poems, his support for
the ritualist and conventual movements, his historical work and his publication of Mediaeval Hymns and
Sequences (which represents a strong Anglo-Catholic
trend to the revival of ancient hymns and prayers),
he tried to instil medieval spirituality into modern
Anglicanism. William Morris judged him to be the
"chief figure" of medievalist Ritualism.[51] His
attitude is encapsulated in a poem in Hierologus,
beginning,

          Oh, the good old times of England! Ere,
                in her evil day,
          From their Holy Faith and their ancient
                rites her people fell away.

Medieval faith ameliorated the lot of the poor with
alms and prayer, while modernism neglects them. But
all is not lost, because Catholic Anglicanism is a
link with the medieval faith, and through her the
power of the medieval faith can regenerate the land :
"S. Cuthbert and S. Edward might alone redeem a
land!" He envisages an imminent struggle between
spirituality and materialism, in which England's
"commerce", "arts, and wealth, and power, and fame, /
Shall melt away", to be superseded by the commerce of
"the daily sacrifice to GOD", the arts of "banner,
cross, and cope", the wealth of "martyrs' prayers",
the power of the Church, and the fame of a dominant,
revivified Catholicism.[52]
      Sebastian Evans (1830-1909) translated medieval
religious and legendary works like St. Francis of
Assisi's Mirror of Perfection (1898) and the High

History of the Holy Graal (1898). The ambiguity of
medievalism is not absent from his poem "How the
Abbey of Saint Werewulf Juxta Slingsby Came by
Brother Fabian's Manuscript",[53] the tone of which is
both affectionate towards the conventuals and
satirically critical. Other poems, written in the
persona of Br. Fabian, continue the mixture of
irreverent and serious medievalism, among them "The
Three Kings of Cologne" and "St. Bernard". Like
Dixon, he has a curiously medieval frame of mind.
Significantly, the Times obituary[54] records that
though he was not a Catholic, he "was interested in
all things connected with the religion of Europe in
the Middle Ages", and that he had an interview with
the Pope shortly before his death.

Catholics and Medievalism

The Roman Catholic response to the medieval
Church was, when favourable, sometimes measured,
sometimes enthusiastic. Seventeenth-century English
Catholics were nostalgic for the Middle Ages : for
example, the Benedictines hankered after the old
monastic sites. In the eighteenth-century, however,
English Catholicism became very Anglicized, and this
heritage lived on into the nineteenth century, so
that even figures like John Milner and John Lingard
were still more "English" than the rising spirit of
Romanism would have liked. There were very few,if
any, English Catholic medievalists in the later
eighteenth century and early nineteenth.[55] Later in
the nineteenth century, while the Catholic authorities tolerated Catholic medievalism, they did not
enthusiastically support it, for it was considered as
nationalist and irrelevant to the dual task of
fitting the Church to meet the threats of the present
day and of re-forging the bonds between English
Catholicism and that of the Continent; and if there
was to be an ambiance expressive of this supra-
nationalist, triumphalist Ultramontanism, it was to
be the Baroque of the Catholic Reformation. What
room there was for medievalism was in the rôle of
asserting the ancient legitimacy of the Catholic
Church in England, and in supporting the conservative
milieu now embraced by the Catholic Church in England
in order to combat all manner of revolutions and to
purge earlier elements of radical,"Whig" Catholicism.
The full-blooded Catholic medievalists Pugin and De
Lisle were out on a limb. There were, nevertheless,
traces of Catholic medievalism which require
consideration.

When Newman became a Catholic, his attitude towards the medieval Church remained substantially the same : he respected it without venerating it, he appreciated it without sentimentalizing it; and in this he represented the mainstream of the Church. In 1848 he ruthlessly satirized "aesthetic" Anglo-Catholicism in Loss and Gain, and in the same year condemned Pugin's revivalism as contrary to the Church's spirit of development in matters of discipline and ritual and the ambiance in which they are set : "in these respects the Middle age was not what the First Centuries were, nor is the Age Present the Middle age".[56] Next year, however, he said he wanted a religion which "addresses the intellect and the heart".[57] And in "The Second Spring" (1852) he pictured the magnificence of the medieval Church in England : "where was there in the whole of Christendom a more glorious hierarchy? ... it seemed destined to stand, so long as England stood, and to outlast, it might be, England's greatness". It was great, but its ending was proper : "it was the high decree of heaven".[58] Then he retails a vision of the rebirth of the Church in England, under the guiding spirit of the medieval Church, with its power to address the intellect and heart : he pictures a building "fashioned upon that ancient style of art which brings back the past", the singing of the chant echoing through the cloisters, and all covered by "the shadow of the saints".[59] But his visionary tone is not so much a paean for the resurrection of the body of the medieval Church, but a celebration that the spirit of the Church is vital in the present day and holds promise for the future. He is clear that the fabric of the medieval Church is - though tragically - gone forever : "we clung to the vision of past greatness, and would not believe it could come to nought; but the Church in England has died, and the Church lives again".[60] The medieval Church was glorious not because it shed a romantic nimbus, or was eternally perfect, but because its achievements were great, it had played a part in God's grand design, and it had been a manifestation of the one, true Church. Correlatively, the modern Catholic Church was the true Church by virtue of its affiliation with the medieval one : "the Roman Catholic communion of this day is the successor and representative of the Medieval Church, ... [and] the Medieval Church is the legitimate heir of the Nicene".[61]

Newman has been mistaken as an anti-medievalist on the grounds that he was a romantic, regarding the mind as "the locus of truth".[62] Doubtless there was

an element of "poetic" appreciation of the medieval
Church in Newman, thereby affording apparent grounds
for the epithet "romantic"; but the word "poetic" in
Newman's vocabulary is specially meant. In his essay
on "Benedictine Schools" (1859) he describes St.
Benedict as poetic; but this has nothing to do with
dreamy sentimentalism, for while he associated
"poetic" with poetry, he connoted by it the transcendent and the sphere of "admiration, enthusiasm,
devotion, love".[63] He believed that it was a Christian duty to view things poetically : "we are bid to
colour all things with hues of faith, to see a Divine
meaning in every event, and a superhuman tendency".[64]
It was this intuition of transcendence which he
valued in the medieval Church, where it was especially evident. In 1836 he had discovered the Breviary
and written a laudatory tract on it, and two years
later published hymns from it. (Newman, it has been
said, was always "in the forefront of Tractarian out-
reach toward forms of devotion".[65] Thenceforward, he
always kept it by him. It is too much to say, as did
Lewis G. Gates, that "one is sometimes tempted to
describe [Newman] as a great mediaeval ecclesiastic
astray in the nineteenth century";[66] but one can
agree with him that "Newman sought to revive in the
Church a mediaeval faith in its own divine mission
and the intense spiritual consciousness of the Middle
Ages".[67]
    Lord Acton's position was not disimilar : he
valued the medieval Church as having successfully
articulated the Christian message, without wishing to
restore the medieval order. The medieval hagio-
graphical legends had illustrated "a supernatural
order of grace"; [68] and he stressed the popular,
universal character of the medieval Church, whereby
"Christian ideas were able to become incarnate ... in
durable forms".[69] He saw the influence of the Church
as emancipating (as had Newman),[70] and the Protestant
revolution as marking an age of secularism.[71] A
medieval revival was out of the question, but the
Middle Ages might have potential as a stimulus to
new life : the Church "must create anew ... and
instil a new life and spirit into those remains of
the medieval system which will bear the mark of the
ages when heresy and unbelief ... had not obscured
the idea of the Christian State".[72] Charles Justin
MacCarthy, a cousin of Wiseman and disciple of the
French liberal Lamennais, also represented this
feeling of the need for something new, mixed with a
sad rejection of Digby's medievalism : Digby, he
wrote,

> is so completely lost in the past that
> he loses sight of the present and the
> future.... I on the contrary, while I
> yield not to him in affectionate vener-
> ation for antiquity am daily more and
> more convinced of the necessity of
> something very different from the hier-
> archy and chivalry of the middle ages
> for the accomplishment of those things
> which under different forms are perhaps
> equally panted after by his breast and
> by mine. ... there must be a complete
> rejuvenescence and infusion of new blood
> into our veins before we can renew our
> youthful exertions. To hold up Tancred
> and St. Bernard to the men of our gener-
> ation is a refinement of mockery.[73]

While rejecting medievalism as such, he nevertheless
looks back to the Church's "youthful exertions", and
clearly wants to see the restoration of Catholicism's
medieval energy, but not in medieval forms : the
medieval message was right, but the language needs
replacing. Manning also fitted into this category of
being both realistic and respectful.[74]

Similarly, Gerard Manley Hopkins was out of
sympathy with contemporary medievalism,[75] and his own
"medievalism" was hard-headed and intellectual rather
than romantic; and yet he was interested in the
German religious medievalists.[76] Specialists say
that his intellectual and spiritual world-view was
formed by either Duns Scotus or St. Bonaventure, and
that this showed in his poetry.[77] In "Duns Scotus's
Oxford" he proclaims that Scotus was he "who of all
men most sways my spirits to peace". Bump, who
speaks of a religious medievalism of form and metaphysical message rather than of historical content,
supposes that Hopkins's intellect and poetic took a
medieval colour from Keble and Pusey, and that this
involved him in poetry with the "typical and the
typological representational modes of medieval art",
in opposition to romantic individualism.[78] He believes that he was aided in loading his images with
specifically transcendental, sacramental and Incarnational significance by the medievalizing action of
the Oxford Movement and the Catholic Revival on the
Romantic imagistic tradition, leading it back to the
typical, typological and structural approach inherent
in medieval writing. Like other Catholics, Hopkins
was not so much interested in the revival of medieval
forms as in the medieval spirit : in 1864 he planned

an essay, "Some aspects of Modern mediaevalism", to
emphasize that medievalism could be much "deeper than
a mere return to middle age forms".[79]
    Lionel Johnson could be mistaken as a merely
aesthetic medievalist; but in fact he represents
the fin de siècle quest for order and certainty. His
entering the Catholic Church in 1891 was not a water-
shed between "aesthetic" medievalism and "serious"
medievalism : he was serious before 1891 and aesthetic after. Though influenced by Pater, he came to
reject aestheticism,[80] and his religion was a
serious concern.[81] In so far as he was always an
aesthete, he wanted the sanction of Catholicism.[82]
Celticism combined with Catholicism to give a serious
inflection to much of his work; and this combination
is represented by his conscious affinity with Robert
Stephen Hawker, expressed in "Hawker of Morwenstow"
(1895), where he says this affinity is based on one
"Catholic faith and Celtic joy", and on their
perceptions of "The voices and the visions of the
Mystery". Then he dwells on Hawker's religious
quest, which by implication he shares.
    Fundamentally, Johnson was critical rather than
escapist. "Lambeth Lyric" (1888) criticizes the
Laodicean theology and compromising spirit of modern
Anglicanism; while "A Sad Morality" (1888, revised
1902) attacks ethical relativism and rationalism :

    So the Thinkers and their crew made
        morality anew,
    Setting everything askew by enlightened
        Thought.

The essays are also critical. When praising Savon-
arola, he speaks of the world he condemned : "an age
of luxurious corruption, renascent paganism, hideous
crime and moral laxity, Christian upon the surface,
indifferent or superstitious within".[83] He could
have been talking about the 1890s, and probably was.
His essay on St. Francis holds him up as a model of
holy simplicity for the "staid and decorous Established Church", and asks how "to make the medieval
spirit a power upon our modern day?"[84] Yet there is
an escapist element : "of life I am afraid", he says
in "Nihilism" (1888). But he sees his medievalist
dreaming as a metaphysical necessity : these are
"necessary dreams", he says in "Vita Venturi
Saeculi"; and "Dreams and desires were made for
man, whereby / They drink eternity".
    These considerations are combined in a pair of
poems of 1890. "The Church of a Dream" presents the

"dream" of a medieval church, with a priest celebrating mass, to combine escapism and reproof to the present :

> There still, although the world autumnal
>   be, and pale,
> Still in their golden vesture the old
>   saints prevail;
> Alone with Christ, desolate else, left
>   by mankind.

"The Age of a Dream" laments the passing of the medieval dream utopia, which consisted in chivalry, faith, beauty and spirit. Throughout, there is no clear distinction between dream and reality, between aesthetics and religion; and this is because his mode of perception and understanding was chiefly through the aesthetic sense. This relationship between the mode and matter of perception is typically embodied in his ambiguous use of the words "gracious" and "grace" in "The Age of a Dream", and in his reference to the beauty of the holiness of a medieval saint, in "Winchester Close".

Johnson's mentor, Robert Stephen Hawker (1803-1875), only became a Catholic on his death-bed, but he was a Catholic in spirit throughout his life. To a great extent he was the poet of his parish of Morwenstow, which retained a medieval flavour, with its legends of Celtic saints, superstitions, ecclesiastical ruins, anchorites' cells, ancient crosses and holy wells. The loneliness of his holy eremites was his own, their fervour his, their vocabulary often his. He was not only separate from his age : he was against it. The material was really spiritual : crusading and chivalry were for God, the seasons were God's dynamic play, the air was holy, the sea was the water of baptism and its voice a hymn to God. He was no pantheist,[85] and no Erastian, for worldly powers were subject to the Church.[86] As he said, "Scenes of the former men my soul surround".[87] By contrast, he ridiculed Protestant "reasoning"[88] : Catholicism was the "Imagination",[89] by which the mysteries of past and present could be reconciled, understood and lived.

Margaret F. Burrows has shown that Hawker's The Quest of the Sangraal (1863) was an intense, mystical, autobiographical outpouring, criticizing the materialist modern age by the light of medieval Catholicism.[90] By contrast with the Quest, Tennyson's "Holy Grail" is a surrender to the confusions of a materialist age. For Hawker the

Grail is "The link that binds to God a lonely land"[91] a sacramental symbol of the Incarnate God, a "Type of the Gospel", which was taken away "when the Land became sinful"; so that its "loss and recovery are emblems of the failure of our light and its Restoration".[92] He identifies himself as priest with Arthur,[93] revealing the mystery of salvation to the round table - and to modern England. The recovered Grail sheds divine light on Saxon and Norman England, but is then lost.[94] The chronology of these lines is vague, but it seems likely that Merlin's third vision covers 1536 to 1863,[95] an age of chaos and warfare. There is also a theological dimension, for it is clear he had no love for post-Reformation Protestant English religious thought.[96] Arthur finally begs England to search once more for the Grail, by which he means it should recover its spiritual vision. Burrows says this vision was undermined by theology,[97] but it was rather underpinned and stimulated by theology : "I have for long been a Man of one Book," he says, "and that the wonderful Summa of Aquinas", to which he turned for the solution to every controversy.[98] Burrows miscalculates the centrality in his world-view of the Church, which was the source of authority, unity and the revelation of the sacramental aspect of nature.[99] The vision is consequently anti-materialist (the emphasis being laid on the "numyne", sacramental essence, the Schechinah and angelic bodies), with man no more than the privileged quester. The irony of the Quest is that if only corrupt England could want salvation, it is to hand; for the divine element, "which pervades the Universe and is called the Holy Catholic Church",[100] like the sea surrounds England as well as Cornwall, the Ocean being his symbol of God.[101] Christian men, who are like fish,[102] need only leap from the cliff to find their natural element. This explains why the sea is so powerfully personified in the last verse.

For Hawker, all this was not dream but life. As he began work on the second part of the Quest, he wrote "Psalmus Cantici" (15 March 1875) on Manning's elevation to the Cardinalate, revealing his faith that the adventure of the Quest continued. Manning is pictured holding "The Rod of Aaron" upon "The throne of Rock amid a quivering Land"; the biblical reference recalling the numerous Hebrew allusions of the Quest, the "Rock" the rock of Cornwall and the Church - especially the "rock" of St. Morwenna's church - and the "quivering Land" the vision of traumatized England concluding the Quest.Additionally,

the cataclysmic hiatuses of English history intimated
in the Quest are symbolically healed :

> A Prince shall reign from the great
>   Gregory's line,
> A Prelate wield Augustine's mighty name;
> They live and breathe again, as though
>   their shrine
> Gave back the buried Saints to Life and
>   fame.
>   . . . . .
> They greet the rescued Realm once more
>   their own,
> Queen of the Lands and Lady of the Sea!

The Cardinal (his "sigill'd Glove, red with symbolic
Blood" - an echo of the symbolic use of red throughout the Quest) is the new knight of the Round Table,
faithful to his fathers, equipped with the Grail and
ready to return England to "the Sea".[103]
    Eccentric though Hawker was, he was a conformist
in medievalism. Conformist though Aubrey De Vere
was, he was sui generis in medievalism. He blended
his discipleship of Digby and Newman with progressivism. Romantically, he believed the Middle Ages
"constituted the devout, joyous though often incoherent childhood of Europe";[104] and the child-like
imagination of medieval man enabled him to perceive
truths beyond the modern "minute philosopher".[105]
Conservatively, he praised their hierarchy, sense of
obedience and humility[106] and non-reliance on private
judgement.[107] People were generally happy because
their lives were dominated by God,[108] and they lived
in "a united Christendom".[109] Yet they were only
important because they matured the seeds of the
primitive age of Christianity,[110] and made Britain
great by bestowing "honour" and "affection" on the
modern age.[111] Unity under "throne and altar",
enlightened by modern achievements was his ideal.[112]
Fearing the day when England would sink into atheistic materialism and be trod by a race of moral
"Pigmies by passion ruled",[113] he looked to the past
for the starting-point of society : Wilfrid Ward
observed that for De Vere Catholicism had "preserved
that unearthly spiritual atmosphere, which the
mediaeval world expressed ... and which the modern
world has so completely lost".[114] Yet he did not
wish to make the Middle Ages live again : rather, to
propagate the spirit which had supported them.[115] He
was also touched - being enthusiastic for science and
politics, and seeking a reconciliation between the

147

religious and the secular - by what has been called
"the superstition of automatic progress".[116] He
thought that the reconversion of England would result
in a true revival of the spirit of progress, as it
had in seventh-century England.[117] The Middle Ages
had lacked "Inductive Science, universal Commerce,
constitutional Freedom," etcetera;[118] so

> the Middle Ages are far from representing
> the height to which human society may reach
> when it has passed through its present
> second transition period; but to that height
> it can only reach if it does full justice to
> the age immediately preceeding it.[119]

De Vere's curious mixture of optimism and pessimism
about the present shows that the medievalist and
anti-medievalist positions were not necessarily so
totally disparate as the parties supposed.[120]

The chief Victorian Catholic religious medievalists commonly identified as "romantic" were Digby,
Pugin,[121] De Lisle and John Patrick Stuart, the third
Marquess of Bute (1847-1900). De Lisle, a disciple
of Digby, was extremely sensitive about those
Catholics who preferred "the most modern developments
of the Church" to the medieval ways.[122] They were
traitors to the Church in an age of crisis, in which
solidarity could bring the millenium of England
reconverted to Catholicism.[123] He looked to that
"vision of Unity and peace, that now opens upon
England",[124] which was given colour by the "revival
of a true Catholick literature ... and Christian
art".[125] Such a conversion, which he thought was
heralded by the restoration of the Catholic hierarchy,
meant a return to the England of St. Edward the
Confessor.[126] He shared with the others in this
group a passion for medieval religious forms, among
them the legends of the saints, which he propagated
in his translation of The Diurnal of the Soul (1864).
Their literal truth was secondary to the sense in
which they reflected the medieval sacramental world-
view; the reader's object being "to seek truth in
the allegory, to learn wisdom from the parable, and
to sift the hidden mystery of the symbol".[127]

Bute shared his emphasis on the religious
"language" of the Middle Ages. David Hunter Blair
summarized the matter thus : the Catholic Church's

> august and venerable ritual, the ordered
> splendour of her ceremonial, the deep sig-
> nificance of her liturgy and worship, could

not fail to attract one who had learned
to see in them far more than the mere
outward pomp and beauty which are but
symbols of their inward meaning.[128]

Aspects of his medievalism included the purchase and
restoration of the priory of Pluscarden, reverence
for saints - especially St. Magnus of Orkney, in
whose honour he wrote a hymn - and his translation of
the Breviary.
     Frederick Faber embodies much of the substance
of this chapter. Until 1845, when he became a Roman
Catholic, he was a Tractarian; and amongst his
influences were Wordsworth, seventeenth-century
Anglo-Catholics such as George Herbert, the medievalist Tractarian Isaac Williams, Continental medievalists such as Guizot, Montalembert and Chateaubriand,
and, it seems, Digby. In his Tractarian period his
attitude to Roman Catholicism was highly equivocal :
his position was that modern Anglicanism was not to
be equated with Catholicism in England, primarily
because its religious practice was wrong, and particularly because it had no adeqaute ritual voice.
But modern Romanism was not true Catholicism because
it had fallen into doctrinal error since the Middle
Ages; and both failed in lack of reverence for
tradition.[129] True Catholicism was to be found in
the medieval European Church, which was truly
Catholic because it united Europe in one faith
consisting in right doctrine, full ritual and
reverence for tradition. This position is explored
in his Sights and Thoughts in Foreign Churches and
Among Foreign Peoples (1842) - which is very similar
in its position and message to Williams's The
Baptistery, of the same year - in which Faber, in the
person of the authorial voice, engages throughout a
Continental tour in dialogue with a medieval figure
called the Stranger, who is his alter ego, much as
Rowley was Chatterton's. The Stranger and the work's
ambiance of vision and dream allow the rational,
educated, Anglican Faber to "safely" voice his
probing anxieties about the mysteries of religion,
which are beyond reason and education, and, he felt,
beyond the Anglican establishment. The Stranger says
"all hearts are turned towards Rome, all eyes fixed
upon her in love, hope, fear, and inquiry" (623); but
in the contemporary climate it was safer to discuss
Rome and Anglicanism vis á vis the Catholic ideal in
medievalist terms; and Faber ratifies his own
medievalism in condemning modern Rome.
     Unlike Digby, Faber here records shortcomings of

the medieval Church; yet the work is strongly reminiscent of Digby. It opens with an image of a
beneficent, sanctified, sanctifying and united
medieval polity, wherein the Church sheltered the
poor (1-3) - whereas Anglicanism does not (214) -
and continues in like manner. The medieval papacy
is defended as the "best possible state of things
for degenerate ages" (385); chivalry was good, but
only while it rested in the Church (151,161); monasticism should be restored to channel the power of
Chartism and Dissent into orthodoxy, to strengthen
episcopal power by encouraging the principle of
obedience, to conform with the practice of Eastern
and Western Churches, to teach and care for the
manufacturing population (358-62. 366-7); medieval
monks were humble, intellectual, pious, and
monasticism brought heaven to earth (86, 164-5);
legendary miracles were valuable (279-81); and the
thirteenth century had marked the zenith (150-1). To
appreciate the Middle Ages, he had to overthrow the
rationalist heritage,and he gladly disowned Voltaire,
Mosheim and Gibbon, finding "the memory of the pious
dark ages ... very soothing after the glare of
enlightened sin" (11, 20, 235, 280).
    His yearning for catholicity, for religious
unity, is a dominating theme : as he pleads for unity
in his own day (598), so he looks back to the Middle
Ages, when "unity and brotherly intercourse ... were
so much prized" (3), and correspondingly deplores
"the transition of Europe from the papal unity to the
individuality of states" (72) and the modern idea of
national churches (114). He firmly blames the growth
of "political individuality" (that is nationalism)
about 1400 for the collapse of European religious
unity, which was until then "so strong, that all
national distinctions and barriers of geography or
language were lost sight of" (57-8). By "language",
Faber means Latin, the disuse of which he takes as an
"image of the present broken and disordered state of
Christendom" (4). On this subject of unity through
language, which is of the utmost significance to
Faber, he quotes Sir Francis Palgrave's Truths and
Fictions of the Middle Ages : The Merchant and the
Friar (1837), which quotation ends with the eponymous
merchant saying "there is one spot where the pilgrim
always finds his home. We are all one people when
we come before the Altar of the Lord" (5). Faber
is the pilgrim who knows where his home is, but is
not yet sure of the language. Latin is but one
aspect of that "language", and represents its
totality naturally. Latin also symbolizes the fact

that his concept of unity is not merely political or
social or even denominational : it is metaphysical.
     Faber anticipates a point implicit in Francis
Thompson's writings : that Dante was the embodiment
of the holy possibilities of poetry, and St. Francis
was the embodiment of the poetic possibilities of
holiness.[130] Faber's love of Latin is not the love
of an antiquarian; nor is his concern with form in
religion a matter of mere aesthetics. His position
recalls Digby describing the medieval "Catholic type
of felicity", which consisted in

> nothing but images of quiet wisdom,
> sanctity, and innocence; symbols of
> infinite love ... the daily sacrifice,
> the evening hymn, the sweet music of
> the pilgrim's litanee.....

All this is not aesthetics, but the result of "the
Christian philosophy" (MC. I, 102). He learnt from
Coleridge and Wordsworth that material form could be
spiritual form : that the mainspring of artistic
genius - imagination (as distinct from mere fancy) -
was related to spiritual insight. He believes that
Romans expressed this by using the same word for poet
and priest, whose common task it was to "penetrate
into and realize the unseen", to "bring back the
unseen into the seen, in the same blending wherein
they existed before man's sin cast them apart" :
imagination is to intellect what prophecy is to the
soul, for both are the "subsidy and succour of the
Infinite within us" (544). Like medieval Catholicism,
imagination is both unifying and spiritualizing
(546);[131]and as imagination brought fire from heaven,
so monasticism realizes heaven on earth (165), saints
give glimpses of heaven (59), and all the forms of
medieval Christianity are a language which give
heaven utterance on earth and earth utterance in
heaven; and are symbols which effect what they
represent and represent what they effect. He
confesses "complete faith in the depth of those meaning times", and recognizes the value of the "symbolical language of Christian art", which even extended
to "a regular system of the mystical meaning of
colors" (37-8). "Christian art" tells a tale, con-
veys a truth, leads the mind to prayer (37, 5-6), and
can be a symbolic offering to God (163-4).
     Another type of language is medieval ritual.
For Carlyle, though medieval missals were now "old
clothes", originally they had spoken successfully to
the soul of the soul, and something new was needed to

speak freshly to it.[132] Faber believed that the
Church still spoke powerfully. The Roman service
books are "so beautiful ... so fitted to the deepest
devotional cravings of which we are capable ... that
we return almost with a feeling of disappointment
and sense of lowering to our own formularies" (155).
Form in medieval Christianity is not art but art as
religious communication :

> all ritual acts must, from the nature of the
> case be symbolical, being either a reveren-
> tial imitation of sacred acts, or the
> sublime inventions of antiquity whereby the
> Presence of God and His holy Angels is rec-
> ognized and preached to the people, or fit
> and beautiful means for affecting the imag-
> ination of the worshipper, and giving inten-
> sity to his devotion.

Anglicans are separated from the Catholic world by
their impoverished ritual and their corresponding
ignorance of the language of Catholic worship (302-
4). The implication is that Anglicanism must restore
its ritual for the sake of unity, and unity is
necessary so that the Church can speak to the world
(609-10). It must also restore its ritual to live
a full spiritual life : having observed parishes all
over England, the Stranger asks "Is England beneath
an Interdict?" (645).
    Faber was engaged in a search for beauty, for he
did not find sufficient beauty in Anglicanism, nor
any understanding of it (351-2, 455); and he found it
in medieval Catholicism (86, 155, 623) : even
ruination could not destroy the beauty of Gothic
(465-6). When he describes a revelatory, medievalist
dream which shows him that beauty and relgion are
inextricably mixed, it almost seems that beauty takes
precedence over religion : "beauty is to be sought
through holiness" (455). But the crucial point about
beauty, which emerges in the dream, is that it is a
pleasing presentation of the principle of order, for
which discipline is a requisite quality. Ritual -
which is the central, representative aspect of the
Catholic language - is the explicitly religious form
of beauty, and is also order; and both orders lead
to God, Who is the creator of order. Two passages
from the dream illustrate this integration of beauty,
ritual and order and the goal to which they tend. The
first refers to liturgical plainsong :

> these sweet sounds are so arranged, knitted

> to such holy words, and incorporated
> into such sublime liturgies, that they
> lead the soul onwards, disciplining it
> for other harmonies in another world (461).

This description anticipates the following vision of
ritual :

> from the mitred patriarch, through the
> priests, and incense-burners, and banner-
> bearers, and choristers ... through the
> Crosses and the pictures ... and the monks,
> and the nuns, and the poor, and the devout
> lay-folk, ... through all that long waving
> line, as it bent and swayed and drew itself,
> like one creature, onward to the Altar, the
> very soul of chastest spiritual beauty ran,
> and thrilled, and circulated (469).

Just as the "sweet sounds" of the first passage have
their fixed place in the liturgy and in the pattern
of salvation, so the individuals of the second are in
order and thereby united in their destiny. This sense
of order is an integral part of the idea of community
: it is the ambiance of communication between
individuals, and it is the bond which unites them
with each other and with God.
    Just as the revival of monasticism - which had
once seemed the "wildest dream" - appeared to be
imminent (353), so Faber hopes his medievalist dream
will shortly become reality; for he regards history
as circular rather than linear (349), and he believes
in resurrection. Consequently he reprimands those
medievalists who unwittingly help to keep the medieval Church in its grave by regarding it as eternally
dead :

> there is a daily and incessant resurrection
> of opinions. The seeds of the Middle Ages
> have been long deposited in the fertile mould
> of neglect and disbelief. They are now be-
> ginning to swell and split underground. You
> will see their green shoots parting the dull
> mould shortly (350).

He continues his anticipation of Newman's vernal
analogy thus :

> you have all of you ceased to believe that
> the deciduous trees can bud and bloom again.
> The best among you have planted ivy at the

> foot of the leafless trunks, as if to
> honor the decay of the venerable stems,
> and to make the dead branches, like the
> influence of a departed Saint, a stay
> unto the living (352).

They speak of revival, Faber speaks of resurrection :
"the pious opinions of the Church are raised out of
their tombs" (353). He is keenly aware of the
follies of mere revivalism (36-7, 151, 161). Having
observed the fact that religious medievalism had
encouraged religious revival in France (114), and
believing that the medieval Church did indeed have
lessons for contemporary Churches (150), he saw
medievalism as a guiding hand amidst the crisis of
the Anglican Church (417-18); a hand more feasible,
appropriate and unifying in the present exigencies
than that of modern Rome (609). In addition, the
medieval Church was a true guide because it was kin
with the primitive Church (279, 609).

The same range of opinions is also displayed in
his Sir Lancelot (1844), an enormous poem which
outlines the lessons of the thirteenth century for
the present. The Anglican Church is barren because
it has neglected its Catholic heritage;[133] whereas
the Middle Ages are a "true gage" by which to measure
"the stammering Churches" and restore "Their unity of
ritual voice".[134] By contrast, the "stream of sacred
liturgy" still flows in Rome.[135] He also significantly develops the Wordsworthian theme of "how to one
in ascetic living nature is a kind of Church",[136] a
book of "Christian science", which the Church could
once illumine because of the harmony between nature
and ritual.[137] (Sights and Thoughts was dedicated to
Wordsworth.) Faber's duality is also evident. He
does not join Rome, which he identifies with medievalism, because he will not idolize "Past / Or
Present", believing that "Christ is always present
with His Spouse";[138] which is to say that Anglicanism
is capable of being reformed, as is the questing
Lancelot. This equivocality points the way to his
realization that medievalist dreaming is not enough,
that "ancient books" have made him want the truth
behind the dream facade.[139] The past must be made to
act for the present.[140] Such dreams are not value-
less, because they liberate the soul by releasing
the imagination, as he says in "The Knights of St.
John",[141] thereby echoing Coleridge on how romance
had accustomed his imagination to the Vast. One use
is in reconciliation, for Christian Rome, sitting on
the ruins of the ancient secular state,

                    draws
        By mediaeval laws
        The Church and World augustly into one.[142]

It is significant that for Catholic Faber it is the
modern Church, not the medieval, which has primacy;
and the series "Thoughts While Reading History"
displays his awareness of the shortcomings as well as
the greatness of the Middle Ages.
        G.K. Chesterton (1874-1936), himself a late-
Victorian, provides an important and appropriate
postscript to Victorian medievalism. Chandler
implies in A Dream of Order that medievalism died
with the nineteenth century, and, indeed, the term
"medieval" is today commonly a term of abuse; but
Chesterton alone is sufficient to gainsay the
implication. He believed in the power of Catholicism
(even long before he became a Catholic in 1922) and
in the superiority of the spirituality and world-view
of the Middle Ages over the modern period. Though
keenly aware of the crudities and cruelties of the
Middle Ages, he believed, in contradiction of the
modern historical tradition, that they had constituted not a dark period but civilization reborn.
Additionally, he believed that medievalism was being
reborn in the face of virulent opposition from
modernists of every hue : from Darwin, Herbert
Spencer and Mill to Dean Inge, H.G. Wells and George
Bernard Shaw: "seldom," he said, "has one whole
period like the present fed so repeatedly and persis-
tently on one whole period of the past".[143]
        "We hear," said Chesterton, "a great deal of
discussion for and against the Middle Ages":[144]
contemporary anti-medievalists were only the latest
in a succession of arrogant, "modernist" generations
stretching back to the Renaissance.[145] There was the
"Cheap Manchester View", which lauded modern material
superiority,[146] and the "Condescending View", which
was smugly self-satisfied at the expense of the
Middle Ages.[147] Modernists wished the Catholic
Church dead, and by that token pretended that it had
virtually died with the Middle Ages;[148] but while it
had given every appearance of dying ever since its
birth, it kept reviving, today standing "erect and
resurrected".[149] Pope Leo XIII embodied the "modern
resurrection of Mediaevalism",[150] while the animating
and supporting force of St.Francis of Assisi reaches
from the medieval to the modern Church.[151] The
Middle Ages had been a visionary, idealistic age, to
which the extant cathedrals bear witness - the same
cathedrals also bearing symbolic witness to the fact

155

that the medieval ideals live on,[152] having been
neither frustrated nor fulfilled.[153] "The modern
world," he proclaimed, "has already been mediaevalized".[154]

Like De Vere, Chesterton combined to some extent
the medievalism of Newman and Digby, although he did
not have anything of De Vere's faith in modernism.
"Everything mediaeval," he believed, "... ramified
back to a root in religion",[155] and this organicism
was the foundation of an age of balance, commonsense
and exhuberant vitality.[156] The Church had come to
its zenith in the thirteenth century with Pope
Innocent III and St. Francis,[157] and Chesterton was
"still dreaming of the dream of Innocent III" about
St. Francis being the pillar of the Church.[158] But
he did not believe in a "Golden Age"; although he
believed the "plain man" has to "find some guidance
in the past if he is to get any good in the future",
after perceiving the "complete collapse of the
present".[159] The "Silver Age" of the thirteenth
century had gone off course before it could evolve
into a Golden Age,[160] because of the decline of the
Papacy, which stood for the "international ideal",[161]
and most of all because of the loss of Jerusalem, the
effect of which had been shattering to a visionary
age.[162] The Middle Ages, then, had been the age "in
which everything went wrong", and most tragically so,
because everything could have gone right.[163] The
Reformation had finally nailed down the coffin of
ideal Catholicism before it had been properly alive :
but medieval Christianity had not been outlived;
rather, it had not lived enough.[164]

Though a medievalist, Chesterton was only one
in so far as he was a Catholic; and he certainly
does not fit the traditional picture of the romantic
medievalist. "Catholicism," he insisted, "is not
medievalism"[165] (although medievalism was sometimes
Catholicism); and "medieval history is useless
unless it is modern history"[166] : that is, it has to
be relevant. "Unless," he wrote symbolically, "a
man understands that Rome is a modern city, he does
not understand that it is an eternal city".[167] He
was a medievalist not because the Middle Ages were
romantic and dead, but because medieval ideals were
alive, quintessentially in the Catholic Church.[168]
As the Church was modern, so, he proclaimed, was he
also;[169] and he even supposed that "the modern world
has been mediaevalized enough".[170]

Chesterton regarded himself as an anti-romantic,
and was conscious of a number of mistakes which had
been made about the Middle Ages and medievalism,

especially in the nineteenth century : the Middle
Ages had been judged to be dead - they were not;
medievalism was thought to be dead - it was not;
Catholicism was thought to be medievalism - it was
not; the British historical tradition had interpreted
the medieval as dark - it was not; the medievalists
had loved the Middle Ages for something they were
not. Modern historians were generally partial and so
told only half the truth[171] : Macaulay had seen only
one half of Digby, failing to see the other, which
was "very far from being merely an amiable old
antiquary haunting Melrose by moonlight".[172] He saw
much to criticize in nineteenth-century medievalism :
"the worst weakness of the medievalists is that they
fall short of the medievals".[173] There was fault on
both sides of the medievalist divide. The Romantics
had been only superficially and ambiguously medievalist : they developed

> a faint and hazy sympathy, if not with
> mediaeval theology, at least with mediaeval
> religion. ... Byron or Hugo probably pre-
> ferred an abbey to be a ruined abbey.... ...
> Scott advised us to see mediaeval Melrose by
> moonlight; with the delicate implication
> that the mediaeval religion was moonshine.[174]

The Romantic liked the medieval as a dead curio :
"his pleasure in the poetic past is as frivolous as
a fancy-dress ball".[175] But medievalists could be
discriminated : there was the "Old Romantic View",
which made a pleasing and comforting fiction out of
chivalry;[176] there was the "Rossetti View", which
made the Middle Ages into a cornucopia of aestheticism;[177] and there was that view which, "seeking only
earnest Churchmanship in a Protestant Church, found
its models in the Saxon Saints and Gothic monkeries
of the Oxford Movement".[178] All these were fictions,
but not entirely false : they were fragmentary views,
and therefore, in differing degrees, superficial.[179]
But Chesterton's whole point is that the medievals
lived not a fragment of a life, but a full one, a
point he expressed by saying that "all the popular
things [were] specially soaked in religion",[180] that
the Middle Ages provides "not a romance of darkness
nor a romance of moonlight, but a romance of the sun
at noonday".[181] And yet he rejected romance for its
fragmentariness. Medievalism need not, however, be
fragmentary, if it was Catholic : it need not be
romantic. True medievalism was wrongly accused of
being "romantic and unreal", wrongly because true

medievalists have reasonably supposed that

>they have taken the wrong turning, because
>they know they are in the wrong place. To
>know that, it is necessary not to idealise
>the medieval world, but merely to realise
>the modern world ... They do not start ...
>with the idea that man is meant to live in a
>New Jerusalem ... but with a strong inward
>and personal persuasion that a man was not
>meant to live in a man-trap.[182]

His poem "Mediaevalism" is a bitter account of the
modern mind realizing that it has taken the wrong
turning and looking wistfully to the past. The poem
is ambiguous, suggesting both that medievalism is
utterly futile, for the past is dead,and that the
dead can rise again; but the scales tip in favour
of resurrection :

>Is it a dream from the dead if your own
>>decay discovers
>Alive in your rotting graveyard the worm
>>of the world's desire?

He ends the poem :

>We went not gathering ghosts; but the
>>shriek of your shame is arisen
>Out of your own black Babel too loud;
>>and it woke the dead.

Had he known about them, Chesterton would have
relished two stories which represent two aspects of
Catholic medievalism. The first is about how Bute,
who had lived like the most beneficent lord from the
pages of Digby, ordained that his heart should be
delivered on his death, in the medieval way, to Mount
Olivet in the Holy Land, where he had so often
pilgrimaged, for burial at the spot where Christ is
said to have wept over Jerusalem, as Bute had figur-
atively wept over the tragedy of modern Britain. The
other concerns the titular Abbot of Westminster - the
then head of the Benedictine Order in England - who
owned the ring of the Abbots of Westminster, and who
suffered a symbolic loss. As he was mounting the
steps of St. Peter's to attend the opening day of
the first Vatican Council in late 1869, his ancient
abbatial ring fell from his finger and rolled down
the steps to oblivion. If some Catholics looked
longingly to the great age of their Church,scorning

the present, Providence decided that the Church would shed the integument of the past and cast off its insulating cerecloth to meet the modern age.

The concerns of the pre-Romantic and Romantic writers emerge frequently in Catholic writings. There is the criticism of their own age, the theme of unity and reconciliation, the interest in forms as sacramentals and aesthetics as a tool of faith, with an emphasis on the importance of imagination. But it is clearly inadequate to identify them all simply as romantics; and it is wrong to suppose that they saw the medieval Church as an object of revival, because they really saw it as an agent of renewal. Architecture was seen in both these ways; it was also seen as a focus of two other ideas: that the material can embody the spiritual, and that it can express different views of what Christianity should be. So many writers considered this subject, and it expresses so much of the whole work, that it must now be considered in detail.

NOTES

1. The History of England from the Accession of James the Second (1858) I, ch.I, 49; 1st.pub.1848.

2. See "The Monk as Civilizer", "The Clergy and the Heathen" in The Roman and the Teuton (1864), and LM II, 213 on chivalry.

3. Eg. Brilioth The Anglican Revival 58-61, Andrew L. Drummond The Churches in English Fiction (Leicester, 1950) 106, Chadwick The Victorian Church I, 174, Storr The Development of English Theology in the Nineteenth Century 1800-1860 256, Fairchild "Romanticism and the Religious Revival in England" Journal of the History of Ideas II (1941) 334-5, Joseph Ellis Baker The Novel and the Oxford Movement (New York, 1965) 50.

4. Cf. supra 76, Alice Chandler "Sir Walter Scott and the Medieval Revival" NCF XIX (1965) 322.

5. Respectively, The Romany Rye (1914) App. 333-4, 339 FM XXXVI (1847) 351, Purcell Life and Letters of Ambrose Phillipps de Lisle I, 169 n.2, I, 170.

6. The Spirit of the Age (1825) in The Complete Works ed. P.P. Howe (1932) XI, 57-8, 65.

7. Digby The Temple of Memory 2nd.ed. (1875) 28, 64, 372.

8. Ecclesiologist VI, 83; qu. James F. White The Cambridge Movement: The Ecclesiologists and the

Gothic Revival (Cambridge, 1962) 8.
    9. Reminiscences of Forty Years, by an
hereditary High Churchman (1868)] qu. Brilioth The
Anglican Revival 58.
    10. Brendon Hurrell Froude and the Oxford
Movement 28.
    11. Keble Occasional Papers and Reviews
(Oxford & London, 1877) 75,76.
    12. British Critic XXV (Apr. 1839), qu. Scott
The Critical Heritage ed. John O. Hayden (1970)378-9.
    13. Apologia Pro Vita Sua ed. Martin J.Svaglic
(Oxford Clarendon Press, 1967) 94.
    14. Newman Lectures on the Present Position of
Catholics in England (1851) 68-9.
    15. The Victorian Historical Novel 1840-1880
(1978) 120-1.Cf. Fairchild Journal of the History of
Ideas II, 334,
    16. Life of Edward Bouverie Pusey 4v.4th.ed.
(1894) I, 253-4.
    17. CW XXXIII 227, 228-9, 512.
    18. Ibid. 104.
    19. The Abbot (Edinburgh, 1886) 7-8. Further
p. refs. in text.
    20. Burke Complete Works (1803-27) V, 122.
    21. Edgar Johnson Sir Walter Scott (1970) II,
1275.
    22. Introduction to the first ed. (Mar. 1813)
of The Bridal of Triermain,parag. 3.
    23. See below ch. VI.179-80, 188-90.
    24. Eg. Storr The Development of English
Theology 256, Kingsley in Apologia 363, 364, 367-72,
Henry Rogers in "Recent Developments of Puseyism" ER
LXXX (Oct. 1844) 314, 343, 365, 366; cf. J. Derek
Holmes "Newman's Reputation and The Lives of the
English Saints" Catholic Historical Review LI (Jan.
1966) 528-38.
    25. Eg. Apologia 72.
    26. Eg. See James Patrick "Newman, Pugin, and
Gothic" VS XXIV No. 2. (Winter 1981) 193.
    27. Bump VP XV (1977) 100.
    28. Apologia 257-8.
    29. Ibid. 34.
    30. Loc.cit., Brendon Hurrell Froude and the
Oxford Movement 31.
    31. Brendon Hurrell Froude 101-2, 135.
    32. Eg. J.W. Burrow "The Sense of the Past" in
The Victorians ed. Laurence Learner (1978) 130.
    33. Apologia 34, 58.
    34. Ibid. 15-16.
    35. Ibid. 190.
    36. See Ibid. 58-9.

37. DeLaura overstates the Tractarian debt to romanticism : Hebrew and Hellene in Victorial Literature xiii.

38. Fairchild's phrase : Journal of the History of Ideas II (1941) 336.

39. L.A. Willoughby has described what he believes to be affinities between German Romanticism and Tractarianism, including religious medievalism, and he implies that one influenced the other : "On Some German Affinities with the Oxford Movement" MLR XXIX (1934) 52-66.

40. The Victorian Church I, 174.

41. John Keble's Literary and Religious Contribution to the Oxford Movement 9.

42. Cf. Stephen Prickett Romanticism and Religion (C.U.P. 1976) 105.

43. George Saintsbury unequivocally believed in the outstanding medievalist influence of the Oxford Movement : A Short History of English Literature (1898) 779.

44. Baker The Novel and the Oxford Movement 104.

45. Frances M. Brookfield The Cambridge "Apostles" (1906) 238.

46. In The Poems of Richard Monckton Milnes 2v. (1838) I.

47. "Archbishop Trench's Poems" in Essays Chiefly Literary and Ethical (1889) 64.

48. Short Studies on Great Subjects I, 571.

49. A Poet Hidden. The Life of Richard Watson Dixon 1833-1900 (1962) 71; cf. Lionel Stevenson The Pre-Raphaelite Poets (N. Carolina State U.P. 1972) 275. On Dixon's medievalism see also Sambrook op. cit. 11-12, 15, 17-20.

50. Op. cit. 6v. rev. 3rd. ed. (Oxford 1895) I, 22, 2 respectively; 1st. ed. 1878.

51. John M. Neale Good King Wenceslas (Birmingham, 1895) introduction by Morris.

52. Hierologus 101-2.

53. In Brother Fabian's Manuscript and Other Poems (1865).

54. 20 Dec. 1909 p.13. And see Georgiana Burne-Jones Memorials of Edward Burne-Jones 2v.(1904) II, 254.

55. See Eamon Duffy "Ecclesiastical Democracy Detected" Recusant History X no. 4 (Jan. 1970), J.C.H. Aveling The Handle and the Axe (1976) ch.15, and "Epilogue".

56. Letters and Diaries of John Henry Newman ed. C.S. Dessain and V.F. Blehl XII 221, letter to De Lisle 15 June 1848.

57. Discourses Addressed to Mixed Congregations (1929) 252.
58. Sermons Preached on Various Occasions (1874) 169-70.
59. Ibid. 175.
60. Ibid.177-8.
61. Essay on the Development of Christian Doctrine (Harmondsworth, 1973) ch.3 sec.I,184-5; 1st. ed. 1845.
62. Harold L. Weatherby Cardinal Newman in His Age (Nashville, 1973) 63; and see ibid. 4, 65, 66. The case is too complex to argue here, but Weatherby underestimates Newman's subtlety and true Catholicity.
63. "The Mission of St. Benedict" (1858) in Historical Sketches v.II.
64. "Poetry With Reference to Aristotle's Poetics" in Essays Critical and Historical; qu. Raleigh Addington "Newman and the Benedictines" Pax LXIV no. 332 (Spring/Summer 1974) 4. And see ibid. 3-5 on Newman and "poetic". See also G.B. Tennyson Victorian Devotional Poetry. The Tractarian Mode (1981) 20, 39-41.
65. Tennyson Victorian Devotional Poetry 48.
66. Qu. Beers The History of English Romanticism in the Nineteenth Century 355. Cruse similarly misjudged him : The Victorians and Their Books 141.
67. Beers op. cit. 356.
68. Essays on Church and State ed. Douglas Woodruff (1952) 203-4.
69. The History of Freedom and Other Essays (1907) 200-201.
70. Letters and Correspondence of John Henry Newman ed. Anne Mozley 2v. (1891) v. I, 454, letter of 8. Sept. 1833.
71. History of Freedom and Other Essays 203, 188 respectively.
72. Ibid. 210-11.
73. Letter of MacCarthy to Lord Houghton 30. Sept. 1833 in Trinity College Library, Cambridge, Houghton Suppl. (2) 4885.
74. See Grennan William Morris : Medievalist and Revolutionary 6, Reilly Aubrey de Vere 98, Shane Leslie Henry Edward Manning (1921) 327, 329.
75. The Correspondence of Gerard Manley Hopkins and Richard Watson Dixon ed. Claude Colleer Abbot (Oxford, 1935) 82-3, Further Letters of Gerard Manley Hopkins ed. C.C. Abbott rev. ed. (Oxford,1956) 148.
76. The Journals and Papers of Gerard Manley Hopkins (O.U.P. London, 1959) ed. Humphrey House, Graham Storey 26, 32.

77. See Jerome Bump "Hopkins, Pater, and Medievalism" VNL L (1976), Leonard J. Bowman, "Another Look at Hopkins and Scotus" Renascence XXIX no. I (1976) 50-6, James Finn Cotter Inscape. The Christology and Poetry of Gerard Manley Hopkins (Pittsburgh U.P., 1972) ch.6 "Scotus and the Scholastic Tradition", Poems and Prose of Gerard Manley Hopkins ed. W.H. Gardner (Harmondsworth, 1978) xxiv-xxv.

78. "Hopkins' Imagery and Medievalist Poetics" VP 15 (1977) 101-3.

79. Journals and Papers of Gerard Manley Hopkins 26, and see 33. Commentators seem united in viewing Hopkins's acquaintance Digby Mackworth Dolben (1848-67) as a medievalist (see Fairchild IV, 297, Ifor Evans English Poetry in the Later Nineteenth Century [1966] 237, Chapman Faith and Revolt 247); and, indeed, not only were several of his poems in a medieval manner, but he joined the English order of Benedictines in 1864, from then on casting himself "in the role of a medieval monk" (Uncollected Poems of Digby Mackworth Dolben ed. Martin Cohen [Reading, 1973] 9; cf. The Poems of Digby Mackworth Dolben ed. Robert Bridges [O.U.P., 1915] xxxi, 1, c). In March 1867 he decided to become a Roman Catholic. His poetry evinces a fierce struggle between the licence and sensuality of the classical and the self-denial and piety of the medieval; and the victory lay with the medieval. This struggle is reflected in "From the Cloister" (1864) and "On the Picture of an Angel by Fra Angelico" (1865).

80. See Gerald Monsman Walter Pater (Boston, Mass., 1977) 166.

81. Cf. Fairchild V. 175, Richard Le Gallienne The Romantic Nineties (1951) 113, Three Poets of the Rhymers' Club ed. Derek Stanford (Cheadle, 1974) 16-17, The Complete Poems of Lionel Johnson ed. Iain Fletcher (1953) xvi-xvii.

82. Cf. Complete Poems xxxvi.

83. Post Liminium: Essays and Critical Papers by Lionel Johnson (1911) 54.

84. Ibid. 94. Johnson also wrote on St. Francis in his poem "Men of Assisi" (1890). Naturally enough Catholic writers were unambiguous in their affection for St. Francis, and other examples of such writings are De Vere's poem "St. Francis and Perfect Joy" (in Mediaeval Records and Sonnets), Faber's Sir Lancelot (Book VII), Chesterton's St. Francis of Assisi (1923); see also below p.151 and n.130.

85. Stones Broken from the Rocks : Extracts from the Manuscript Note-books of Robert Stephen

Hawker Vicar of Morwenstow,1834-75 selected and arranged by E.R. Appleton, ed. C.E.Byles (Oxford,1922) 3.

86. Footprints of Former Men in Far Cornwall ed. C.E. Byles (1903) 6, "Psalmus Cantici" in Cornish Ballads and Other Poems by R.S. Hawker Vicar of Morwenstow ed. C.E. Byles (1904).

87. "Minster Church on the Confirmation Day August 17, 1836" in Poetical Works of R.S.Hawker ed. Alfred Wallis (1899) 43.

88. Stones Broken from the Rocks 99.

89. Ibid. 84.

90. Robert Stephen Hawker : A Study of His Thought and Poetry (Oxford, 1926) 70-4.

91. Quest of the Sangraal in Cornish Ballads 185.

92. The Life and Letters of R.S. Hawker C.E. Byles (London, New York, 1905) 412, letter 22 Nov. 1863.

93. Ibid. 410.

94. Cornish Ballads 188-9.

95. Cf. Burrows Robert Stephen Hawker 124.

96. Eg. Stones Broken from the Rocks 87, 98, 99, 100.

97. Robert Stephen Hawker 98.

98. Byles Life and Letters of R.S. Hawker 384, letters to J.G. Godwin Feb., Mar. 1862.

99. Stones Broken from the Rocks 44.

100. Ibid. 83.

101. Ibid. 54, 47.

102. Ibid. 53, 54.

103. Another eccentric, Frederick Rolfe (1860-1913), is reminiscent of eighteenth-century medievalists, despite his Catholicism. A Chattertonian shade writing poems with titles like "Sestina yn honour of Lytel Seynt Hew", he in a sense "played" at being a Catholic; and "Seeking and Finding : A Sequel to 'The Lost Chord'" and "The Waits : A Yule-Tide Carol" return to Warton's "Pleasures of Melancholy" by using the catalyst of an ancient abbey to produce religious dream visions. He wrote a crusading novel, Hubert's Arthur (finished 1908), and planned another on St. Thomas of Canterbury.

104. Qu. S.M. Paraclita Reilly Aubrey De Vere : Victorian Observer (Dublin, 1956) 111.

105. Mediaeval Records and Sonnets (1893) xii.

106. Ibid. xiii.

107. St. Thomas of Canterbury (1876) xxiii.

108. Mediaeval Records and Sonnets x.

109. Legends and Records of the Church and the Empire (1887) xii.

110. Legends and Records of the Church and the

Empire vii-viii.

111. Mediaeval Records and Sonnets ix, Legends of the Saxon Saints (1879) xlix, De Vere Recollections of Aubrey de Vere (1897) 367.

112. Legends and Records of the Church and the Empire "The Crowning of Charlemagne; and the Holy Roman Empire" st. IX.

113. Legends of the Saxon Saints 26.

114. Aubrey de Vere (1904) 148.

115. Cf. Calvert Alexander The Catholic Literary Revival (Milwaukee, 1935) 41.

116. William R. Inge Outspoken Essays, Second Series (1933) 3.

117. Legends of the Saxon Saints xlviii.

118. Legends and Records of the Church and the Empire xxv.

119. Mediaeval Records and Sonnets viii.

120. Cf. below 228.

121. See below 181-4.

122. DR No. 463 (1st. Quarter, 1954) 325.

123. Dormer MSS. : letters to Digby Oct. 1829, 22 April 1830, 27 April 1842.

124. Magdalen College Archives MS. 459 MS. Letters. Ambrose Lisle Phillipps De Lisle to Bloxam 25 Jan. 1841.

125. Ibid. De Lisle to Bloxam 31 Mar. 1841.

126. See De Lisle Letter to the Earl of Shrewsbury on the Re-establishment of the Hierarchy (1850).

127. Diurnal of the Soul (1864) Preface 21.

128. John Patrick Third Marquess of Bute, K.T. (1921) 40-1.

129. Faber Sights and Thoughts in Foreign Churches and Among Foreign Peoples (1842) 609. Subsequent p. refs. to this ed. given in text.

130. Eg. "Dante" and "Sanctity and Song". See R. L. Mégroz Francis Thompson : The Poet of Earth in Heaven (1927) ch. XI, especially 209.

131. Faber quotes Arthur P. Stanley's Prize Essay on how the medieval Church erected "a new Christian literature out of the corrupt dregs of Byzantium and Rome", 59.

132. Past and Present II, ii, 43.

133. Sir Lancelot (1844) 454.

134. Ibid. 475, 38.

135. Ibid. 455.

136. Faber Poet and Priest. Selected Letters... 92.

137. Sir Lancelot 50, 51, 156-8, 473-4.

138. Ibid. 465.

139. Faber Poems (1857, 2nd.ed.) 210.

140. Ibid. "Use of the Past" 517.
141. Ibid. espec. 115, 116, 124.
142. Ibid. "New Rome" st.IX, 496.
143. The Resurrection of Rome (n.d. [1930])119.
144. "What Might Have Been" The Glass Walking-
Stick (1955) 113.
145. The New Jerusalem (n.d. [1920] 260-1.
146. "History versus the Historians" Lunacy and
Letters (1958) 130.
147. Ibid. 131.
148. The Resurrection of Rome 111. Henceforth
cited as R.R.
149. Chaucer (1962) ch. IX 292; 1st. ed. 1932.
150. R.R.116-17, 121.
151. Ibid. 132-3.
152. Ibid. 119.
153. "The Riddle of Restoration" Lunacy and
Letters 172.
154. R.R.119.
155. "The Chartered Libertine" A Miscellany of
Men 4th. ed. (1926) 251.
156. Eg. Chaucer 59, 70, 266, 288, 293, Lunacy
and Letters 132, 133.
157. R.R. 109, 132.
158. Ibid. 131, 109.
159. The New Jerusalem 239.
160. Glass Walking-Stick 115.
161. Chaucer 47.
162. New Jerusalem 245, 246, 247, 249.
163. Ibid. 241, 244-5.
164. What's Wrong With the World 8th. ed.(1910)
38-39.
165. Chaucer 290.
166. Ibid. 46.
167. R.R. 123.
168. Lunacy and Letters 172.
169. R.R. 116.
170. Ibid. 120.
171. Lunacy and Letters 129.
172. "A Grammar of Knighthood" The Well and the
Shallows (1935) 218. The ref. is to Scott.
173. "Baroque and Gothic" Glass Walking-Stick
103.
174. "If they had believed" The Thing (1929)
240-1.
175. Lunacy and Letters 172.
176. Ibid. 130, R.R. 118.
177. Lunacy and Letters 131, R.R. 119.
178. R.R. 118-19.
179. See also "Robert Bruce and His Age" Glass
Walking-Stick 108-10, New Jerusalem 255.

Chapter VI

ATTITUDES TO MEDIEVAL ECCLESIASTICAL ARCHITECTURE IN
THE EIGHTEENTH AND NINETEENTH CENTURIES

Thou who Thy tabernacle mad'st of old
To be a type of things invisible,
And didst within Thy temple come to dwell
Making it holy ....

Isaac Williams The Cathedral

Medievalism has been perceived as mere aesthet-
ism : Walter Pater and Heine saw the Middle Ages as
a store of poetic inspiration;[1] but the latter also
saw that medieval culture was essentially religious,
a "passion-flower which had blossomed from the blood
of Christ", and that consequently medievalists were
engaged in a religious quest.[2] Catholicism was, he
said, a "concordat between ... the spirit and the
senses"; and Catholicism, according to Lord Macaulay,
excelled in the art of "striking the senses and
filling the imagination".[3] It was perceived to be
artistic - sacramentally so - and conversely its art
was thought to be religious, so that the evocation of
its medieval art was an equivalent for the evocation
of its spirituality. Medieval Catholic art was,
therefore, the natural resource of artists searching
for a deeper spiritual language; moreover, Digby,
for example, believed that it could convey faith to
modern youth.[4] All this was in close alignment with
the Romantic desire to deepen art by imbuing it with
a religious dimension.[5] The revival of interest in
medieval religious art and architecture was a mental
chameleon, expressing both vague romantic and precise
partizan religious aspirations, a subject which
focusses the general response to the Middle Ages,
illustrating its depth and range, and depicting the
process whereby it became more profound.

168

I : The Eighteenth Century and Romanticism

The eighteenth century was rationalist and anti-Catholic, classicist and anti-Gothic, and, typically, James Thomson regarded Gothic buildings as "heavy monuments of shame".[6] But in 1733 Thomas Gent wrote that Kirkstall Abbey "produc'd in me an inward Veneration" and was "enough to strike the most harden'd Heart, into the softest and most serious Reflexion".[7] In 1783 John Pinkerton said : "the rude effusions of the Gothic Muse are like the monuments of their architecture. We are filled with a religious reverence, and, forgetting our praise of the contriver, adore the present deity."[8] This striking epiphany of sublimity and divinity is echoed by Coleridge. It has been noted that when the romantics talked of the sublime, they were talking as much religiously as aesthetically, and "sublimity merged with mystical religious experience" for Coleridge;[9] so the following collocation of the sublime, the religious and the medieval is not surprising :

> When I enter a Greek church, my eye is
> charmed, and my mind elated; I feel
> exalted, and proud that I am a man. But
> the Gothic art is sublime. On entering
> a cathedral, I am filled with devotion
> and with awe; I am lost to the actualities
> that surround me, and my whole being expands
> into the infinite; earth and air, nature and
> art, all swell up into eternity, and the
> only sensible impression left is, 'that I am
> nothing!'[10]

This is a locus classicus of medieval culture taking precedence - and to a religious degree - over rationalism and classicism; and that the Romantic "I" is obliterated cannot be overestimated. How did such "heavy monuments of shame" become great religious experiences?

Such questions are hardly susceptible of answer; still less is proof available. One can only surmise that the earlier set of norms became inadequate to cope with the anxieties produced by the unending search for truth, anxieties which had been coaxed into new grooves by the introduction of new vogues to the cultured classes. From this it was but a step to seeing afresh the religious dynamism of the products of the age of faith, and constant exposure to Gothic naturally resulted in its deeper absorption,

a process reinforced by the fashion of looking to the
(increasingly medievalist) Continent. The French
Revolution and the social revolution at home doubtless brought anxieties to a head, and thereby
accelerated cultural movements already in the air for
fifty years and more. Certain signposts, all pointing the same way, and stamped with originality, can
be picked out as evidence of the change.

Just as poetry allowed an escape from rationalist thought, so the "poetic" medieval evoked an
unbuttoning of restraints. In Warton's "The
Pleasures of Melancholy" (1747) there is a significant model of release from reason, and of the entire
religious appeal to the Middle Ages, in the
narrator's falling asleep in the ruins of a
monastery. Sleep is the romantic symbol of contact
with the id or the divine, and the monastic ruins
seem to induce this sleep (ll.41-2); that is, they
open a channel to divine depth, itself a waking.
The idea of waking in sleep is produced by a confusion between sleep and wakefulness, itself produced
by the omission of the information that the narrator
falls asleep, by the phrase "noon / Of night" (50-1),
and by his waking when the rest of nature is asleep
(55). In sleep, says the analogy, there is possible
an enlightenment usually associated with day : "let
the sacred Genius of the night / Such mystic visions
send, as Spenser saw" (62-3). In this state he is
not afraid of enthusiasm, and he wants religious
experience "Till all my soul is bath'd in ecstasies,
/ And lapp'd in Paradise" (200-1). He is after
religious ecstasy, which he associates with Spenser,
whom he in turn equates with Gothic; so what better
place to recreate Spenser's 'Gothic' mystical
experience than in the 'Gothic vaults' of a monastery?[11] Poetry emancipates his medievalist imagination from the constraints of his classical consciousness.

The ground for alignment with this Gothic dream
was partly laid by Burke and Hurd. Burke said of
Westminster Abbey : "the moment I entered I felt a
kind of awe pervade my mind which I cannot describe :
the very silence seemed sacred".[12] As J.T. Boulton
points out, Burke's Philosophical Enquiry into the
Origins of our Ideas of the Sublime and Beautiful
(1756) provided principles by which subsequent
writers found Gothic preferable to Grecian.[13] In
1762 Hurd made the simple but very significant
suggestion that Gothic should be viewed on its own
terms, and that if it was it would be seen to have
merits just as much as the Grecian.[14] Walpole seems

to have taken note of this idea, or of the cultural
direction of which such a comment was the sign, and
came positively to prefer Gothic to Classic.
   Horace Walpole (1717-97)[15] wrote "Verses in
Memory of King Henry the Sixth, Founder of King's
College, Cambridge" in 1738. In the chapel

> mild Devotion bends her pious knee,
> Calm and unruffled as a summer sea;
> Avoids each wild enthusiastic tone,
> Nor borrows utt'rance from a tongue unknown.
> O Henry! from thy lucid orb regard
> How purer hands thy pious cares reward;
> Now Heav'n illuminates thy godlike mind,
> From Superstition's papal gloom refin'd.[16]

His "mild", Enlightenment, Anglican devotion does not
rest easily in a Catholic Gothic structure built with
"impure" hands in "papal gloom"; but his mind was
clearer when he gothicized Strawberry Hill (a villa
he bought in 1747) and when he wrote the Anecdotes of
Painting (1762-71). Here he writes that the Gothic
builders,

> who had not the happiness of lighting on
> the simplicity and proportion of the Greek
> orders, were however so lucky as to strike
> out a thousand graces and effects which
> rendered their buildings magnificent, yet
> genteel, vast, yet light, venerable and
> picturesque. ...[the priests] exhausted
> their knowledge of the passions in
> composing edifices whose pomp, mechanism,
> vaults, tombs, painted windows, gloom, and
> perspective infused such sensations of
> romantic devotion....[17]

He identifies with "magnificent", "vast", "venerable"
Gothic; though his conscience suggests that it was
really classic, "genteel" and "light". It is
noteworthy that priestly passion is thought to be the
basis of religious creativity : there speaks a true
romantic, passion being romantic fire from heaven, a
fire which, in a sense, is returned to heaven in the
phrase "romantic devotion". (It may be that passion
- or perhaps passion-with-imagination - in the
romantic is secularized grace.) He has mythified
Gothic, for he suggests imagination and the sense of
the quasi-religious sublime are most at home with
Gothic. He then says that passion is the channel
through which the Gothic can be received. Such

reception takes the form of a reluctant epiphany :

> In St. Peter's one is convinced that it
> was built by great princes - in Westminster
> Abbey, one thinks not of the builder; the
> religion of the place makes the first
> impression; and though stripped of its
> altars and shrines, it is nearer converting
> one to popery than all the regular pageantry
> of Roman domes. Gothic churches infuse
> superstition - Grecian admiration.[18]

"Though stripped" is very telling, since it implies
that "altars and shrines" would effect a final
conversion within the setting; and the setting is
important because, as he says, "gloom and well-
applied obscurity are better friends to devotion than
even wealth!" He continues,

> Cato is a regular drama, Macbeth an
> extravagant one; yet who thinks the
> genius of Addison equal to Shakespeare's?
> The one copies rules, the other the
> passions. A Gibbs and money, a French
> critic and English schoolmaster, can make
> a building or a tragedy without a fault
> against proportion or the three unities....
> It required a little more genius to write
> "Macbeth," or to establish the Roman
> Catholic religion....[19]

He admires Grecian tastefulness, but Gothic for something other and deeper than taste. Passion, which is
both the hand of spiritual expression and the eye of
transcendental observation, creates it and responds
to it; it infuses superstition and devotion; it is
the proper expression of Catholicism; indeed, Gothic
emerges as missionary, acting as a rallying-point for
the spiritual appetite, whether secularized, as in
Walpole's case, or not. Walpole likes Shakespeare
and savage scenery for the same reason he is
attracted to Catholicism through its architectural
expression : not because they touch his escapist
instinct, but because they appeal to his thirst for
greater depth, which is to say, because they bring
him, as he thinks, nearer to reality. The age, he
implies, is astray. Though rationally opposed to
Catholicism, he momentarily 'plays at' being a
Catholic, and Walter Scott supposed that Walpole
liked to give his fiction readers a similar imagin-
ative-spiritual thrill to the one he extracted from

Gothic, that it was his object

> not merely to excite surprise and terror,
> by the introduction of supernatural agency,
> but to wind up the feelings of his reader
> till they became for a moment identified
> with those of a ruder age, which 'Held each
> strange tale devoutly true.'[20]

This imaginative-religious leap was operative in much religiously-oriented medievalist literature, and is the factor on which the tension between disbelief and the desire for belief (or at least depth) operates.

Walpole's view of 'gloom' in the Anecdotes contradicts that of the much earlier 'Verses in Memory of King Henry the Sixth' : in one it is corrupt, in the other it leads to devotion. This is emblematic of the change which has taken place in the man and his age. Earlier, King's Chapel was beautifully religious because it was not Catholic; later, the Gothic is awesome because it induces a feeling for Catholicism, whose genius he is now prepared to acknowledge. Walpole, a man representative of his age,[21] exemplifies the growth in appreciation of the Middle Ages as an age of faith, which, in the face of prejudice, habit and circumstance it was not yet possible to recognize or openly acknowledge, so that he and others had to transfer their appreciation to the vehicles and expressions of that spirituality.

Like an echo of Walpole, Vicesimus Knox (1752 - 1821), also something of a classicist, was probably influenced by the poetry of Gray and Warton, sharing the latter's attitudinal ambiguity. He liked to think that Gothic taste was dead, but conceded that medieval virtues continued to be "proper objects of imitation" and felt that the Gothic excites "a species of emotions peculiarly adapted to the purposes of the cathedral". Medieval ecclesiastical buildings were hallowed by "the enlarged benevolence and unaffected piety of our forefathers", and he believed that "the pious heart has poured forth its animated devotion at the rude Gothic shrine, with a fervor not to be surpassed in the Grecian temple".[22]

By contrast, in 1773 William Blake wrote an explicitly favourable inscription to an engraving : "this is One of the Gothic Artists who Built the Cathedrals in what we call the Dark Ages, ... of whom the World was not worthy; such were the Christians in all Ages". Blake's independent mind ignores traditional anti-medievalism, readily identifying the medieval church builders with the spirit of Christ.

About 1810, he made a Gothic church a symbol of
"true Art", which he identified with Christ, just as
ten years later he identified Gothic with "Living
Form [which] is Eternal Existence". This was
contrasted with Grecian, which is "Mathematic Form",
itself "Eternal in the Reasoning Memory". There is
little doubt which he considered superior, for he
despized the Classical : "the Classics! it is the
Classics, & [sic] not Goths nor Monks, that Desolate
Europe with Wars".23
     In 1783 Hugh Blair anticipated Coleridge by
associating Gothic with sublimity.24 The Roman
Catholic prelate John Milner advocated the abandonment of classical for church-building and, in an
influential work, supposed that a man experiences in
Gothic a "frame of mind that fits him for prayer and
contemplation", and that it "produces an artificial
infinite in the mind of the spectator"25 : Gothic
evokes religiosity, which, by the end of the
eighteenth century, classic is increasingly thought
not to do. By the end of the century the Gothic star
was rising and perceived to be a focus for transcendent experience, while medieval Catholicism, by
virtue of its association with Gothic, was darkly
supposed to be a possible source of enlightenment.
     In the early nineteenth century many Continental
medievalists interpreted Gothic religiously. It led
Chateaubriand to reflect on "the insignificance of
man.... Everything," he wrote, " in Gothic churches
recalls labyrinthine forests, everything evokes
religious awe, the mysteries and the deity".26
Heine said it exalted the spirit and abased the
flesh, that its stone was an "exponent of Christian
spiritualism", its cathedrals revealing the "fundamental idea of the Church" : in it "everything tran-
substantiates itself".27 These sentiments have much
in common with Pugin's idealist Christianity and his
ultimately Platonic notion that manufactured objects
can embody the spirit in which they are produced.
Frankl believes that on the Continent Gothic "was
regarded as the symbol of Christianity because it
represents the infinite immediately",28 which is to
say that Gothic - and this is particularly true of
Coleridge - was viewed as the real symbol (which
Coleridge thought "always partakes of the reality
which it renders intelligible")29 of the spiritual;
that is, that it was thought to sacramentally embody
the religious, to express the numinous in the
physical.
     Such ideas were transmitted to England by
writers like Digby and Carlyle.30 Coleridge relied

heavily on the works of A.W.von Schlegel, although
he had had a long-standing empathy with the medieval
spirit, for, as he said, he was of the opinion that
medieval romances had "habituated [him] to the Vast"
- that is, to the transcendent - and given him a
"love of the Great and the Whole".[31]   According to
the Green report of his lecture on the "General
Character of the Gothic Mind in the Middle Ages,
given in 1818, Coleridge preferred Gothic to classical architecture because there complexity and
variety are unified into a whole, a quality also
wondered at by Goethe,[32] and which had for some
romantics a mystical significance. In 1833 he said
"the principle of the Gothic architecture is
Infinity made imaginable",[33] and whereas ancient art
was finite and material, Gothic art "entirely
depended on a symbolical expression of the infinite,
- which is ... whatever cannot be circumscribed within the limits of actual sensuous being".[34] Moreover,
"a Gothic cathedral is the petrifaction of our
religion", by which he meant "the material expression
of our religion",[35] a sacramental-type view which is
at one with medieval Catholic reverence for the
physical as an expression of the spiritual. According
to the Cawardine report of the same lecture, he spoke
of the "intensity of the emotions which had been
produced by a view of the cathedral at York, and the
interior of King's College Chapel", and adds that
this enthusiasm was "evidently associated with feelings of religion".[36] His tenor is one of anti-
romantic, Christian humility, "that I am nothing";
and while classical art excites "exalted notions of
the human self", "Gothic architecture impresses the
beholder with a sense of self-annihilation; he
becomes, as it were, a part of the work contemplated".[37] "Could you ever," he asked, "discover
anything sublime, in our sense of the term, in the
classic Greek literature? I never could. Sublimity
is Hebrew by birth",[38] and Gothic is more sublime
than Greek[39] : Gothic expressed the Hebrew spirit.
Comparing Knox and Coleridge one sees that the
appreciation of Gothic moved from the more aesthetic
category to an almost purely religious one, and that
via the demotion of the classic. For Coleridge,
Gothic was a statement of faith, was itself mystically spiritual, and had the power to evoke a mystical
response. In him the preceding trend was clarified,
while the succeeding developments were anticipated.
    Organicism was important to the Romantics be-
cause it symbolized integration and represented the
essence of nature, which itself represented the

transcendent and infinite; and many Romantics
appreciated Gothic for its affinity with organic
nature. Continental writers such as Schlegel, Georg
Forster and Goethe used the analogy between Gothic
and nature and thereby extracted a religious message
from Gothic.[40] In England, Wordsworth used the same
analogy in The Excursion (Bk.V, ll.148-9), and
Coleridge spoke of the great cathedrals, with their
"pillared stems and leaf-work", as a petrified wood-
land "symbol of the everlasting gospel".[41] This is
pantheism becoming Catholicism, whereas Heine
suggested religious medievalism was pantheism in
disguise. If Keble could regard nature poetry as a
discreet way of discussing Catholic doctrine, it is
likely that nature seen in Gothic was potentially
Christian. Organicism figures in an essay by John
Sterling on Netley Abbey (1828), which he pictures
in the days of its aesthetic glory, its "venerable
forms, and awful symbols", when ritual gave a
"purport and meaning and heavenward application to
the whole". The ruin calls to his mind the organicism of history, and in its oneness with nature, he
sees it as a shrine, because through nature it leads
one to God and symbolizes the closeness and harmony
of man and God. Coleridge preferred the pristine
Gothic of the past, Sterling - here the more romantic
- the destroyed Gothic of the present; and he is not
a true medievalist because he admires man too much.[42]
    By contrast, Wordsworth regretted the destruct-
ion of the monasteries and looks on them with
humility:

          Once ye were holy, ye are holy still;
          Your spirit freely let me drink, and live.

Medieval churches lead one to heaven and are "Types
of the spiritual Church". In the 'ecclesiastical
sonnet' 'Inside of King's College Chapel Cambridge'
and in the sonnet which follows it, he implicitly
explains why he does not criticize the extravagance
of medieval ecclesiastical architecture : because the
resulting aesthetic experience leads the soul to God;
which was, indeed, the object of the buildings :
"They dreamt not of a perishable home / Who thus
could build".[43] The perception of King's has totally
changed since Walpole's poem on it, wherein piety is
associated with present Protestant worshippers, and
not with the building or its builders.[44] John
Nicholson's Airedale in ancient times, William Lisle
Bowles's 'Restoration of Malmesbury Abbey' and John
Wilson's 'Melrose Abbey' and 'An Evening in Furness

Abbey' are other Romantic examples showing an ill-formed nostalgia which forces a compromise between the Catholic past and the Protestant present.[45]

II: The Victorians

Such precedents led naturally to a Victorian surge of enthusiasm for medieval architecture, which developed variations on a long-established theme, but with the parties polarizing and explicitly displaying deep feelings, although these did not arrange themselves on obvious lines, of pro-Gothicists being all Catholics and anti-Gothicists being all non-Catholics. Four parties present themselves for consideration in this period : Catholic and non-Catholic anti-Gothicists, High Church and Catholic Gothicists. Coleridge's dictum that Gothic was the "petrifaction of our religion" was mainly accepted, and it was interpreted as the vehicle of Christian ideology and spirituality. In The Last Romantics, Hough supports the notion that medieval arts were interpreted and appreciated in this period as spiritual expressions, although he over-emphasizes Ruskin's initiatory rôle in this respect, mistakenly believing that "earlier romantics ... had visited history as spectators, intelligent tourists, not as exiles from a lost paradise". He also notes that stimulus was given to Gothicism by the consciousness of the industrial revolution's failure; and he further believes that corroded, Tractarian-style devotional sentiment shifted, in the middle of the century, into aesthetic channels.[46] Digby certainly displays discontent with the industrial scene; but the second point is an over-simplification, because while Pater, Arnold and the Pre-Raphaelites made something of a religion out of aesthetics, and cocasionally strayed into the ambiguous realm of medieval art, Ruskin did not become an aesthete - his religion was too sincere for that - and there was within the High Church ample room for religious aestheticism, so there was no need for it to be diverted into another movement.

The years adjacent to 1840 saw an attitudinal shift towards medieval ecclesiastical architecture; and since such buildings provided a palpable link with an alien faith, the prevailing prejudices were also affected. Lord Acton said (with only slight exaggeration) that during the period from the Reformation to the Revolution "the remains of mediaeval art were not even curiosities" and the great Gothic churches "had to be discovered again";[47] until, as has been remarked, Gothic became for Pugin and De Lisle "a living embodiment of Catholicism,

almost Catholicism itself".[48] By 1843 both Pugin and
Neale felt just cause to hail the rapidly increasing
appreciation of what they both referred to as
Catholic art.[49] Carlyle, the curser of Catholic
paraphernalia, praising the medieval spirit,suggested
that St. Edmund's Abbey had 'crystallised' that
spirit.[50] Even the Catholic-hater Charles Borrow
weakened in 1843 before the sight of St.James of
Compostella;[51] and by 1849 it could be conceded
even by Kingsley that medieval art "has now become
a reigning fashion among us".[52] William Rushton
commented in 1863 on the "phase of revived mediaevalism" of the "last thirty or forty years", particularly referring to the interest in medieval literature
and art, which had led "ardent young men", medievalist enthusiasts, "further than they originally
intended to go".[53] In 1842 Wordsworth could write an
almost Puginesque sonnet,[54] acclaiming the 'Papal
Unity' of the Middle Ages, which gave rise to
glorious and graceful art, and hailing the churches,
which take

> Form spirit and character from holy writ,
> Give to devotion ...
> Pinions of high and higher sweep, and make
> The unconverted soul with awe submit.

But the Middle Ages were really whatever
individuals wanted them to be, and some swam against
the tide. In 1843 Kingsley insisted that Gothic
architecture is "dumb", "raising a semi-selfish
emotion; that is, having its beginning and end in
us",[55] a view directly opposed to that of the
'transcendentalists'. But his attitude romantically
softened, obtaining a primitivist twist, for in a
lecture of 1871 he admires Gothic as latently Protestant. He clearly means English Gothic, interpreting its indigenous, national style as a harbinger of
religious independence, an idea possibly taken from
the Ecclesiologists. He also reproduces the romantic
tradition of the primitive and arboreal derivation of
Decorated Gothic, with its reminiscence of God. In
the thirteenth century, he supposes, architecture
"received, as it were, a soul" and signified
aspiration, while its architects are attributed with
earnestness, care and reverence.[56] Like Neale, then,
he believed in the spirituality of Gothic, the goodness of its builders, and its spiritual influence,
but on his own primitivist natural-supernaturalist
terms. By contrast, in 1844 the Rev. Francis Close
published two books which uncompromisingly attacked

the Ecclesiologists and condemned Gothic as Popish
and too aesthetic to be used by Protestants.[57]

Catholics

To understand religio-aesthetic disagreements
within Victorian Catholicism one has to be aware of
the basic party divisions. The discreet, conformist
Cisalpines ("Old Catholics"), disliked both the Ultramontanes, who looked uncompromisingly to Rome and
favoured Roman baroque, and the group of aggressive
"English Catholics", who favoured the architecture of
the foremost Catholic Gothic-revivalist Augustus
Welby Pugin (1812-52). The Cisalpine Joseph Berington, while viewing twelfth-century abbeys as
"monuments of the piety, the magnificence, and the
taste of the age", believed that "superstition" was
the "animating principle" behind their erection.[58]
The English Catholics promoted English Gothic partly
because they thought it patriotic (and therefore
"safe") because national,[59] and partly from a notion
that the antiquity of the Catholic Church was proof
of its present truth. Ultramontanes supposed that
Gothic was Anglican, and Charles Eastlake noted that
"it is a common error to suppose that the Church of
Rome has encouraged to any great extent, or for any
special purpose, the Revival of Gothic Architecture",
for Rome was not medievalist in either architecture
or ritual.[60] Wiseman, though ultramontane, at first
encouraged Pugin's medievalizing activities, despite
his personal preferences,[61] because he realized that
while the taste for Gothic had not been formed by the
end of the 1830s, the "_feeling_ or love" for it had
fructified; so that the extension of Gothic would
help to "awaken those dormant religious sympathies,
which once were the causes, but must now be the
results of such sublime conceptions".[62] Uneasy that
classical churches might be confused with dissenters'
chapels, he even recommended Gothic,[63] though he disliked slavish imitations, the development of a new
truly "Christian art" being the proper pursuit of the
Catholic architect.[64] Later, however, he reverted to
the pursuit of his own classical taste.[65]
This shift of sympathy from Gothic was a feature
of the Catholic intelligentsia. As a young man,
Frederick Faber had been "caught up in dreams of
medieval chivalry and monasteries", but the later
1840s saw his emancipation from Puginesque Gothicism.[66] Newman had also been interested in Gothic in
the later 1830s, but abandoned it by 1842.[67] Like
most other High Church Anglicans of the time, Newman

had faith in his Church because he believed it
preserved intact a primitive doctrine, and through
its antiquity had the divine cachet of approval. He
wrote :

> People shrink from Catholicity and think
> it implies want of affection for our
> National Church. ... In order to kindle
> love of the National Church, and yet to
> inculcate a Catholic tone, nothing else
> is necessary but to take our Church in
> the Middle Ages.[68]

Thus he was drawn to the Gothic style. As he became
more Catholic, however, his emphasis on the principle of antiquity waned, since he then placed more
stress on the authority of the present-day Church.[69]
Also, when he became a Catholic, he did so keenly
aware of the principle of Catholicity, and this led
him to shun the national aspects of the Church in
England, in favour of the international, which in
turn led him to favour the international baroque
style.[70] A third reason for his abandonment of
Gothicism is that he was consumed by ideological
principles and the inculcation of holiness, to the
virtual exclusion of eccelsiastical aesthetics.
Basically, his interest in Gothic was little more
than indulgence in the current fashion, for at a
deeper level his view of religious expression was
rather stern : in a sermon of 1842, given at the end
of his 'Gothic' period, he warned against indulging
in the beautiful side of religion while neglecting
the severe.[71]
　　Newman set the seal on his drift from Gothicism
when he built his Catholic Oratory in the baroque
style,[72] which led to conflict with De Lisle and
Pugin, who shared the aim of re-uniting Anglicans and
Catholics on a platform of English Gothicism,[73] and
felt they were under attack from Newman, though he
denied it.[74] De Lisle accused the 'Romanists' of
decrying the Middle Ages and of having no sympathy
with medieval saints.[75] Though untrue, Newman and
others realized the Church could not rely fundamentally on the past, so he rejected Pugin's equation of
Gothic and orthodoxy as the cause of a narrow
extremist,[76] condemning his preference for style over
the proprieties of modern ritual.[77] Newman disliked
the partizan or extreme spirit, so always shied from
such religio-aesthetic movements as the Camden
Society.[78] While he preferred 'Grecian' to Gothic
detail, nevertheless he saw that English Catholics

loved Gothic through familiarity, and even thought
Gothic a more beautiful architectural idea than
Grecian, believing its adaptability should be put to
good use, for it had become like "an old dress" which
no longer fitted the rubrics and should be altered to
take account of them: "I wish to wear it," he said,
for he had "the greatest admiration of the Gothic
style". Just as he criticized Pugin for confusing
the faith with an architectural period, he also re-
buked him for confusing "the principles of his great
art with the details".79 So while he was not a
medievalist in the sense of wanting to restore in
every detail the architecture of a particular century,
he criticized Pugin not for being a Gothicist but for
being an antiquarian, and condemned not the Gothic
idea or the principles of the Gothic style, but the
modern use of Gothic details. It is noteworthy, however, that he did not correlate the Gothic style with
the spiritual or transcendent, as romantics did.
     In works like Contrasts (1836) and The True
Principles of Pointed or Christian Architecture
(1841) Pugin promoted the triune notion that Gothic
was quintessentially Christian architecture because
medieval Catholics had embodied their faith in it,
that the Middle Ages were the source of salvation for
modern society, and that beautiful Gothic required
good Catholics to build it. With Wiseman he believed
the general feeling for Gothic could be used for the
restoration of the old faith,80 and with Neale he
felt the neglect and destruction of the Reformation
had brought a curse on those who had benefited from
it, the restoration of God's favour being dependent
on repairs.81 He stood the eighteenth-century position on its head : whereas the classicists condemned
medieval taste by condemning the superstition which
produced it, he defended it by defending the faith
behind it; and he answered the late eighteenth-
century romantic anxiety for a metaphysical-religious
ideal by proclaiming the beauty of the Catholic
Church and its material works.
     Contrasts, with its irony, sarcasm, metaphor,
epigram and rhetoric is more literature, more Catholic propaganda, than architectural treatise. His
theme is that classicism and the Reformation ruined
architectural standards, and that the only way to
restore them was to restore the medieval Catholic
frame of mind. In the first edition he says Protestantism was the primary cause of architectural ruin,
but tones this down in the second, attributing it to
the "decayed state of faith throughout Europe in the
fifteenth century, which led men to ... forsake, the

principles and architecture which originated in the
self-denying Catholic principle, and admire and adopt
the luxurious styles of ancient Paganism". Later, he
hails the "faith, the zeal, and above all, the unity,
of our ancestors" as the means by which their buildings were conceived and erected,[82] a theme passionately iterated five years later.[83] This is anti-
romantic in its anti-individualism, as is his
absolutist tone. Medieval architecture,"so glorious,
so sublime, so perfect", sprang from "men who were
thoroughly embued with devotion for, and faith in,
the religion for whose worship they were erected"[84] :
restore the perfect faith to England and then you can
restore the perfect architecture.[85]

Correlatively, present architectural corruption
is the fruit of modernism, especially Protestantism.
"I seek," he wrote, "antiquity not novelty. I strive
to revive not invent", for he despized "the monster
innovations so powerful at present".[86] Contradicting
Neale's insistence that the Anglican Church was one
with the medieval while Rome was not, yet capitaliz-
ing on his patriotic rhetoric, he asks, "What! an
Englishman and a protestant! Oh, worse than parric-
ide, to sever those holy ties that bind him to the
past".[87] He also capitalized on the recent romantic
heritage :

> can a man of soul look on the cross-crowned
> spire, and listen to the chime of distant
> bells, or stand beneath the lofty vault of
> cathedral choir, ... and yet protest against
> aught but that monstrous and unnatural
> system that has mutilated their beauty and
> marred their fair design?[88]

Yet in the eyes of the Ultramontanes, the Gothicizing
Catholics were perilously close to High Church
Anglicanism, with its emphasis on the national
character of the English Church throughout the ages,
its reliance on the principle of antiquity and its
attempts to restore medieval English liturgies and
practices. Indeed, Pugin, who was friendly with the
Tractarian John Rouse Bloxam (who almost certainly
encouraged Newman's Gothic interest), complemented
the "Oxford men" on their ecclesiological proclivit-
ies,[89] seeing in this common ground for ecumenical
advance. As it became increasingly clear that the
Catholic Church in England was not favouring the
national style, Pugin turned his back on modern Roman
Catholicism and looked to an ideal, non-Protestant
Anglicanism, freed from the fetters of the State : at

182

the end of his life he began work on An Apology for
the Separated Church of England, wherein he said
that, as a nation, Britain had preserved its liberties and fundamental Christianity by virtue of separ-
ation from Rome. It was 'Englishmen', rather than
Catholics, who had helped to restore "pious and
glorious Catholic principles and art". His feeling
was that medieval Gothic had testified to Rome's
purity, but that the revival of classical architecture by the Church signified Rome's apostasy. Even
here, however, he was not forsaking the romantic
feeling for unity : he believed that post-Reformation
Catholicism was not truly Catholic, being used by the
separate European states, while pre-Reformation
Catholicism was truly united; so that an evocation
of the medieval Church was an evocation of religious
unity.[90]
 Newman's implicit critique of Pugin, contained
in his work on university education (1853), singles
out the intrusion of ideas into the practice of
architecture for condemnation: he wants a commonsense ecclesiastical architecture, rather than a
romantic one, fitted to the present, as the following
comment (which, incidentally, gives a rare glimpse
of his own mild idealization of the Middle Ages)
shows :

> We are not living in an age of wealth and
> loyalty, of pomp and stateliness, of time-
> honoured establishments, of pilgrimage and
> penance, of hermitages and convents in the
> wild, and of fervent populations supplying
> the want of education by love, and appreh-
> ending in form and symbol what they cannot
> read in books. Our rules and our rubrics
> have been altered now to meet the times,
> and hence an obsolete discipline may be a
> present heresy.[91]

The revival would lead to serious error if it was
viewed and advertized as the "emblem and advocate of
a past ceremonial or an extinct nationalism". Wiseman also expressed the fear of emphasis being laid on
the national character of English Catholicism, the
fear lest

> the revival of medieval studies should lead
> to the undermining of religious union, by
> the setting of nationalities in opposition
> to the universality of Christianity, points
> of the circumference in rivalry with the

centre, admiration of the branches to
the contempt of the trunk.[92]

As late as 1875 there was observed to be a confront-
ation of "Ultramontane and Roman, versus old and
national".[93]
    In an ironic parallel to Newman's position, to
quasi-Catholic Hawker, an axious delving after the
Church into the age of faith was in a sense unnecessary, since it existed for those with eyes to see in
the present:

        Let not the Dreamer-of-the-Past complain -
        The Saints, the Sanctuaries, the Creed, this
            very day remain![94]

This notion of the medieval-in-the-present is contemplated in the church of which he was rector: in
"Morwenna Statio" he suggests intimacy with "My Saxon
shrine", which is "a daughter of the rock": that is,
it shares the spirit of nature, the genius of the
locality and is affiliated to the rock which is the
Church catholic, and a refuge from the world; and
since the medievals built it with firm faith, wise
hearts and thoughtfulness, its form still proclaims
Christian truth. Hawker, always keenly aware of
doctrine - and therefore no mere aesthete - saw the
Eucharist as the vivifying force in Gothic churches,
as can be seen from "Morwenna Statio" and "The Cell
by the Sea".[95] Though he does not want antiquarian
revivalism, he still uses the Gothic as a model.
    Sources of Contrasts included Saint-Simon's Le
Nouveau Christianisme (1825), which had found the
Reformation wanting and noted the secularization of
religious experience which had eliminated art and
made the Church prosaic, and Digby, for Pugin's knowledge of volume III of Mores Catholici (1833) can be
verified from his diary of 1837.[96] Some of Digby's
comments (which were themselves largely based on such
as Dugdale, Chateaubriand, Friedrich von Schlegel[97]
and even Victor Hugo) sound very like Pugin's, while
pre-dating Contrasts. Digby regarded the Gothic
cathedral, in its vastness, variety, plenitude and
unity in diversity, as a source of wonder, a glimpse
of the sacred sublime, a figure of the infinite God.
Gothic "showed a free and boundless imagination",[98]
and imagination was a path to the transcendent.[99]
Medieval churches encouraged community worship and
depicted "harmonious concord" in "variety", while
Catholicism could determine the character of whole
towns; and because the will of the medievals

conformed with God's will, their works resembled
His. [100] Medieval churches were a "hymn or act of
praise to God", rather than man-centred - as is the
case with modern architecture - a living testimony to
the faith of medieval man, as well as a symbolic
statement. He even suggests the Puginesque idea that
Catholics are needed to produce satisfactory Christian architecture, when he says England would now have
nobler buildings if she had continued Catholic. By
contrast, paganism and Protestantism have spawned
wretched modernism, "decomposition and disunion".[101]
Ruined monasteries speak of the destruction of
medieval order, the start of alienation and the
sweeping away of much medieval ecclesiastical architecture by the "spirit of sedition and schism which
set up the private judgment of every individual ...
against the general judgment of the Church".[102]
Digby is both romantic in his Platonism and feeling
for the sublime, imagination and transcendence, and
anti-romantic in his opposition to individualism and
egotism, in his reverence for order, discipline and
obedience.
    In 1859 Lord Acton significantly commented that
Gothic art declined because the modern (post-Renai-
ssance) age was fatal to medieval ideas, of which art
was the "instrument and symbol"; and that Gothic
art, especially in church buildings, was "part of the
mediaeval revival which distinguishes our age and
seems to me as important as the revival of pagan
learning in the fifteenth century".[103] Here is an
eminent, intellectual, liberal Catholic accepting the
Puginesque principal of the extra-aesthetic significance of art and its subjection to ideological
change, and observing the significance of the Gothic
revival.

Anglicans

    The ecclesiologists, who are to be chiefly
identified with the Cambridge Camden Society, and who
were romantic, nationalist, High-Church Gothicists,
basically distinct from the Tractarians, believed in
the divinity of the Church as Christ's body, and
wished to reverse the tide of secularization of
church services and architecture. With Pugin, they
believed Gothic was the only Christian architecture,[104] presumably because they thought that men were
"more spiritually-minded and less worldly-minded" in
the Middle Ages than in the nineteenth century.[105]
For them, Gothic architecture and ritual were re-
assuring totems of the validity of their Church

in the face of the Roman Catholic challenge : if the
paraphernalia were Catholic, they themselves were
Catholic, for their roots in antiquity were thereby
re-emphasized. Roman Catholics regarded this stance
as self-deception : Gothic without Roman Catholicism
was a mere shell, and Pugin was a constant reminder
of this.[106] The honorary secretary of the Cambridge
Camden Society, F.A. Paley, illustrates the instability of the Camdenian position. In 1844 he published
The Church Restorers : a Tale Treating of Ancient and
Modern Architecture and Church Decoration, tracing
the history of a medieval church from its Saxon
origins to the nineteenth century, the preface of
which points out that he contrasts the faith, devotion and discipline of the medieval Church with the
dispiritedness of the modern Church, using the architectural contrast as the point of focus. Disowning
alleged tendencies to Romanism, he says he intends to
remind Protestants of "the great days of the Church".
The security of this position was retrospectively
undermined when he converted to Rome in 1847.[107]

John Mason Neale was one of the Society's leading members, and he expressed many of his beliefs
about Gothic in Hierologus (1843). Like Digby and
De Lisle, he wanted "communion with bygone ages",[108]
fellowship with the "holy men of old",[109] and
believed that respect for the medieval was a scale of
religious progress,[110] respect for Gothic a guarantee
of orthodoxy. With Wiseman and Pugin, he believed
Catholic art would "win some to Catholick truth" but
unlike them he studied religious aesthetics because
he saw it as a prerequisite to winning souls from the
Roman communion in England; for, in Neale's view,
modern Anglicanism is one with the pre-Reformation
Church in England, despite the religious upheaval
initiated by "that monster" Henry VIII, the mal-
effects of the Dissolution of the Monasteries[111] and
the despoilment and ill-treatment of medieval
churches.[112] Gothic "nationality of style" proclaims
and underwrites the distinctness and patriotism of
Catholicism in England. He is also a romantic, as
when he complains : "how lamentably unromantic is
every thing and every one becoming", and how the
railways are "cutting up by the root hearty old
English associations, superstitions, attachments" :
roots being of prime importance for the validity of
Anglican claims. This semi-assent to superstitions -
he believed that beauty accrued to Gothic through
legend[113] - is reminiscent of Hurd's romantic assent
to the marvellous and fable. The poetry which Hurd
and Warton saw in the Middle Ages, Neale now sees in

Gothic and associates with Catholicity:[114]

> Imagine an abbey church, newly dedicated -
> rood-screen, tapestry, stall, frescoed
> vault, gilt capital and pier in their first
> lustre ... a mighty band of priests, in
> copes and chasubles blazing with gold and
> gems ... deacons with the sacred banners,
> the silver staves, or crozier....[115]

Is this aestheticism or religion? Pugin, on whom the
Camdenians greatly relied, also lists the glory and
joy of Gothic, with its stoups, rood, screen, relics,
and where "the albs hang in the oaken ambries, and
the cope chests are filled with orphreyed baudekins;
and pix and pax, and chrismatory are there, and
thurible and cross".[116] Again, is this aestheticism
or religion? Pugin thought he and his work were
religious, and he cannot be convincingly gainsaid.
Like the medieval church itself, everything in it was
invested with sacramental power, and the explication
of medieval symbolism by the medieval Durandus was of
corresponding importance to the Camdenists, as to
Digby.[117] The ecclesiologically-oriented Rev. George
Ayliffe Poole makes the point about sacramentalism in
The Appropriate Character of Church Architecture
(1842) :

> So entirely did this [Gothic] style arise
> out of the strivings of the church to give
> a bodily form to her teaching, that it
> seems to have clothed her spirit, almost
> as if the invisible things had put forth
> their energies, unseen, but powerful and
> plastic, and gathered around them on all
> sides the very forms and figures which
> might best serve to embody them to the eye
> of sense.[118]

This is the veneration of Gothic as a totem of
spirituality, the veneration of the Gothic-builders;
and by mental sleight-of-hand it is the foundation-
stone of the intuition that the restoration of Gothic
would, if perfectly achieved, like a charm unite the
present with the past and thereby open a channel by
which the spiritual energies of the past could flood
into the present. Neale and the ecclesiologists were
anti-Erastian but patriotic, 'Catholick' but anti-
Roman : a mirror image of Pugin, with the same
features, but reversed. Their view was satirized by
G.G. Coulton, who pictured their movement as a

pathetic mistake, a confusion between art and religion and a misrepresentation of the ascetic Middle Ages.[119]
    Though the Tractarians were distinct from the ecclesiologists, the Oxford men did share their interest in the medieval and the Gothic, but to a far lesser extent. Since they believed that poetry was religious, that nature was God's instructive art and that the Church itself is a work of art, it is not surprising that they could regard Gothic in a sacramental light.[120] One Tractarian, Thomas Mozley, supposed that Pugin had got his ideas from the Oxford Movement, and so gladly accepted what he took to be Pugin's argument, that "a relish for the beauty of Catholic architecture is a symptom of Catholic soundness".[121] Pugin agreed that the Oxford men had "greatly contributed" to the revival of Catholic antiquity.[122] In Kenneth Clark's judgement, they were mistaken by their antagonistic contemporaries as sentimental medievalists : they were not mere romantics, but because Tractarianism and Gothicism "were very similar in aim and temper", and connected by ritualism, Tractarianism did have "its strong, if unconscious, romantic side".[123] This suggestion - excepting the first part - is questionable : reference to the medieval Church is not necessarily romantic; the fact that medievalism was not essential to Tractarianism makes it unlikely that one can call their "romanticism" "strong"; their "romantic" interest was anything but unconscious. Clark seems to equate the Tractarians with the Camdenians, and this is wrong : Tractarian Newman deliberately did not join them, and Neale himself made the distinction in 1844 in a letter to Benjamin Webb : "the Tract writers missed one great principle, namely the influence of Aestheticks, and it is unworthy of them to blind themselves to it".[124] While anti-Erastian and emphasizing the principle of Catholicity, like the Tractarians, the Society was much more medievalist, ritualist and less concerned with doctrine : James White characterizes its members as torn between Tractarianism and Romanticism.[125]
    Bloxam, Pugin's Tractarian friend, introduced him to other Oxford men, was the most ecclesiologically learned amongst them, and was a founder of the Oxford Society for Promoting the Study of Gothic Architecture. His interest in Gothic architecture and ritual was gained from three other Catholics: De Lisle, Dr. Rock and Digby. Bloxam owned a set of Digby's Mores Catholici,and therefore knew his volume on Gothic architecture.[126] It is tempting to

speculate that Bloxam lent his copy of volume III of
Mores Catholici to Edward Bouverie Pusey, who iter-
ates several of Digby's ideas in an article of 1835
- the year before the publication of Contrasts. The
medievals, he says, built "noble" churches, but now
"their spirit is fled : we have come to the dregs of
time"; and while their churches hallowed the landscape as "a continual memorial of things unseen,
infusing holy thoughts", the moderns fill the sky
with chimneys and smoke. "Which of these," he asks,
"exhibits the picture of a 'wise and understanding
people?'"[127] This anticipates the very core of
Contrasts, using medieval architecture both as a
scale of condemnation and as a religious ideal.

The Tractarian Isaac Williams was a founder of
the Oxford Society for Promoting the Study of Gothic
Architecture, and in keeping with this enthusiasm
wrote The Cathedral (1838) and The Baptistery (1842-
4). Here he depicts Gothic as eloquent of divine
mysteries; and just as Ruskin was to read Amiens
Cathedral both as a sermon in stone and as a
sacramental embodiment of the Faith, so Williams, in
The Cathedral, read into the form of the cathedral
the range of Christian prayer, and described its
sacramental significance. God sanctifies the
cathedral by His direct presence in the sacrament,
and by allowing Christian culture to have sacramental
significance. G.B. Tennyson - who believes that
Williams's Gothicism was a medievalizing influence on
the Tractarians - describes the importance for the
Tractarians of typology, which flourished in the
Middle Ages, and Bishop Butler's teaching on
'Analogy' : that is, that there are vital correspondences between nature and the supernatural; and says
that consequently the material world was held to be
"a mode of communicating religious knowledge".[128]
Newman discovered from Butler that

> the very idea of an analogy between the
> separate works of God leads to the conc-
> lusion that the system which is of less
> importance is economically or sacrament-
> ally connected with the more momentous
> system....[129]

The material could speak directly and symbolically
of the spiritual; so art could be missionary and
incarnational: "things that seem'd of earth, of
Heav'n are found to be". In his "Advertisement" to
The Cathedral, Williams stresses that Christ's
teaching was based on "visible objects"; so medieval

art could speak of religious truth, since it was
informed by the Gospel : "What is the long Cathedral
glade, / But Faith ...?" His tone is not optimistic,
however, for "rude change" appears to be having its
way, instilling a spirit of "canonized Regret" in the
observer. Without conviction he says the battered
tabernacle "might yet be eloquent for a nation's
good". The speech metaphor recurrs, for the
cathedral holds that "Love" which "Speaks peace to
fall'n humanity" - that humanity which is nevertheless "Dwarf'd to a speck" by the mountainous
building.[130]
     The Cathedral may have provoked accusations of
Romanism, which in The Baptistery he was eager to
disavow : in the courts of Rome "Imagination holds
too high a place" and charms hearts "To sense from
spirit". The other evil is puritanism, which "Clogs
up heart-easing Heaven-born poesy". This work is
more optimistic than The Cathedral, observing that
the Church is "wakening through the land", freshly
breathing life into ancient worship and calling on
the arts to serve her. Thus Williams is keenly aware
of how art can be religious and how the external
manifestations of religion are sanctified art.
Momentarily he returns to the flavour of eighteenth-
century medievalism, when describing a Gothic church,
likening its elements to "giants in enchanted tale",
and calling the ancient superstitions which accumulated around it "Blest wisdom,dress'd in fancy's hue",
judging that "such holy dreams" are "More true than
life". The feeling is one of anti-Enlightenment,
with the "alms and prayers and penitence" of the
medieval worshippers preferred to "things of sense".
And the church they worshipped in embodies this
rejection of arrogant, egotistical worldly wisdom,
for it is a witness "Of self that died to live to
God".[131] So pronounced was his Gothic enthusiasm
that in 1825 Froude wrote that "Canterbury Cathedral
has converted Williams to be a Roman".[132] Thus it
was clearly an exaggeration for Neale to say the
Tractarians "blind themselves" to Gothic.

Retrospect

     In the pre-Romantic and Romantic period Gothic
was an equivalent for the transcendent, evoking a
more colourful religious style than the puritanical
one which prevailed. In the Victorian period it also
became an equivalent for particular sectarian
positions, focussing feeling for Catholicity, the
universal Church, individualism and national pride.

190

For some, Gothic remained a byword for superstition, or an anachronism. In the manner of Catholic sacraments and sacramentals, it was thought by others to invite the Divine Presence on earth in physical form, and even to have a proselytizing capacity. As early as 1826 Digby expressed belief in the possibility that medieval ecclesiatical buildings could convince people of Catholic beneficence,[133] and De Lisle at least, thought this partly came to pass.[134] Indeed, some Catholics so closely identified their faith with Gothic that, along with many Anglicans, they engaged in large-scale Gothic building projects, as it were, in a vain attempt to reconstruct the medieval scene which they thought was their proper element. In literary circles Gothic was seldom a focus for solely aesthetic discussion.

Towards the end of the century, however, Francis Gasquet declared when speaking of monastic ruins, that

> it is to be feared to most Englishmen the desecrated sanctuary calls up one thought above all else - the thought of wasted, wanton or vicious lives, and of the sad necessity which compelled king Henry to proceed to drastic measures of reform.[135]

This was the harsh reality of the non-literary world, and essentially nothing had changed in this respect since the Enlightenment : Gothicism had been revived amidst great suspicion in the Catholic and Anglican Churches, a few had leaned towards, or been converted to, Catholicism and many neo-Gothic churches had been built only to be derided in succeeding generations. To John Ruskin, however, Gothic art was all in all, and perhaps he can stand as a model for those - he certainly influenced many - who, attracted by Catholicism (and he was, in a sense, converted to it), transferred their outlawed feelings to Catholic externals, shying away from the theological substance behind them.

NOTES

1.   Pater "Postcript" Appreciations (1901) 248, Heine Religion and Philosophy in Germany (1834) in Prose Writings 150.
2.   The Romantic School (1833) in Prose Writings 70.

3.   Religion and Philosophy in Germany in Prose Writings 155, Lord Macaulay's Essays and Lays of Ancient Rome "Hallam" 60; and see ibid. "Milton" 10, II.

4.   MC I (1831) 28.

5.   See Honour Romanticism 281-2, 295, 300.

6.   Works of the English Poets ed. Johnson, Chalmers XII, 476. Also see B. Sprague Allen Tides in English Taste 1619-1800 2v. (New York, 1958) II, 43-74, Peter Quennell Romantic England: Writing and Painting 1717-1851 (1970) ch.I.

7.   Ancient and Modern History of the Loyal Town of Ripon (1733) qu. E.F. Carritt A Calendar of British Taste, From 1600 To 1800 (n.d.) 208.

8.   Introduction to Select Scotish Ballads (1783) I, xxxv, qu. Merriman The Flower of Kings 98. William Woty (1731?-1791) found exactly the reverse was true of classicist St. Paul's Cathedral, where he thought more of Wren than God. At Ely, Lincoln or York, however, "all the God comes rushing on the soul" : "Church-Langton", qu. Fairchild II, 275.

9.   Clarence DeWitt Thorpe "Coleridge on the Sublime" in Wordsworth and Coleridge ed. Earl Leslie Griggs (New York, 1962) 206.

10.   Coleridge's Miscellaneous Criticism ed. Thomas M. Raysor (1936) 11-12.

11.   For Warton's emotional pro-Gothicism see John Nichols Literary Anecdotes (1812) III, 699; letter 2 July 1789.

12.   Letter to M. Smith 1750, qu. Carritt A Calendar of British Taste 252.

13.   Preface to The Sublime and Beautiful (1958) cvii.

14.   Letters on Chivalry and Romance 118.

15.   B. Sprague Allen, in Tides in English Taste II, 44, and R.W. Ketton-Cremer, in Horace Walpole (1964) 137, think his part in the Gothic Revival is overstressed.

16.   Qu. Fairchild II, 16.

17.   Anecodotes of Painting in England ed. Ralph N. Wornum 3v. (n.d.) I, 117-118.

18.   Ibid. v. I, 119.

19.   Ibid. v.I, 120.

20.   Biographical Notices of Eminent Novelists (1820); essay on 'Horace Walpole' in Sir Walter Scott On Novelists and Fiction ed. Ioan Williams (1968) 89.

21.   Cf. Kenneth Clark The Gothic Revival (John Murray, 1975) 41.

22.   Essays Moral and Literary 2nd.ed. (1779) "On Architecture" v.I, 329-339. 1st.ed. 1778.

23.   Poetry and Prose of William Blake ed.

Geoffrey Keynes (1967) 667, "A Vision of the Last
Judgement" 644, "On Virgil" and "On Homer's Poetry"
583 respectively.
    24.   Lectures on Rhetoric and Belles Lettres
(Dublin, 1783) v.I, 62.
    25.   Essays on Gothic Architecture Milner et
al (1802) xvi-xvii, xviii. 1st. ed.1800. And see
Milner History of Winchester, qu. Carritt A Calendar
of British Taste 415.
    26.   Génie du Christianisme, qu. Georg Germann
Gothic Revival in Europe and Britain: Sources,
Influences and Ideas (1972) 77; and see Honour
Romanticism 157-8.
    27.   The Romantic School, Religion and Philos-
ophy in Germany in Prose Writings 79-80, 150 respect-
ively.
    28.   The Gothic 460.
    29.   Statesman's Manual.
    30.   J.A. Froude Thomas Carlyle (1882) v.I,372,
Nikolaus Pevsner Some Architectural Writers of the
Nineteenth Century (Oxford, Clarendon Press, 1972)
12, 13, 15.
    31.   Collected Letters of Samuel Taylor
Coleridge ed. E.L. Griggs (Oxford, 1956) v.I, 354.
    32.   Pevsner Some Architectural Writers of the
Nineteenth Century 11.
    33.   Table Talk for 29 June 1833 in Complete
Works of Samuel Taylor Coleridge ed. W.G.T. Shedd 7v.
(New York, 1854) VI, 461.
    34.   See above 19.
    35.   Raysor Coleridge's Miscellaneous Criticism
7.
    36.   Ibid. 9.
    37.   Ibid. 7.
    38.   Qu. Clarence DeWitt Thorpe Coleridge on
the Sublime 208; from Table Talk and Omniana of
Samuel Taylor Coleridge (1917) of July 25 1832 (191).
    39.   Shedd Complete Works of Samuel Taylor
Coleridge VI, 461.
    40.   See Frankl The Gothic 444, 460, Honour
Romanticism 157.
    41.   Qu. Honour Romanticism 347 n.4.
    42.   Essays and Tales, by John Sterling v.II,
58, "A Meditation at Netley Abbey" pub.in Athenaeum
1828.
    43.   Ecclesiastical Sonnets III, xxxv, xlii,
xliii, xlv respectively.
    44.   For further comments on King's see Milner
et al Essays on Gothic Architecture xvi-xvii, Shedd
Complete Works of Samuel Taylor Coleridge VI, 641,
Winthrop Mackworth Praed's 'Stanza Written Under a

Picture of King's College Chapel, Cambridge' (1830).
45.   Nicholson's title poem was written c.1822.
In 1835 Bowles wrote Annals and Antiquities of Lacock
Abbey. Scott is said to have developed a love of
Gothic, which may have helped its revival: see
Drummond The Churches in English Fiction 106, White
The Cambridge Movement 8, and Scott's The Monastery
and The Abbot.
    46.   The Last Romantics (1961) xv-xvi; see
Introduction.
    47.   'The Catholic Academy' The Rambler V
(Sept. 1861) in Essays on Church and State ed.
Douglas Woodruff.
    48.   Ronald Chapman Father Faber (1961) 182.
    49.   Pugin in DR X, 301,342, DR XII, 182-3;
Neale in Hierologus; or The Church Tourists (1843)
viii.
    50.   Past and Present (George Routledge & Sons
1893) II, iii, 49.
    51.   The Bible in Spain (Everyman, 1926) ch.
XXVII, 245; 1st. ed. 1843.
    52.   Literary and General Lectures and Essays
196.
    53.   'The Classical and Romantic Schools of
English Literature' in Afternoon Lectures on Liter-
ature : a course under the presidency of Maziere
Brady (1863) 87, 89.
    54.   Ecclesiastical Sonnets II, ix.
    55.   LM I, 99.
    56.   'Grots and Groves' Literary and General
Lectures and Essays 275, 278, 283, 292, 293. See
also LM (1885) 48-9.
    57.   See S.L. Ollard A Short History of the
Oxford Movement (1915) 228.
    58.   A Literary History of the Middle Ages 322,
325-6.
    59.   For this patriotism see Pugin True
Principles and Revival of Christian Architecture
(1853) 4, 50, and Louis Allen "Letters of Phillipps
de Lisle to Montalembert" DR no. 463 (1st.Quarter,
1954) 60, 450.
    60.   A History of the Gothic Revival ed. J.
Mordaunt Crook (Leicester U.P., 1970), reprint in
"The Victorian Library" ser. of 1st. ed. 1872 (Old
Woking, Surrey) 118.
    61.   Ward Life and Times of Cardinal Wiseman I,
359; and see Letters and Diaries of John Henry Newman
XIV 294 n.I.
    62.   Wiseman "Church Architecture of the Middle
Ages" DR VII (Aug. 1839) 250, 251, respectively; and
"Christian Art" DR XXII (June,1847) 486-7.

63.   Wiseman "Pugin on Modern and Ancient" DR
III (Oct. 1837) 384, DR VII, 252.
64.   DR XXII 490-3.
65.   Eastlake A History of the Gothic Revival
347.
66.   Faber Poet and Priest. Selected Letters by
Frederick William Faber 1833-1863 ed. Raleigh
Addington (Glamorgan, 1974) 11, 22, 177-8.
67.   See Patrick 'Newman, Pugin, and Gothic'
VS XXIV no. 2 (Winter 1981) 188-96.
68.   Letters and Correspondence of John Henry
Newman letter to J.W. Bowden 4 Apr. 1841 v.II, 345.
69.   See Patrick op.cit. especially 192-6. It
should be noted that Patrick does not prove the
direct relationship between Newman's principle of
antiquity and his attitude to Gothic, although his
evidence is persuasive. More importantly and
damaging to his thesis is the fact that Newman's
stress on the principle of antiquity, apropos the
question of authority, was not exclusive in the later
1830s, as his Prophetical Office of the Church (1837)
shows. Additionally, he does not take into account
Newman's overriding interest in the primitve Church.
70.   A point neglected by Patrick.
71.   Sermons on Subjects of the Day (1869) 391.
Pevsner exaggerates when he says Newman wanted
"gorgeous Italian churches and services" : Some
Architectural Writers of the Nineteenth Century 118.
72.   See Letters and Diaries of John Henry
Newman XII, 221; cf. Eastlake History of the Gothic
Revival 347.
73.   Purcell Life and Letters of Ambrose
Phillipps de Lisle II, 222.
74.   Letters and Diaries of John Henry Newman
XII, 220-1.
75.   Letter of 19 Nov. 1851 'Letters of
Phillipps de Lisle to Montalembert' ed. Louis Allen
DR no. 463 (1st.quarter 1954) 325.
76.   Letters and Diaries of John Henry Newman
XII, 220, XIII, 461.
77.   Ibid. XII, 221-2, XIII, 461-2.
78.   Ibid. XII, 222.
79.   Ibid. XIII, 460-61, XII, 221 respectively.
80.   'Elevation of the Cathedral Church of St.
Chad, Birmingham' DR X (May,1841) 302.
81.   'Ecclesiastical Architecture in England'
DR XII (Feb. 1842) 182.
82.   Contrasts 'Victorian Library' reprint of
2nd. ed. (1841) Leicester U.P. (Old Woking, Surrey,
1969), Preface iii, 6.
83.   DR X (May, 1841) 301.

84.   Contrasts 2, 5.
85.   For this sentiment see also Pugin DR X
(May, 1841) 301, 302, 309, 342, and DR XII (Feb.1842)
181, 182.
86.   Letters to J.R. Bloxam Item 9 and Item 15,
3 Feb. 1841 MS. 528 MS. Letters Pugin
Magdalen College Archives.
87.   An Apology for the Revival of Christian
Architecture in England in (spine title) True
Principles and Revival of Christian Architecture
(1853) 50; cf. DR X (May, 1841) 311.
88.   An Apology for the Revival of Christian
Architecture in England 50-1. De Lisle was Pugin's
ideological twin. His letters to Digby show how
important a place the style of ritual had in his
faith (eg. Dormer MSS. Letters from De Lisle to Digby
22 April 1830, 11 Jan. 1835),and felt with Pugin
that there was something immoral in Catholic churches
built in other than Gothic, for he believed it
embodied the spirit of Catholicism. In a letter to
Lord Shrewsbury (1840) he urges the "Xtian origin,
meaning and destination" of Gothic, so that
preference for it is not a matter of mere taste, but
of "principle" (Purcell Life and Letters of Ambrose
Phillipps de Lisle II, 209).
89.   DR X (May, 1841) 342, 348; and see Purcell
Life and Letters of Ambrose Phillipps de Lisle I,268.
90.   Benjamin Ferrey Recollections of A.N.
Welby Pugin (1861) 438-9. Pevsner comments mislead-
ingly on Pugin's Apology,in Some Architectural
Writers of the Nineteenth Century, p.120: it is not
Ferrey who quotes Pugin's Apology,as Pevsner says,
but E.S. Purcell, in a work called "An Appendix: in
Which the Writings and Character of Augustus Welby
Neale Pugin are considered in their Catholic Aspect",
printed in the same volume as Ferrey's. Pevsner
gives the impression that Pugin reverted to Anglicanism, which as Purcell emphasizes (op.cit.), was not
the case. Also, Pevsner says that Pugin arrived at
the above-described position "in the end"; but in
fact it is certain that he was expressing exactly
this view as early as 1839, since his close associate
De Lisle then held it: see Purcell Life and Letters
of Ambrose Phillipps de Lisle II, 221.
91.   The Idea of a University (New York, 1959)
113.
92.   Qu. Holmes More Roman than Rome 70.
93.   J. Fowler Richard Waldo Sibthorp : A
Biography (1880) 283-4.
94.   "The Saintly Names" from Reeds Shaken in
the Wind (1843) in Poetical Works of R.S.Hawker 50.

196

95.   From Ecclesia (1840) in Poetical Works
of R.S. Hawker 47-9, 72.
96.   Phoebe Stanton "The Sources of Pugin's
Contrasts" in Concerning Architecture: Essays on
Architectural Writers and Writing presented to
Nikolaus Pevsner ed. John Summerson (1968) 138; cf.
Pevsner Some Architectural Writers of the Nineteenth
Century 108.
97.   See Schlegel's Lectures on the History of
Literature, Ancient and Modern (1859) 190-1. Lectures delivered 1812 and first pub. 1815.
98.   MC. III, 73.
99.   See BS II. lii-liii and 149, BS. Morus
(1848) 163, Compitum II, 329.
100.   MC. III, 8 and 108, 14-15 and 177, 31
respectively.
101.   Ibid. 23, 33, 73-4, 103-6, 128.
102.   Morus (1826) 48 and 14-18.
103.   Lord Acton and His Circle ed. Francis
Gasquet (n.d. [1906]) 58.
104.   See A.G. Lough The Influence of John
Mason Neale (1962) 32-4.
105.   Report of the Cambridge Camden Society
for MDCCCXLII (Cambridge, 1842) 14, [qu. White The
Cambridge Movement 29.]
106.   See Letters of Archbishop Ullathorne eds.
anon (1892?) 89, letter of 19 July 1857; Phoebe
Stanton The Gothic Revival and American Church
Architecture (Baltimore, 1968) 20; Pugin DR XII
(Feb. 1842) 181, 182, Montalembert DR XVII (Sept.
1844) 244-5, Purcell Life and Letters of Ambrose
Phillips de Lisle II, 239.
107.   See Drummond The Churches in English
Fiction on Paley.
108.   Hierologus 17.
109.   A phrase used in the Ecclesiologist II,
21, qu. White The Cambridge Movement 32.
110.   Hierologus 24.
111.   Ibid. xii-xv, 5-6, 29-30.
112.   Ibid. 9-12, 21-3, 116-117. There was
still room for complaint about the misuse of medieval churches as late as 1865 : then Digby Dolben
wrote of his disgust on the matter : The Poems of
Digby Mackworth Dolben ed. Robert Bridges (O.U.P.,
1915) xci-xcii.
113.   Hierologus vi, 90, 92.
114.   Ibid. 44.
115.   Ibid. 19; cf. Neale Agnes de Tracy (1843)
3-6.
116.   Remarks on Articles ... in the Rambler
(1850) qu. Ruskin Stones of Venice I, App. 12.

117. Neale and Benjamin Webb pub. a translation of Durandus : William Durandus, The Symbolism of Churches (Leeds, 1843). Digby often mentions Durandus.
118. Qu. Stanton The Gothic Revival and American Church Architecture 9.
119. Friar's Lantern 15-16.
120. See G.B. Tennyson Victorian Devotional Poetry ch. II "Tractarian Poetics".
121. Rev. of Pugin's Contrasts, British Critic XXV (Oct. 1839) 498.
122. DR X (May, 1841) 342.
123. The Gothic Revival 153.
124. Letter of 2 Feb. 1844 Letters of John Mason Neale ed. Mary Sackville Lawson (1910) 87-8.
125. The Cambridge Movement 26.
126. Bloxam to De Lisle 3 April 1841, item 151 MS. 335 Reunion : Ambrose Lisle Phillipps Magdalen College Library. This set is in the possession of the present writer.
127. See British Magazine VIII (1835) 582-5.
128. Victorian Devotional Poetry 145-7, 172.
129. Apologia Pro Vita Sua 23.
130. The Cathedral, or the Catholic and Apostolic Church in England 2nd. ed. (Oxford, 1839) iv-v, 2, 18-19, 143-4.
131. The Bapistery, or the Way of Eternal Life 2nd. ed. (Oxford, 1844) ix-x, 194-5.
132. Qu. Brendon Hurrell Froude and the Oxford Movement 54.
133. Morus (1826) 159.
134. Letter of 5 June 1852, DR 463 (1st quarter 1954) 445.
135. Henry VIII and the English Monasteries I, xiii.

Chapter VII

JOHN RUSKIN AND MEDIEVAL ART IN THE NINETEENTH
CENTURY

> Its glory is in its Age, and in that deep
> sense of voicefulness, of stern watching,
> of mysterious sympathy, nay, even of
> approval or condemnation, which we feel in
> walls that have long been washed by the
> passing waves of humanity.

John Ruskin Seven Lamps of Architecture

Background : Sages and Influences

The so-called Victorian sages did not neglect
the metaphysical significance of medieval Catholicism.
The most deeply medievalist of them in the religious
sense was John Ruskin. Since he learnt much from the
contemporary intellectual ethos, and since he is
always grouped with the other sages, it is worth
discussing the context provided by them.
It is as if Thomas Carlyle and Ruskin were
addressing themselves to the anxiety articulated by
John Stuart Mill in The Spirit of the Age (1831),
that modern society suffers from "intellectual
anarchy", that no new doctrine has arisen to equal
the now-abandoned ancient ones in unanimity of
assent.[1] Under the influence of Saint-Simonism, he
thinks that firm belief in a positive creed is
necessary for the progress of society, that classical
polytheism and medieval Christianity had been such
positive creeds, and that European society has been
in an increasingly incoherent state of "transition"
ever since the Reformation.[2] Medieval Christianity
had uniquely produced, in the jargon, an "organic"
age, in which a dominating, and basically beneficent,
creed had brought about progress, a "natural" state
of society, in which power and ability coexisted in
the power élite. Modern impotence is occasioned not

199

only by credal incoherence, but, he emphasizes, by
lack of that strength of belief so evident in the
Middle Ages, when the ascendancy of the Catholic
clergy was beneficial, being a "potent cause ... of
the present civilization of Europe". Not only did
they know the wisdom of the ancients, but they were
holy.[3]
     Medieval Catholicism provided Carlyle with a
scale of reference for, and a method of exploring, an
invigorated means of metaphysical communication which
was not hamstrung by the inappropriate tools of
rationalist discussion and philosophical enquiry. A
truer medievalist than many, since he definitely did
not wish to resurrect merely the forms of medieval
Catholicism, but instead its spirit (as he perceived
it),[4] his attitude was influential : Kingsley noted
that the monastic world "was all but inconceivable to
us till Mr. Carlyle disinterred it in his picture of
Abbot Sampson, the hero of 'Past and Present'".[5]
Ruskin thought him Catholic-minded and always just to
the spirit and virtue of Catholicism;[6] yet he was no
papist : Carlyle the radical truth-seer perceived the
greatness of medieval Christianity through the fog of
Protestant and rationalist propaganda; Carlyle the
radical Protestant and Saint-Simonian progressivist
had to reject its substance if not its spirit; which
led him to the inconsistency of condemning Catholic
paraphernalia while upholding the propriety of
spiritual 'materiality'.
     In 'The Hero as Poet', in Heroes and Hero-
Worship (1841), Dante figures as the great poet of
the soul, great because concerned in The Divine
Comedy - the "sincerest of all Poems"[7] - with the
spiritual. His spiritual, earnest intensity is the
source of his greatness, which is the actualizing of
his soul, a soul which contains "the soul of the
middle ages" : "no light task; a right intense one :
but a task which is done". The heroic act of incarnating the spiritual is of primary importance, the
spiritual essence itself seems to be of secondary
importance, while the nuance - the Catholic "clothes"
- is tertiary. The hero is the man who "pierces ...
down into the heart of Being", the man who acts in
relation to the depths of existence, who has a
special relationship with Truth, thereby incarnating
the Divinity. Dante, the "spokesman" of the Middle
Ages, "for rigour, earnestness and depth, ... is not
to be paralleled in the modern world; to seek his
parallel we must go into the Hebrew Bible". Medieval
symbolism is also perceived to be about depth :
Dante's Inferno, Purgatorio - "an emblem of the

noblest conception of that age" - and Paradiso "make up the true Unseen World, as figured in the Christianity of the Middle Ages; a thing forever memorable, forever true in the essence of it, to all men". But Carlyle is no medieval, for he rejects the literal truth of the allegory of the Divine Comedy, as held by medieval Christendom, interpreting it as a way of talking about human duty, morality and the "Practical Life". Sincere Dante was, in himself, his work and his religious language, a symbolic bridge between the seen and the unseen, a mode of communication and reconciliation : sincerity is the catalyst of unity.

In 'The Hero as Priest' he adopts Mill's idea that "a man who will do faithfully, needs to believe firmly"; and firm belief is, for Carlyle, concerned with essence, "unconscious", sincere and thereby organic with daily life : Methodism and Puseyism are condemned for their self-consciousness.[8] Failure in this regard is one reason why the Catholic age ended, another being that its symbolism, its "clothes", ceased to fit the wearer. But there was indeed a Catholic golden age, a spiritual one : "the Old was true.... It was good then; nay there is in the soul of it a deathless good".

The medievalism of Past and Present (1843) demonstrates these views, and criticizes the failure of the modern world to match act to "the eternal inner Facts of this Universe",although he does not call for a return to the past, but for a re-assumption of medieval spiritual sincerity and vitality. So while he fully draws the spirit of Abbot Samson, he contradictorily insists on the foreignness of the medieval chronicle and its "life-furniture" on which Past and Present draws. His medievalism argues against his 'modernist' self : he disliked Catholic paraphernalia,[9] yet believed symbolism to be the very means and element of religious knowledge,[10] and, possibly, he was attracted to medieval Catholicism by its sacramental understanding of the material as symbol; certainly, his idea of the hero supernaturalizing the natural by transmuting the world into truth is not unlike the Catholic theology of sanctification through Christ, the Church and her sacraments and the saints. The quest for spiritual unity was also something he shared with Catholicism, holding the Romantic view of the Middle Ages as an age of unity and seeing the medievals as spiritually sincere, while believing that "only in a world of sincere men is unity possible".[11]

Despite his self-conscious rejection of the Middle Ages Past and Present idealizes them as the

age of total, all-embracing and uncompromising
religion, which bore great fruit, contrasting them
with modern sterile doubt. The abbey and its abbot
are representatives, even crystallizations, of the
spirit of the age: the Abbot is elected by a heroic
people with a "reverence for worth". He is chosen
because he is a symbol of divine order and coherence,
and man most properly fulfils his rôle when he is
"the Missionary of Order", the reconciler. Carlyle
viewed the medieval establishment - especially the
hierocratic, hierarchic establishment - as admirably
manifesting the Divine Order. This sense of
religion's proper place being in the world and of
society is the essential point of his apotheosis of
medieval Catholicism beginning "the great antique
heart : how like a child's in its simplicity, like a
man's in its earnest solemnity and depth". The
passage ends with insistence on the truth of medieval
spirituality : "the 'imaginative faculties?' 'Rude
poetic ages?' The 'primeval poetic element?' Oh, for
God's sake, good reader, talk no more of all that!
It was not a Dilettantism this of Abbot Samson. It
was a Reality...."[12]
    Matthew Arnold was also sensitive to the need
for a new metaphysical language, and though agnostic
deeply valued the medieval Church's "magical",
imaginative capacity to enhance life, which, because
he equated profound culture with religion, was, in
his own terms, a spiritual capacity.[13] He confessed
that the period "has poetically the greatest charm
and refreshment possible for me",[14] and its
'language' had, in his view, a spiritually catalytic
power. In 'Eugénie de Guérin', he explains that the
"accessories", "style" and "circumstance" of
Catholicism (he means especially medieval Catholicism), while not essential to it as a religion, are
certainly not "indifferent" : they are "European,
august, and imaginative". By contrast, Protestantism, in its "signal want of grace and charm", is
seriously weak.[15] Arnold, who believed in a 'relig-
ionless Christianity' based on a balance of the
'Hebrew' and 'Hellene' temperaments, supposed in
1864 that St. Francis of Assisi embodied the Hebrew
side of this 'religion', for he - "a figure of the
most magical power and charm" - was able to "fit
religion for popular use",[16] which was what was
needed in the nineteenth century. Francis interpreted life through "the heart and imagination",
through the "inward symbolical side", "drawing from
the spiritual world a source of joy so abundant that
it ran over upon the material world and transfigured

it".[17] In other words, Arnold believes that St.
Francis had reconciled the separated worlds of matter
and spirit, as Ruskin believes it had been achieved
by the medieval Church, especially in its art. He
also values the medieval Church for its orderly
authority, meritocracy and unity.[18] He oscillates
between the twin poles of Hebrew and Hellene, spirits
which "reach the infinite, ... - the Greek spirit by
beauty, the Hebrew spirit by sublimity",[19] and hence
his uncertainty about medieval Catholicism, which is
part of Hebraism. Although the weight of his
sympathy is with rationalism and beauty, he is deeply
nostalgic for the Age of Faith : "Oh hide me in your
gloom profound", he cries to the Carthusian monks,
the "Last of the people who believe!"[20] Again, he
agrees with Joseph Joubert that the Catholic Church's
success was the result of her making herself loved
rather than feared, and quotes Joubert on the cause
of this being her beauty, which was "the result and
the proof of her incomparable excellence".[21]
     Ruskin repeatedly echoes Arnold and Carlyle,
and goes further : at the end of the tenth century
there were, he proclaims, fifteen thousand Abbot
Samsons.[22] In 1853, when he is supposed to have been
furthest from Catholicism, he distinguished three
cultural periods : "Classicalism, Mediaevalism, and
Modernism" (XII, 136): and "Mediaevalism began ...
wherever civilisation began ... to confess Christ....
Modernism began and continues, wherever civilisation
began and continues to deny Christ" (XII, 139). Three
years later he protested that it was not the Middle
Ages which were dark but the present, with its weary
sadness, "jaded intellect, and uncomfortableness of
soul and body"; and "the profoundest reason of this
darkness of heart is ... our want of faith" (V,321-
2).
     The monastic spirit embodied his approval. Like
Arnold, he believed the value of St. Francis lay in
his vision of religion as in the world and for it;
but he also valued his emphatic Christianity. Work
well done "is the only sound foundation of any religion", and Francis is the "Apostle of Works", teaching
men how to behave, how to live a "Universal Monasticism", wherein renunciation does not mean abandoning
the world. Eventually he felt himself to be a
Franciscan tertiary.[23] The years 1000 to 1500 saw,
he said, many good works in the Church, done "beyond
any bettering", works inspired by the regular clergy.
The lecture "Mending the Sieve" is a panegyric on
monastic vitality and goodness, a prophetic plea -
not hysterical, but couched in ironic and sarcastic,

anti-Protestant, anti-modernist terms - showing how
a broken world might be mended. The title is taken
from St. Benedict's first miracle, when he mended a
corn-sieve, which Ruskin takes as a symbol of the
fertile results of Benedict's ministry. Ruskin coyly
invites his audience to "break" the myth, thereby
symbolically disowning Europe's Benedictine and
Cistercian heritage, knowing that the myth is already
broken, and with it the heritage renounced.

With ironic deference to his audience's
attitudes, he calls the lives of Saints Benedict and
Bernard "fairy tales", then twists the knife, insisting that they are "the basis of things real and
visible around us", later chiding the audience's
"vulgar Gibbonian theory of pious imposture", as
applied to the lives of the saints. Instead, the
monks were "devoted to all the arts and labours which
are serviceable to mankind", and Benedict's gospel
incorporated "useful labour as man's duty upon earth",
with total faith as the dynamo. Medieval Christianity was great because faith was translated into
"deed" as a necessary part of the religion. The
medievals had life to the full because they lived it
to the full : "the King, the Monk, the Knight, the
Craftsman, all are doing, all being, the best that
Manhood may".[24] Dante, "the great prophetic exponent
of the heart of the Middle Ages, ... declared the
mediaeval faith, - that all perfect active life was
the expression of man's delight in God's work" (V,
279). All this is opposed to the modern spirit of
"Liberty, Reason, and Science","gainful commerce, and
luxurious civilization", with its heart of pessimism.
Benedictine monasticism healed social agonies after
the collapse of the Roman Empire, and Bernard came to
the rescue when barbarism rose again.[25] In Ruskin's
view, Victorian society was similarly distraught, and
the implication is that only medieval spirituality is
capable of "labouring in calm and rational strength
against the fever of the world" (XXIII, 204).

Victorian society was too far gone to believe
the "fairy tales" of the saints, to build their lives
on the legend of St. Ursula, as had a Venetian Doge,
to comprehend the medieval "Imagination" which
resulted in "Deed" (XXXIII,507-8, 518). By "Imagination" he means the eye of the soul,[26] by which the
"Old Catholics" perceived the transcendent through
the material, which constrasts with Protestantism as
"the appeal of Truth against wanton or impious
imagination", which attracts those who "will not look
for the things they have not seen" and prefer "the
material to the spiritual"; and the truth to which

Protestantism "narrowly consents, [is] a totality of lie". The key they cannot grasp is "Fancy". Fancy, which meant "all imaginative energy", was a "universal power", which, when informed by the Christian faith as it had been in the Middle Ages, gave spiritual insight. Indeed,

> in the Middle Ages, this action of the Fancy ... was the happy and sacred tutress of every faculty of the body and soul; and the works and thoughts of art, the joys and toils of men, rose and flowed on in the bright air of it, with the aspiration of a flame, and the beneficence of a fountain.

Such insight enabled the medievals to live the truth behind their legends. So Ruskin cannot scorn the "mythic saints", who were "the baptized resuscitation of a Pagan deity, or the personified omnipresence of a Christian virtue"; nor does he scorn the "affectionate traditions" surrounding the 'real' saints, which should be properly interpreted, while the rôle of the saints in moulding the Church should be appreciated: for these are the scale by which to measure the Church and the "directness of spiritual agency by which she was guided".[27] Marianism, for instance, was always "productive of true holiness of life and purity of character".[28]

Ruskin resolved the Hebrew-Hellene tension in Victorian culture by continuing to value the ancient world, while judging that the Middle Ages had sustained, transformed and fulfilled whatever had been valuable in paganism. While suggestively linking Amiens Cathedral with the ancient world, he says "Paganism" could not die in the human soul, and the reaction of the medieval Church was not to reject but absorb and use it : "every great symbol and oracle of Paganism is still understood in the Middle Ages"; and this is a matter for praise : "quite the most beautiful sign of the power of true Christian-Catholic faith is this continual acknowledgement by it of the brotherhood ... of the elder nations who had not seen Christ".[29] The culpable folly of the modern age was that it had abandoned the tradition of metaphysical symbolism, just as it had turned its back on the tradition of medieval art. Gibbon had been wrong : it was not Christianity that was guilty of breaking with tradition, but modernism. So much for the personal background to Ruskin's approach to art, but what of the general cultural background? Ernst Gombrich has well summarized the mechanism

by which medieval art came into favour:[30] in the
second half of the eighteenth century nationalism
encouraged people to look at the heritage special to
themselves, which meant going back to the Middle
Ages. Rousseau, Winckelmann, Herder and Goethe were
instrumental in the shift, Herder having been
influenced by Percy and Ossian. A cultural theme
developing from Vasari to Chateaubriand propagated
the notion of modern, rationalist artistic decadence,
and the corresponding preferability of late-medieval
art. The moral dimension of this aesthetic preference came to the fore with the group of German Romantic painters of the early nineteenth century called
the Nazarenes, who "where Winckelmann had preached
the noble simplicity of the ancients, ... were cap-
tivated by what they saw as the devout simplicity of
the age of faith". The changing current led to the
ousting of classicism and the large production of
medievalist devotional art which was more concerned
with the expression of a state of mind rather than
with form.

The Nazarenes were a quasi-religious order,
founded in 1809 by Johann Friedrich Overbeck and
Franz Pforr. Ulrich Finke's reference to "Pforr's
nostalgic admiration for the Middle Ages ... when
consciousness had not yet been split into the two
extremes of the individual ego and the world, and
religion was still the universal basis for life and
art"[31] reminds us that the reconciliation theme is
operative here also. How much the Pre-Raphaelites
took from them is disputed,[32] though initial interest
suffered from diverging ideals; and though they were
important medievalists, even their few religious
products in art and literature were merely imitative,
nostalgic or only incidentally religious.[33]

In 1836 Alexis François Rio declared in The
History of Christian Art that true art was impossible
without Catholic piety and mysticism, and condemned
the Renaissance for abandoning pure medieval art and
becoming naturalist and pagan: Christian art was a
language which testified to faith via emotions and
imagination.[34] He clearly influenced Lord Lindsay's
Sketches of the History of Christian Art (1847), and
both influenced Ruskin. Lindsay believed Christian
art superior to Classic because one represented the
spirit, the other the intellect, and that Christian
artists had conveyed "the highest and holiest
spiritual truths and emotions". He hoped for some
sort of revival of "Imaginative Christianity", as he
called it, for he believed the modern world was still
suffering in every sphere - including the theological

206

and moral - from the Cinquecento inception of
rationalism and paganism.[35] Ruskin reviewed the
Sketches in 1847, agreed with Lindsay's depreciation
of Fra Angelico and used this point to make anti-
Catholic and anti-medievalist gibes. Wiseman also
reviewed it, plucking quite a different fruit : that
medieval artists displayed "absolute sanctity become
the guarantee of success in its perfection",[36] that
the spirit of Christian art should be revived, but
the old forms abandoned.

In Sacred and Legendary Art (begun in 1842 and
published in 1848) Anna Jameson suggested that
religious art was spiritually educational and admired
the spirit of the legends depicted in it. She
testifies that

> of late years, with a growing passion for
> the works of Art of the Middle Ages, there
> has arisen among us a desire to comprehend
> the state of feeling which produced them,
> and the legends and traditions on which they
> are founded.[37]

Perhaps in response to Wiseman's jeer that

> Protestantism presents no types of Christian
> art. It has destroyed the types of the past.
> It excludes as legendary all the most beaut-
> iful histories of the early saints : it has
> quenched all sympathy for the favourite
> themes of mediaeval painting,[38]

Kingsley reviewed Sacred and Legendary Art (1849),
accepting that Protestantism had failed to meet a
religious hunger by neglecting the heroic, the
romantic, the marvellous, and by having "nothing to
do with the imagination". The young were finding
through histories that the Middle Ages were not so
thoroughly decadent as they had been taught :

> they are looking for themselves at the ante-
> Raphaellic artists, and when we tell them
> that Fra Angelico's pictures are weak ...
> they grant it, and then ask us if we can
> deny the sweetness, the purity, the rapt
> devotion, the saintly virtue, which shines
> forth from his faces. ... 'You say that
> Popery created these glorious schools of
> art; how can you wonder if, like Overbeck,
> we take the faith for the sake of the art
> which it inspired?'[39]

207

He answers by claiming that the "ante-Raphaellic"
artists are good because they are latently Protestant, a point which, if it had been made more boldly
over the last fifteen years, would have reduced the
losses to Rome.

Digby, who knew Ruskin, influenced him:[40] both
influenced by Rio, they interpreted medieval architecture sacramentally; both spoke of the medieval
craftsman's joy and saw the Gothic as a sermon in
stone, both emphasized the spirit of generosity and
plenitude embodied in Gothic and thought Renaissance
art signalled civilization's decline. This proximity
is evident in their similar statements of 1849 :
Digby's that the medieval churches still "admonish a
wandering benighted people, and point the way to
truth, ever ancient, and ever new";[41] Ruskin's that
the glory of buildings was in their "lasting witness
against men, in their quiet contrast with the transitional character of all things".[42] They were also
similar - and in this different from Pugin - in that
while they shared the greatest admiration for medieval religious expression, neither actually advocated
a complete medieval revival : Ruskin taught that the
essential values of medieval art - and thereby of
medieval society - should be isolated and applied to
the present, while Digby constantly praised modern
Catholic society, thereby demonstrating that he was
a medievalist because he sought the application of
medieval principle - namely Catholicism - rather than
medieval form.

Ruskin on Art

The religious divisions of Ruskin's career
have been remarked elsewhere:[43]until 1848 he was a
firm evangelical; until 1858 he had increasing
doubts, then lost his faith; until 1874[44] he was a
confused agnostic; from 1874 onwards he held a
personalized Christianity. Whatever his current
religious position, however, he consistently viewed
art in moral terms, always seeking to relate artif-
acts to the moral or spiritual disposition of the
artificer and his society.[45] His attitude can
perhaps best be appreciated through discussion of his
opinions in five areas: the ideas of Pugin, the
paintings of Fra Angelico and Giotto, and St. Mark's
and Amiens Cathedrals.

As Rosenberg says, in his first period Ruskin
was in conflict with himself, aware of the disjunction between his Evangelicalism and his love of
medieval Catholic art. Since he always felt that

great art spoke of great spirituality in its
creator,[46] his problem was to show that there was a
disjunction not in his own sympathies, but between
medieval art and the Catholic faith (XII, lxxii). He
tried, like Kingsley, to show that the Gothic revival
was not to be associated with Catholicism but with
nationalism (for English Gothic was in many respects
indigenous), and claimed[47] that Gothic was Protestant
in so far as it was good, vital, true and free.
Additionally, he shifted the weight of the religious
significance of Gothic on to its naturalism, which he
associated with Protestantism.   Ruskin, however,
supremely favoured not English but Italian Gothic,
while he preferred thirteenth-century French architecture to English (XII, 491), and never liked Protestant architecture.

    These tensions were reflected in his attitude to
Pugin, for it seems that he absorbed Pugin's association of goodness with good architecture, through him
inheriting the Romantic sacralization of Gothic,
while ostentatiously rejecting his doctrine, which
was generally taken to be quintessentially Catholic:
the obvious way to salvage Gothic by dissociating it
from Romanism was to deliberately ignore Pugin.[48]   He
could claim they were opposed on the well-known
grounds that Pugin was a revivalist and he was
against revival as such.   In 1855 and 1856 he denied
having read Pugin's major works; but if he read
nothing else of his, he knew his ideas through the
publications of the Ecclesiologists and certainly
knew Contrasts and Remarks on Articles in the Rambler.
He also knew enough about him to know - or think he
knew - that he had become a Catholic because of the
Church's art.   It was to combat this (to him)
insidious tendency to be seduced by the "glitter" of
the Whore of Babylon, which Pugin represented, that
he criticized him so harshly.   By 1851 he was
suggesting that beauty neither necessarily proceeded
from beautiful faith nor issued in it, and urging the
starving of people's imaginations if credal truth
were at risk.[49] Yet, generally in his career, art was
an expression of religion because art expressed and
interpreted God's natural world.   In Edward T.Cook's
words, "according to Mr. Ruskin, Art is Religion",
and

        it is the decadence of the art of archit-
        ecture, corresponding with a decay of vital
        religion, that he finds written on the
        "Stones of Venice;" the clearness of early
        faith that he finds reflected in the

brightness of the pictures of Florence....[50]

Ruskin's criticisms of Pugin were all the more
bitter because he himself felt drawn by Catholicism :
he was persuaded by a service at Rouen Cathedral in
1848 of the propriety of material and ritual
splendour in religious services, though he told himself that this was merely a matter of taste, vulgar
and unnecessary.[51] By 1853 he deflected his religious anxiety by emphasizing the secular value of
Gothic : "The Nature of Gothic" (X) is concerned more
with the romantic and the humanist than the religious,
as are other parts of the second volume of The Stones
of Venice (e.g. X, 118-119), where he specifically
rejects the posited sacredness of the Gothic style
(X,120).

It is difficult not to feel that the extent and
insistence of Ruskin's lament for the death of
Venice, his neurotic desire to record everything
there in precise detail,[52] argues a personal and
symbolic concern with Venice in particular and
medieval architecture in general: he calls himself
"a foster-child of Venice". Just as the patron of
Venice, St. Theodore, represents to him the "heavenly
life of Christ in men, prevailing over chaos and the
deep", so the death of Venice seems to represent the
death of the Middle Ages, and the asphyxiation of
beauty, culture and religion in the modernist air:
indeed, he blames the "destruction" of St. Mark's on
the "modern system".[53] St. Mark's Cathedral, as the
essence and peak of Venetian Gothic, seems to
symbolize his soul, and its poor treatment in the
nineteenth century the battering of his beliefs and
the contemporary spiritual collapse. It is "an
epitome of the changes of Venetian architecture from
the tenth to the nineteenth century"; its style
reached a peak in the thirteenth and fourteenth
centuries, and then declined with the "extravagances
of the incipient Renaissance; and, finally ... [the]
utterly barbarous seventeenth or eighteenth-century
work" (IX,6). it was also "a type of the Redeemed
Church of God" (X,140).

In 1851 and 1853 it is a matter of style, but in
his 'Catholic' period its symbolism is clear: "St.
Mark's is not ... a piece of architecture, but a
jewelled casket and painted reliquary, chief of the
treasures in what were once the world's treasuries of
sacred things, the kingdoms of Christendom". "Beyond
all measure of value as a treasury of art," he adds,
"it is also, beyond all other volumes, venerable as
a codex of religion". So in his last period he

turned to the Puginesque belief in the alignment of
art and religion, which he summarized in 1877, when
he remarked the "eternal difference" between the art
of men "who worked in the joy of their art, for the
honour of their religion, and the mechanical labour
of those who work, at the best, in imitation, and,
too often, only for gain". In 1884 he looked back
with contempt to 1853 and the second volume of The
Stones of Venice, which, with its "pert little
Protestant mind", failed to ask "what the Church [of
St. Mark's] had been built for!" and consequently saw
it only as a secularized, pleasing artifact. It is,
he says, only by casting off Protestantism, which
still intimidates him - and originally by reading
Lord Lindsay - that he is able to see St. Mark's in
its true religious light, as opposed to its merely
secular value.[54] Too much should not be made of
this simultaneous denial of Protestantism and
secularism, though this would support the notion of
the then-supposed secularizing aspect of Protestantism.

Ruskin's "strong" and "bigoted" Protestantism of
the years adjacent to 1850[55] should not be taken at
face value. In 1845 he was deeply moved by Catholic
painting and architecture, and probably the conflict
to which this feeling gave rise led to his period of
revitalized Protestant bitterness and subsequent
agnosticism. When in 1853 he criticized the solemn
music, incense, etc. of St. Mark's, he was directly
contradicting his earlier impression of Rouen. Even
in the second volume of The Stones of Venice, where he
attacks the ascription of a religious base to great
art, he describes in detail the religious aspect of
St. Mark's, and protests too much in denying its
validity, leaving doubts as to his true feeling.
Also, he contradicts himself when he criticizes
"inferior means of exciting religious emotion" such
as "preciousness of material easily comprehended by
the vulgar eye", then asks "was it not fitting that
neither the gold nor the crystal should be spared in
the adornment of it ...?" Quite out of character
with the rest of that volume, he calls the mosaics of
St. Mark's "the most effective" of "all works of
religious art whatsoever".[56] The weight of Ruskin's
disapproval vis-à-vis St. Mark's (X, 89-93) is not
on the cathedral or its builders, but on the modern
Venetians who do not understand it. We have his
admission that then "the old Protestant palsy still
froze my heart, though my eyes were unsealed" (XXIV,
278), the eyes being those of his soul. Finally,
there is a clear continuity of thought between 1853

and 1884 (the year of the very Catholic St. Mark's
Rest), a constant element of the religious appreciation of St. Mark's, symbolized by the fact that while
in 1853 he - with interesting denominational duality-
calls it "a Book of Common Prayer, a vast illuminated
missal" (X, 112), in 1884 he uses exactly the same
metaphor in the phrase "the scripture of St. Mark's"
(XXIV,282).

His Protestant diatribes were designed more for
public consumption, to please society, than to
express the true complexity of his inmost feelings.
Even in 1853, in the midst of his aggressive Protestantism and his attempt to secularize Gothic, he holds
St. Mark's as a testimony over increasingly materialistic centuries to "the word and the statutes of God"
(X, 140, 142). In his lecture on "Pre-Raphaelitism"
of the same year (1853), his distinction between
medieval and modern art is absolute: "ancient art
was religious art; modern art is profane art; and
between the two the distinction is as firm as between
light and darkness" (XII, 143); and modern "art is
the impurer for not being in the service of Christianity" (XII, 143).[57] Conversely, thirteenth century
art "was great because it was devoted to such
religion as then existed" (XII, 144). Landow
stresses the secular aspect of Ruskin, that as he
became more interested in social problems he became
less interested in the Middle Ages, and he praises
Chandler for recognising that for Ruskin the medieval
ideal "is only an ideal, a myth, a mental construct";[58] but the overwhelming evidence is that he was
not a secularist, that even in his humanist period he
was a medievalist, albeit covertly; that medievalism,
far from being a mere mental construct, was at the
centre of his world-view, as his later works make
plain.

Just as he thought eleventh-century Venetian
Gothic supreme, so thirteenth-century French Gothic
was far superior to English (XII, 491); and, as with
St. Mark's,he admired Amiens Cathedral from one religious stance to another: in 1853 he called it "a
work justly celebrated over all Europe" (XII, 35),
and in 1880 he began work on The Bible of Amiens,[59]
wherein he called it "the Parthenon of Gothic Architecture" (XXXIII, 121) . Cook suggests that here is
found "the final phase, and the central truth, of
Ruskin's religious views" (XXXIII, lxi); and,
tellingly, he attuned himself to the theology of the
stones of Amiens by sinking his mind in stories of
the medieval saints and medieval hymns (XXXIII, xxv),
while finally utterly rejecting rationalism,

Protestantism and modernity in general (XXXIII, 73-5, 77, 104, 106, 123, 124). No longer interested in romantic metaphysical naturalism, he eschews the symbolical interpretation of Gothic, beloved by so many romantics, and stresses the immediacy of Christ to medieval man and its literal embodiment in the cathedral as the house of God. And for Ruskin, the cathedral is not only the house of God, but was also built by Him. It speaks of Christ's present life as the "Incarnate Word", describing "what His life is, what His commands are, and what His judgement will be"; it also embodies the suffering of Christ's mystical body as represented by the martyrs. The Christian teaching which is Amiens was the strength by which "all beautiful things were made".[60] For him, it is not merely a path to God, as hitherto in the romantic perspective; it is also God Incarnate. So by the 1880s he was in love with Catholicism, and in 1888 told a friend that if he fully believed he would become a Catholic at once.[61] Finally he spoke like Pugin: "the visionary faith of the Franciscans purified and animated the art of painting", while

> the modesty and valour of the Cistercians, subdued by the severe lessons of St.Bernard ... produced types of rational and beautiful structure of which the remains, in our age of iron, are still held sacred to the memory of the Catholic Church, and can scarcely be used in a civil building without a sense of profanity.[62]

One writer, who truly says that Fra Angelico was for Ruskin and his audience the type of the Christian artist, gives the impression[63] that in 1844 Ruskin ignorantly and naively thought religion was the basis of great art and believed Fra Angelico evinced this; that a few years later he overthrew the "Christian" aesthetic, and became devoted to progressivism and humanism, thus preferring the Venetian, non-Christian "Naturalists" to the Florentine, Christian "Purists"; that in 1860 he condemned "Christian" art for its pride, enthusiasm and irrelevance, for its neglect of mortality, suffering and social injustice. There is some truth in this, but the neatness of the thesis is destroyed by Ruskin's in 1853 calling Fra Angelico's painting Christian and moral, Titian's unchristian and immoral (XII, 145); while in 1860 he stressed the purity of the Purists, preferring it to carnality (VII,370). Fourteen years later, Fra Angelico was "unmatchable", the "Faithfullest of the Faithful ...

the painter of the felicities of heaven", his
"Madonna and Child, with St. Lawrence and other
Saints" (the San Marco Altarpiece) supreme (XXIII,
253, 259, 262-3). He could even apotheosize Catholic
art in a Catholic way :

> the scriptural teaching, through their art,
> of such men as Orcagna, Giotto, Angelico,
> Luca della Robbia, and Luini, is, literally,
> free from all earthly taint of momentary
> passion; its patience, meekness, and quietness
> are incapable of error through either fear
> or anger; they are able, without offence,
> to say all that they wish; they are bound
> by tradition into a brotherhood which rep-
> resents unperverted doctrines by unchanging
> scenes ... (XXXII, 113-114).

By 1876 he had come more than full circle from the
Angelico eulogy at the end of the second volume of
Modern painters (1846) :

> the Middle Ages are to me the only ages, and
> what Angelico believed, did produce the best
> work. That I hold to as demonstrated fact.
> All modern science and philosophy produces
> abortion. That miracle-believing faith
> produced good fruit - the best yet in the
> world (XXXVII, 189).

So, as with Carlyle, the intensity of medieval faith
was extremely important as a dynamo for good action.
In 1877 he condemned his earlier distorting prism of
Evangelical Protestantism which, he implied, led him
to prefer the "worldly" Turner,Tintoretto and Titian
to the Catholic Cimabue, Giotto and Angelico.[64]
     When in 1874 Ruskin perceived the strength and
greatness of Giotto, he recognized at last his
Catholic sympathies : "I am a 'Catholic'", he said
(XXIX, 86-92). In 1877 he commented that then he
had discovered the

> fallacy that Religious artists were weaker
> than Irreligious. I found that all Giotto's
> "weaknesses" ...were merely absences of
> material science. ... the Religion in him,
> instead of weakening, had solemnized and
> developed every faculty of his heart and
> hand; and ... his work, in all the innocence
> of it, was yet a human achievement and
> possession, quite above everything that

Titian had ever done! (XXIX,91)

Thus he was quasi-converted to Catholicism by perceiving Giotto's greatness of soul through his
paintings, by loving the religion in his work. And
even Giotto's "human achievement" is far greater than
Titian's, because of his Incarnational theology: the
touching of the human with the divine by the grace of
the Incarnation. According to his 1853 introduction
to Giotto and his Works in Padua he saw Giotto even
then as the prime painter interpreter of religious
truth of his time, as the chief exemplar of a time
when painters achieved greatness through conscient-
iousness, faithfulness and abiding with sacred
subjects (sec. 13-16).
    Ruskin's irony was that he was immensely
influential when giving out those views he finally
rejected or found wanting. His 'Catholicism'
influenced no one; his reverence for medieval art
and architecture - latterly entirely religious -
continued to be seen through socialist and aesthetic
prisms. Just as he had made his myth out of medieval
art, so others made their several myths out of him,
picking - along with modern critics - what he himself
came to regard as dead bones. Perhaps Walter Pater
exemplifies this transmogrification, for he seized
upon Ruskin's concentration on beauty and the
indulgence of his sensibilities. Pater, however,
vaguely parallels his development: as a boy he played
the priest, in the 1860s he was enthusiastically
sensuous and even anti-Christian, in the 1870s he
became more conciliatory towards Christianity and the
medieval religion. His essays "Notre-Dame D'Amiens"
(1894) and "Vézelay" fall into his period of Christian rapprochement, and Cook thought Ruskin provided
the starting point for his essay on Amiens (XXXIII,
lx). But Pater insisted on the secularity of Amiens,
its humanism, and for this reason preferred it to the
more religious Romanesque (as he held it) of Vézelay.
In fact, his position was much nearer to Kingsley's,
viewing the abbey as inhuman and "very exclusive",
having "turned its back upon common life". It
represents for Pater the "iron tyranny of Rome, ...
its tyranny over the animal spirits", and is the
"completest outcome of a religion of threats".[65]
Here speaks the shadow of humanist Ruskin, who also
saw in medieval art the spirit of élitism.[66] Ruskin
was a true medieval, for he despized the Renaissance;
Pater was a true modern, for he valued the Middle
Ages only for their subterranean classicism and
latent Renaissance spirit. Pater's scale of value

was pagan, whereas Ruskin believed that in the Middle
Ages, the Christian faith was "Tutress" to the seeing
imagination" which perceived truth and enabled "the
Christian painters" to create "the perfect types of
the Virgin and of her Son; which became, indeed,
Divine, by being, with the most affectionate truth,
human" (XXXIII, 483-4). The last statement
emphasizes his belief in the incarnational aspect of
medieval art: not the romantic faith in man's
divinity, but faith in the goodness, the worthwhile-
ness of man and creation because it has been shared
by God. Chesterton greatly sympathized with Ruskin,
seeing Gothic as Christian art, reconciling the
multifariousness of life into a unified prayer; and
for Chesterton (who was certainly a romantic in the
loose sense of the word) this was a romantic concept,
because it was instinct with a sense of magical joy
which vibrated just beneath life's surface. His
verdict on the revivalists, however, was that they
omitted the great medieval theme of reconciliation,
so the "real objection to revivals of medievalism is
that they are not medieval enough".[67]

NOTES

1. Mill's Essays on Literature and Society ed.
J.B. Schneewind (New York, 1965) 34. The Spirit of
the Age 1st. pub. in Examiner 1831, in 6 installments.
2. Autobiography of John Stuart Mill 125.
3. Mill's Essays on Literature and Society 70.
4. Cf. Albert LaValley Carlyle and the Idea of
the Modern (1968) 204.
5. 'Hours With the Mystics' Literary and
General Lectures and Essays 307-8; 1st. pub. FM Sept.
1856. It is worth noting that Past and Present
exemplifies the increasing faithfulness to medieval
documents, which characterized the 1830s and 1840s :
Grace J. Calder The Writing of Past and Present
(1949) 25-31.
6. CW XXXIII 'The Pleasures of England' 506
n.I, 512.
7. Op. cit. Lecture III in On Heroes... 3rd.
ed. (1846) 143.
8. Past and Present (George Routledge & Sons,
1893) Bk. II ch.xv, 92. Cf. On Heroes ... 152 on
Dante's (and through him medieval Christianity's)
"unconscious" and true "embleming".
9. Past and Present I, ii, 13, I,iv,26 and II,
ii,43, II,i,38, III,i,108 respectively.

10. On Heroes ... 190-1.
11. Ibid. 197.
12. Past and Present II,iv,52, II,iv,50, II, iii,49, II,ix,70, II,vii,63, II,ix,71, II,x,74 and II,xv,91 respectively.
13. See J.P. Farrell "Matthew Arnold and the Middle Ages" VS XIII (March 1970) 332-5.
14. Qu. ibid. 320 from On the Classical Tradition.
15. Essays in Criticism. First Series v.III in Complete Prose Works of Matthew Arnold ed. R.H.Super (Michigan U.P., 1962) 96ff.
16. "Pagan and Mediaeval Religious Sentiment" Complete Prose Works ... III 223.
17. Ibid. 225, 230.
18. Schools and Universities on the Continent v. IV Complete Prose Works (1964) 36.
19. "Heinrich Heine" Essays in Criticism. First Series.
20. "Stanzas from the Grande Chartreuse".
21. 'Joubert' Complete Prose Works III 199.
22. 'Mending the Sieve' (1882) in The Library Edition, The Complete Works of John Ruskin XXXIII, 240. This ed. henceforth cited in text by v.no. and p. See Bibliography.
23. CW XXIX, 88, XXIII, 299, XXIII, 254-9, XXIII, xxxviii, xlvi-xlvii respectively.
24. CW XXXIII, 222-3, 231-9, 245-6, 517-518.
25. CW XXXIII, 233, 518, 249, 239, 254 respectively.
26. CW XXXIII, 484 Ruskin uses the phrase "the seeing imagination".
27. CW XXXIII, 483-5, 493, 509, 520.
28. Fors Clavigera Letter 41 (May 1874) CW XXVIII, 82.
29. CW XXXIII, 121, 131, 136, 238.
30. "The turn of the tide" The Listener CI no. 2599 (22 Feb. 1979) 279-81.
31. German Painting from Romanticism to Expressionism (1974) 50. Also see Keith Andrews The Nazarenes (Oxford at the Clarendon Press, 1964) 12, William Vaughan Romantic Art (1978) 108-110.
32. Landow Modern Philology LXX (1972-3) 366-9, Andrews The Nazarenes 78-81.
33. On Rossetti's fundamental irreligiousness see Jerome McGann "Rossetti's Significant Details" VP VII (1969) 41-54, Beers History of English Romant- icism in the Nineteenth Century 302, Fairchild IV 347-50. But see Humphrey House All in Due Time (1955) "Pre-Raphaelite Poetry" especially 155 and William Sharp's Dante Gabriel Rossetti (1882) 40-1, which

suggest a religious aspect.

34.   Cf. Ferguson The Renaissance in Historiaal Thought 141-2, J.R. Hale England and the Italian Renaissance (1963) 152-3, 156 and Rio The Poetry of Christian Art (1854) I.

35.   Op. cit. 2v. (1885) I, 1-4, 307, 309 respectively.

36.   "Christian Art" DR XXII (June, 1847) 495.

37.   Op.cit. 2v. (1890) I, 17, 1-2 respectively. Kindred spirits included Louisa Twining, who wrote Symbols and Emblems of Early and Mediaeval Christian Art (1852) and the Catholic priest Frederick Charles Husenbeth, who wrote Emblems and Saints(2nd. ed. 1860).

38.   DR XXII (June, 1847) 510.

39.   Literary and General Lectures and Essays (1890) 190, 191 - cf. ibid. "Alexander Smith and Alexander Pope" (1853) 84 - 192-3.

40.   See CW VII, 361, XXVII, 545, The Diaries of John Ruskin ... 1848-1873 ed. Joan Evans and John Howard Whitehouse (Oxford, Clarendon Press,1958) 702; cf. Grennan William Morris 28, Merriman Flower of Kings 125, Holland Memoir 77-8.

41.   Compitum II, 329.

42.   Seven Lamps of Architecture "The Lamp of Memory" sec.X.

43.   George P. Landow The Aesthetic and Critical Theories of John Ruskin (Princeton, 1971) 243-4.

44.   Landow says 1875, but Ruskin himself says he was a humanist until only 1874 : CW XXIX, 90.

45.   Since John D. Rosenberg has already dealt with the ambiguities of his first 2 periods, this aspect is not recounted in detail: The Darkening Glass (1963) 50-61. See also Clark The Gothic Revival 195-7.

46.   A belief anticipated by the partly medievalist Sir Francis Palgrave: see Hale England and the Italian Renaissance 125, 128.

47.   "The Nature of Gothic" in Stones of Venice v.II (1853) CW X.

48.   Cf. Hough The Last Romantics 90, Michael Trappes-Lomax Pugin. A Mediaeval Victorian (1932) 317. Trappes-Lomax thinks Ruskin was jealous of Pugin : 316.

49.   CW V, 428-9, IX, 436-40.

50.   Studies in Ruskin (1890) 15-16.

51.   The Diaries of John Ruskin ... 1848-1873 15 Oct. 1848, I, 369.

52.   Eg. Ruskin in Italy. Letters to his Parents 1845 (Clarendon Press, Oxford, 1972) ed. Harold I. Shapiro 61,62,85,219 and preface to 2nd. ed.Seven

Lamps (1855).
53. CW XXIV 405, sec. 23, 407 respectively.
54. CW XXIV, 277-8, 406, 414-415.
55. E.T. Cook's words, CW XII, lxxii.
56. CW X, 89-92, 130,133-41.
57. He expressed the same view in the same year in the introduction to Giotto and his Works in Padua.
58. Review of Dream of Order Modern Philology LXX (1972-3) 368.
59. 1880-85, part of Our Fathers Have Told Us. On the proposed construction and intent of Our Fathers Have Told Us see Cook's introductory remarks and Joan Evans John Ruskin (New York/London,1954) 387-8.
60. CW XXXIII, 123-4, 131, 169-73.
61. Evans John Ruskin 403.
62. CW XXXIII "Mending the Sieve" 244,245-6.
63. Richard J. Dellamora "The Revaluation of 'Christian' Art : Ruskin's Appreciation of Fra Angelico 1845-60" UTQ XLIII (1973-4) 143-50.
64. Catholics viewed Fra Angelico in the same way as Ruskin: for Aubrey de Vere see Reilly Aubrey de Vere 98, Wilfrid Ward Aubrey de Vere (1904) 148-9; for Wiseman see DR XXII (June, 1847) 495.
65. "Vézelay" in Miscellaneous Studies (1901, 1st pub.1894) 141,131,133 respectively.
66. Eg. XVI, 337-42.
67. "Baroque and Gothic Architecture" (1927) in The Glass Walking-Stick 104. And see "Introductory : On Gargoyles" in Alarms and Discursions.

CONCLUSIONS

> True views on Mediaevalism, Time alone will
> bring ...
>
> W.S. Gilbert _Patience_

While there was no "school" of literary religious medievalism, there is clearly a viable subject
for study,which, for want of a more comprehensive
phrase, can be called "religious medievalism"; and it
is a viable subject, with integrity and a sense of
purpose, because of the large number of writers who
subscribed to it, their seriousness - they were not
escapists but critics - the phenomenon's correlation
with attitudinal developments and patterns, and its
effect on people outside of the literary religious
medievalist sphere.

That literary religious medievalism had an
effect is not susceptible of unequivocal proof : one
must deduce the causal relation by observing the
phenomena. It was certainly an important element in
the polemical battle for the dignity of English Roman
Catholics, although this aspect was largely nullified
by the High Anglicans arrogating whatever was good in
the medieval Church to themselves. There are numerous evidences that medievalism stirred people's
consciences : Ruskin's lectures on "The Pleasures of
England" were said to have had a considerable effect
on his audience.[1] Mere observation of the growth of
medievalism is sufficient to suggest that earlier
medievalists had an effect on later ones, and
"converted" some. The Tractarians took a grain of
encouragement from the medievalist ambiance, and
Anglo-Catholic Ritualism initially took more than a
grain. Digby's influence has only lately been given
serious credit,[2] and, though quiet, it was indeed
not inconsiderable. Firstly, his influence favoured
Roman Catholicism : before his conversion, Bute was

familiar with his writings, and the priest historian
T.E. Bridgett was converted by them, the vision of
the Church he thus received being of

> the Church of the Middle Ages, with which I
> believed the modern Church to be identical,
> and that the Church of the Middle Ages was
> the legitimate development of the Apostolic
> Church.[3]

Significantly, Bridgett was struck by the "isolation
and insularity of the Church of England".[4] Secondly,
Digby indirectly influenced High-Anglican society via
Young England. Kingsley (who knew of Digby[5]) witnessed the good effect that such Anglo-Catholicism had
had on the aristocracy.[6] Such ideas also influenced
architecture and the revival of Anglican monasticism
in the 1840s.[7] Medievalists also had an effect on
Catholic monasticism.[8]
    Observation of the fact of medievalism, its
character and results, strongly suggests the conditions which stimulated its origin and growth. This
phenomenon was a response to the late-eighteenth-
century crisis of confidence in the Enlightenment, to
an indefinable malaise and insecurity; and when the
boil burst in 1789, the response was quickened. Just
as the Revolution was both symptom and agent, so too
was the historiographical development which enabled a
reappraisal of past epochs. This catastrophe made it
finally clear to many that the present was not the
best of all possible worlds, and thereby unbolted the
psychological barrier to the past. The revolutions
of 1820, 1830 and 1842 and the Industrial Revolution
must also have stimulated the quest for a new authority to guide society and cure its ills: at the end
of the century the Catholic historian Wilfrid Ward
reflected that "a century of revolution has done
something towards renewing mediaeval dreams".[9] Dissatisfaction with a spiritually impoverished Established Church was especially acute in the 1820s and
1830s. Ruskin spoke of how St.Bernard had rescued
Europe after the collapse of the Roman Empire : the
Roman Empire had collapsed again with the fall of the
Enlightenment, and so Ruskin naturally preached St.
Bernard. One minor stimulatory factor must have been
that with the ending of Continental warfare, Englishmen were able after 1815 to travel freely through a
largely Catholic world, which impressed many of
those, like Ruskin, Newman, Digby, Bute and Faber,
wealthy enough to undertake the enterprize.
    Religious medievalism is neither adequately nor

properly described as a romantic phenomenon, since
romanticism was fundamentally a rejection of
Europe's traditional "Christian religion-culture",[10]
while religious medievalism was at least an attempt
to return to that heritage. To some extent a seman-
tic point has been discussed, which is the use of
the word "romantic"; the point being that there are
not just different types of romanticism, but different degrees of romanticism : romanticism which is
more or less romantic, or which is more or less satisfied with itself. Religious medievalism is, in
most instances, a romanticism dissatisfied with itself, and is therefore not exhaustively defined when
described as romantic. Religious medievalism is
doubtless romantic when compared with the Enlightenment, which is generally regarded as the apotheosis
of classicism. But this does not affect the problem
of the "essence" of romanticism. In one sense, the
application of the epithet "romantic" depends on the
person applying it, for those observers with a
"mechanistic" or "scientific" - one might say, with
an Enlightenment - view of life, will judge the
visionary, the idealist, the man with faith in
vision, to be a romantic. Such a judgement is not
only subjective, it is a two-edged sword; for the
case could be made that all versions of Enlightment -
inductivism, social Darwinism, historical cyclism or
progressivism, libidinism, materialism and rationalism - are coloured by romanticism, since all world-
views are "visions". It is not, therefore, necessarily useful to describe religious medievalists as
romantics on the grounds that they had a vision of
a Middle Ages vital, thrusting, positive, creative
and integrated by virtue of their own vision. Indeed, such an appellation might be seriously obfus-
cating, since it hides a multiplicity of different-
iations and inhibits discrimination. Religious
medievalism was clearly connected with the revival
of interest in the imagination, itself a matter of
crediting the visionary faculty, with its attendant
paraphernalia of new means of communicating itself.
One would not wish to quarrel with the common view
that it was romantic in the sense of its revival
being contemporary and allied with the development
of romanticism : it is romantic in the chronological
sense, in the sense that it was in the romantic
orbit. Religious medievalism definitely shared the
element of imagination with romanticism; but there
is only limited use in the syllogism : romanticism is
imagination, religious medievalism is imagination,
therefore religious medievalism is romanticism. So

many things outside of the romantic period are to do
with imagination : scientific discovery, for example,
and the search for new language which it implies.
And religious medievalism existed before pre-Romanticism : one need only name Spenser, the metaphysical
poets and those Protestants, such as Sir Henry
Spelman, who anticipated Neale's belief that the
Dissolution of the Monasteries had been a catastrophe.[11] Because romanticism means more than a particular period and imagination, further discrimination
is necessary.

It has been suggested (in Chapter 1) that the
word romantic is most appropriately applied to
writers of the Romantic period, where there is a
tendency for writers to be profoundly egotistical,in
the sense of being introspective, concerned with the
self's vision to the extent of constructing a "language" or system of imagery peculiar to themselves :
each becomes his own prophet, his own hero, his own
god, and his own imagination becomes the divine reconciler - hence Coleridge's concept of the imagination as the human reflection of divine creativity.
Put crudely, imagination plus individualism equals
romanticism par eccellence. This equation issued
naturally from rationalist and Protestant individualism. Imagination as reconciler was the equivalent of
religious medievalism's religion-culture as reconciler. But the romantic formula of reconciliation plus
individualism was highly unstable and bound to
provoke a reaction, for it was preponderantly atomistic, with its cults of the hero and the genius, the
glorification of the personal Weltanschauung, nationalism and relativism, thereby exacerbating the disease it was intended to cure. By contrast, religious
medievalism was imagination plus the desire for a
communal language, a shared metaphysical understanding and experience. The emphasis of the Protestant/
rationalist/Romantic syndrome was on personal salvation; that of the Catholic/mystical/non-romantic
syndrome on communal salvation. The Enlightenment
and Romanticism were variations on the theme of the
modernist divinization of man (or the tendency which
led that way), the first being the divinization of
the "light" side, the second being the divinization
of the "dark"; and the Catholic Revival, to which
medievalism was a contributory factor, was a radical
alternative to this tradition.

This view of religious medievalism as the search
for a unifying and reconciling communal language of
spirituality, which was symptomatic of the desire for
metaphysical unity, can be elucidated by reference to

an anthropological work called <u>Natural Symbols</u>
(1970) by Mary Douglas, who argues that ritual -
which is symbol-in-action - derives from a cohesive
society, and in so doing helps to preserve its
cohesion. Thus ritual cannot be regarded as merely
aesthetic frippery, a religious redundance, or an
optional extra. In essence, Douglas argues the
profound power of ritual. Alienation from society
leads to anti-ritualism, to

> exaltation of the inner experience and den-
> igration of its standardized expressions; pre-
> ference for intuitive and instant forms of
> knowledge; rejection of mediating institut-
> ions, rejection of any tendency to allow habit
> to provide the basis of a new symbolic system.

This is a close description of the Protestant revolt
against Catholicism; it is also a good description
of romanticism and its revolt against Enlightenment
formalism and propriety, and indeed against the traditional religion-culture. If romanticism has this
much in common with Protestantism, it is unlikely
that religious medievalism, which must of its nature
always be tending towards Catholicism, can be satisfactorily described as simply romantic. Douglas
continues :

> after the protest stage, once the need for
> organization is recognized, the negative
> attitude to rituals is seen to conflict
> with the need for a coherent system of
> expression. The ritualism re-asserts itself
> around the new context of social relations.

If pre-Romanticism is the initial protest stage,
then Romanticism is the secondary protest stage,
combined with the attempt to construct new, personal,
mental or cultural "rituals"; but "personal ritual"
is oxymoronic. Religious medievalism is also part of
the re-assertion of ritual, but is more successful
as such, because it seeks a common ritual or symbolic
language. (It cannot be more successful in the sense
of being great art, however, because the imagery is
necessarily second-hand.) But despite its efforts,
continues Douglas, the new, anti-ritualist sect has
lost something from the "original cosmic ordering of
symbols"; and "... just as revolutionaries may evict
kings and queens from the pages of history, the anti-
ritualists have rejected the list of saints and popes
and tried to start again without any load of his-
ory".[12] It may be supposed that the analogy breaks

down here, because romanticism included the recovery
of history and its celebration, unlike the "new
sect". But this would be erroneous, because romantic
history was in fact as warped and partial as that of
the sect : it was historicist, in the bad sense of
supposing that history followed a design or set path,
a path which was usually Whig, progressivist, nationalist and Protestant; and it was doubly deficient
because it was usually smothered by the egocentricism
of the Enlightenment view. Such historicism disowned
much of history and fragmented it, whereas the medievalists, such as Ruskin, Digby and Lionel Johnson,
had a propensity to reconcile history, to see the
Middle Ages in filial relation to the ancient world.
 The "new sect", then, prefers personal symbol to
ritual, which is not only symbol-in-action but comm-
unicative symbol : "ritual," says Douglas, "is pre-
eminently a form of communication."[13] And the alienated rebel

> by rejecting ritualized speech ... rejects
> his own faculty for pushing back the boundary
> between inside and outside so as to incorpor-
> ate in himself a patterned social world. At
> the same time he thwarts his faculty for
> receiving immediate, condensed messages
> given obliquely along non-verbal channels.[14]

All this may account for the striking virtual absence
of religious medievalism from English Romanticism, an
absence which was encouraged by England's being Protestant, and therefore not exposed to Catholic sacramentalism, which dignifies ritual in the highest degree. The Eucharistic doctrine, which informs the key
ritual of Catholicism, assumes, as Douglas points
out,

> that humans can take an active part in the
> work of redemption, both to save themselves
> and others, through using the sacraments as
> channels of grace ... whose very possibility
> was denied by Protestant reformers.[15]

The Protestant emphasis is on the superiority of
spiritual over material, which is "to insist on the
liberties of the individual and to imply a political
programme to free him from unwelcome constraints";[16]
and it is noticeable that revolution was a feature of
Romanticism. But the Catholic emphasis on the close
relationship between spirit and matter "implies that
the individual is by nature subordinate to society

225

and finds his freedom within its forms",[17] and it is
noticeable that religious medievalism was conservative. Romanticism is notoriously equivocal, and so
not surprisingly, romantics reached towards the
sacramental position in their ambiguous view of
nature. Coleridge spoke volumes on the instability
of the relationship between Romanticism and sacramentalism when he said, "every season Nature converts
me from some unloving heresy, and will make a
Catholic of me at last".[18] Newman was given a strong
push in the direction of Catholicism by this type of
sacramentalism, in the shape of Keble's The Christian
Year (1827).[19] In his account of it, Newman strongly
implies that Keble's sacramentalism was not typical
of the preceding period : "Keble struck an original
note ... a new music, the music of a school, long
unknown in England". This music was the "Sacramental
system; that is, the doctrine that material phenomena are both the types and the instruments of real
things unseen".[20] R.S, Hawker, the arch-medievalist,
believed that "every visible Thing is an embodied
Thought of God", a matter of communication between
man and God, and he speculated that "all material
things are but sacraments of God".[21] This outlook
was very near the core of religious medievalism.

The elements of religious medievalist "ritual",
of their "language", were obviously images, themes
and subjects taken from medieval Christianity, which
had the advantages of being Christian, varied, comprehensive, pan-European and "poetic". Medieval forms
clearly stimulated what might be called the "spiritual imagination", and in this sense, those looking for
a new cultural-cum-metaphysical language found a soul
mate : this is why some writers have vaguely seen
romanticism as a return to the Middle Ages. This
search for a spiritually more competent language
began with the early days of pre-romanticism :
Beattie, Hurd and Warton were engaged in an unconscious quest for a language which would reconcile
culture and religion, and thereby regenerate society.
Chatterton embodied the ambiguity of religion-in-
culture and incarnated the theme, as it were, by
actually reverting to pseudo-medieval language. The
stimulation of these efforts enabled men like Burke,
Coleridge, Southey and Cobbett to unwrap the aesthetic packaging (one would not wish to press this
metaphor) and look at the religious core in relation
to society. Though they were all consciously non-
Catholic or anti-Catholic, they could not help
elevating their subject by the seriousness of their
attention. This set the stage for Digby and

CONCLUSIONS

Wordsworth to present the "cultural" language of
medieval religion in a blatantly religious light :
the balance of the scales tipped from aestheticism to
religion. In a sense, Digby picked up Chatterton's
idea of letting the medievals speak for themselves;
for he realized that the historical view was so
polluted by fiction and histories which only masquer-
aded as fact,[22] that fresh insight was needed : his
solution was to quote medieval writings often and at
length. Medieval art and architecture were aspects
of the Church's language, and there is ample evidence
that they were seldom viewed in eighteenth and nineteenth-century English literature as anything but the
repositories of ideology and spirituality, the
cultural sacraments of Catholicism, by which medieval
Catholicism could be vitally communicated to men of
later centuries. In fact, ideology and form came to
be so closely identified that Gothic art became a
focus of religious dispute. Gothic symbolized unity
in diversity and ecumenism. Victorian sages,
Catholics and Anglo-Catholics were also deeply concerned with medieval Catholicism as a way of reconciling culture, society and religion and articulating
a spiritual world-view. The sacramentalism of
culture was an appropriate embodiment of the communal
shared language and its implicit quest for community,
since it reconciled the cultural - and, indeed, the
material - with the religious.
     Other aspects of this medieval language were the
legends of the saints and monasticism. The legends
were regarded as symbolic and true at the same time,
and many understand them as also literally true.
They were educative, like Gothic architecture and
art. Monasticism - also like Gothic architecture -
was regarded as an incarnation of the organic,
united, brotherly, orderly, vital and free society,
as an embodiment of the ideal, religiously-based
society, to which the whole of medieval society was
regarded as having aspired. Because a monastery was
a religiously-based society, it was a total contrast
to the modern individualistic and materialistic
society, which imposed social order without consent.
Monasticism produced order with consent. The abbot
stood for the medievalist ideal of spiritually-
enlightened, monumental authority, the alternative to
atomistic relativism. Visions of ritual were often
depicted in the monastic context, and quintessentially depicted the need for a new language within a
new society.
     Just as the function of the new language was as
reconciler and unifier, so the vision of medieval

society was of one united and yet free. (The very
idea that one age might be better than all others
was itself anti-relativist.) For Digby, the sense of
social duty founded on religion was both unifying and
liberating; the anti-Erastians, like R.H.Froude and
Neale, wanted to see the Church restored to medieval
freedom; and Chesterton believed the medievals
constantly "attempted freedom", and attempted it
"always through division and definition, rights and
privileges, orders, guilds, colleges".[23] This was
the Digbeian vision of a hierarchical society informed by Christianity, in which liberty and equality
under the yoke of Christ were practised. The medievalists suspected that Protestantism, partly because
of its individualism and partly because it was in
England established, conspired to support the status
quo; and that all contemporary materialist ideologies were useless as moral systems, because they
eliminated the divine sanction for morality. Wiseman,
for example, said he preferred medievalism to the
"delirious ravings of sickly phantasies" produced by
materialist reformers.[24] The vision was of wholeness,
both in the sense of fraternal unity and fullness of
life. But the anti-medievalists were also concerned
with the state of society, and also searched for new
language to carry new ideas; but they looked down
the same telescope from the opposite end. They were
"supernatural-naturalists", while the medievalists
were natural-supernaturalists. Kingsley thought
communication with God would be easier if human society and progress were elevated into the language of
spirituality; so he stressed the immanent God,
whereas materialists like Huxley abolished the transcendent God, elevating science into a quasi-metaphy-
sical language. Both groups were looking for a language to describe a world-view; but they were as
exiles from Babel, one party, as it were, speaking
Middle English, the other modern. Kingsley attacked
an Aunt Sally of etiolated pietism and élitism,
whereas Digby, Arnold, Ruskin and Carlyle believed
the medieval Church to have been of the people, for
the world and in the world, a view which had its
theological-cultural equivalent and expression in the
sacramental outlook of medievalism.

The ambiguity, duality, equivocality and
confusion inhering in virtually every manifestation
of religious medievalism, is a function of the
exploration of new perspectives, periods of transition, complexity of influence, conflict between the
Protestant/rationalist tradition and the Catholic
ethos, the vicarious satisfaction of Catholic tastes

through literary fantasy, the conflict between
reason and conditioning, the religious desires
(which meant that two answers could be given to the
same question by the same individual) and the trav-
ersing of the shadowy borderland between culture and
religion, where fantasy transmutes into faith, dream
becomes reality and culture becomes religion. In
this regard, it is fitting that several manifestations of religious medievalism involve dreams or
visions; and one recalls that Hypnos, the god of
sleep, was thought to give man the gift of communication with the gods through his son Morpheus, the
god of dreams. In this sense, the Middle Ages were
a dream-world which facilitated the liberation of
religious musings, and mediated between the super-
ficialities of the physical world and the depths of
the spiritual.

The great paradox is that while non-Catholics,
and even anti-Catholics, were drawn towards Catholicism by the study of the Middle Ages, Catholics
themselves were not (with one or two exceptions)
obsessed by the medieval language: they were more
interested in the spirit and propaganda value of the
medieval Church. Morris, while judging Neale to have
been the chief medievalizing Ritualist, observed that
Ritualism had become divorced from medievalism when
secularists cultivated an interest in medievalism.[25]
As Chesterton said, "Catholicism is not medievalism",
by which he meant that Catholicism was of every age,
modern as well as medieval and primitive. Since the
Catholic Church had a difficult job to do in the
present, it could not afford to luxuriate in its own
language : it was too busy simply surviving. Additionally, Catholicism did not need to be self-consciously medievalist, since the Middle Ages were part
of the Church's living tissue. This does not mean,
of course, that the Church did not love its own past.
Pugin and De Lisle are the exceptions which prove the
rule : even Digby did not suppose that the language
was more important than the message; although there
was a grain of truth in Pugin's belief that "it's not
what you say, but the way that you say it" which is
important, for the linguists and sociologists appear
to be agreed that language has a determinative rôle
in the development of society, and presumably this
also applies to ritual forms. Ruskin, Digby, Carlyle
and Chesterton had this in common : that they wanted
to revive not the medieval corpse, but the spirit
which had informed medieval society.

Nor is Catholicism romanticism : in this, this
thesis agrees with Fairchild; but where it disagrees

CONCLUSIONS

with him is in his implication that religious medievalism was not properly serious, not even potentially
truly Catholic.[26]   Often, as with Neale and the
Camdenians, where medievalism appeared to be merely
antiquarian it had a truly religious aspect, and no
clearly-defined boundary between this type of antiquarianism and religion can be fixed. Nor can one be
fixed between Tractarian and post-Tractarian sacramentalism and pre-Tractarian medievalism, for it too
had a symbolic religious dimension. It was a child
of romanticism, but in radical rebellion against its
father. It shared romanticism's seriousness of quest
but not its characteristic individualism or its
frequent attraction to the strange, exotic and
ultimately superficial. It was orthodox, while
romanticism was often a desperate and even degener-
ative form of religion - "spilt religion", in T.E.
Hulme's phrase. To return to the initial image, it
was truly a cuckoo's egg, incubated by the unsuspect-
ing sparrow Romanticism, and even nurtured by it;
but despite the times in which it developed, the
shared nutriment of the imagination and the quest,
and their similar shapes, the cuckoo was undeniably
itself and not a sparrow.
     The conclusions, then, are that because of its
Catholic quality, religious medievalism cannot
adequately or properly be described as a romantic
phenomenon; that literary religious medievalism was
a serious, and ultimately metaphysical quest, involving the search for a more adequate spiritual language; and that the medieval Church was widely viewed
as having, in its very forms and vitality, like
Prometheus, brought fire from heaven, a sacred fire
which had lit and cleansed a decadent and barbarian
world, and which could light and cleanse an individualistic and materialistic world.

<u>NOTES</u>

     1.   CW XXXIII liii.
     2.   Mark Girouard <u>The Return to Camelot.
Chivalry and the English Gentleman</u> (Yale U.P., New
Haven and London, 1981) ch.5, 132, 142.
     3.   Cyril Ryder <u>Life of Thomas Edward Bridgett</u>
(Burns & Oates, 1906) 15.
     4.   Ibid. 14.
     5.   Ch. XXIII of <u>Two Years Ago</u> is called "The
Broad Stone of Honour".
     6.   <u>Yeast</u> (1878) Preface to 4th.ed. v, ix-x.

230

7.   Peter Anson's The Call of the Cloister describes the development of Anglican monasticism, and gives a list of novels which touch on this quasi-medievalist theme, including twenty twentieth-century titles.

8.   See Heyer The Catholic Church From 1648 to 1870 144, Daniel Rees "The Benedictine Revival in the Nineteenth Century" in Benedict's Disciples (Leominster, 1980). ed. David H. Farmer.

9.   Ward The Life and Times of Cardinal Wiseman 11, 583.

10.   The phrase is E.I. Watkin's : Catholic Art and Culture (1947) 158. Watkin gives a traditional account of the relationship between Christianity and Romanticism : op.cit. 157-8.

11   Aveling The Handle and the Axe 35.

12.   Douglas Natural Symbols: Explorations in Cosmology (Harmondsworth, 1978) 40-1.

13.   Natural Symbols 41; cf. ibid. 60.

14.   Ibid. 76.

15.   Ibid. 70.

16.   Ibid. 195.

17.   Loc. cit.

18.   Coleridge Anima Poetae ed. Ernest Hartley Coleridge (1895) 26.

19.   On naturalism as sacramentalism in the Tractarians see G.B. Tennyson "The Sacramental Imagination" in Nature and the Victorian Imagination ed. U.C. Knoepflmacher and G.B. Tennyson (U.P. California - Berkeley/LosAngeles/London, 1977).

20.   Apologia 29 (italics mine); cf. ibid. 23 on Bishop Butler's Analogy.

21.   Stones Broken from the Rocks 44; cf. Isaac Williams' Tract 80 on Reserve.

22.   Chesterton was to write on this problem and suggest Digby's solution : "History versus the Historians" Lunacy and Letters.

23.   "Robert Bruce and His Age" Glass Walking-Stick 111.

24.   "Montalembert's St. Elizabeth" DR III (Oct. 1837) 386-7.

25.   Introd. to J.M. Neale Good King Wenceslas (Birmingham, 1895).

26.   Cf. Tennyson on Fairchild Victorian Devotional Poetry 248 n.6.

BIBLIOGRAPHY

MANUSCRIPTS

Cambridge : Charles Justin MacCarthy letters to Lord
    Houghton, Trinity College Library, Cambridge,
    Houghton Suppl. (2).
Oxford: Magdalen College Archives : MS.335 Reunion:
    Ambrose Lisle Phillipps,MS.459 MS. Letters.
    Ambrose Lisle Phillipps,MS.528 MS.Letters Pugin.
Dormer MSS. (in the possession of Michael Dormer) :
    letters from Ambrose Phillipps de Lisle to
    Kenelm Henry Digby.

TEXTS

Place of publication is London, unless otherwise
indicated.

PRIMARY

Dates in square brackets are those of first editions.

Acton, Lord John Essays on Church and State ed.
    Douglass Woodruff (1952).
Acton, Lord John Lord Acton and His Circle ed.Francis
    A. Gasquet (n.d. [1906]).
Acton, Lord John The Correspondence of Lord Acton and
    Richard Simpson ed. Joseph L.Altholz etc. 3v.
    (C.U.P., 1971-5).
Acton, Lord John The History of Freedom and Other
    Essays (1907).
Alison, Archibald Miscellaneous Essays in Modern
    British Essayists ser. (Philadelphia, 1846).
Arnold, Matthew Essays in Criticism. First Series v.
    III (1962 [1865]) of The Complete Prose Works
    of Matthew Arnold ed. R.H. Super (Michigan U.P.)
Arnold, Matthew Schools and Universities on the

232

Continent v.IV (1964) Complete Prose Works.
Arnold, Matthew The Poems of Matthew Arnold ed.
    Kenneth Allott (1965).
Ashton, John, ed. Chap-Books of the Eighteenth
    Century (1882).
Ayre, Joseph The Christian Philanthropist's
    Pilgrimage, ... and Other Poems 2nd. ed. (1851).
Bagshawe, Henry "Compitum" DR XXV (Dec. 1848) 463-78.
Barbauld, Anna L. The Works of Anna Laetitia Barbauld
    2v. (1825, Ist.ed. of poetry 1773).
Barham, R.H. The Ingoldsby Legends Everyman ed. (1960
    Ist. ed. in 3 ser. 1840-7).
Beattie, James On Fable and Romance v.III The Philos-
    ophical Works (1970 facsimile reprint of 1783
    original).
Belloc, Hilaire Europe and the Faith (1962 [1920]).
Berington, Joseph A Literary History of the Middle
    Ages Ist. ed. (1814).
Blair, Hugh Lectures on Rhetoric and Belles Lettres
    2nd. ed. 3v. (Dublin, 1783 [2v. 1783]).
Blake, William Poetry and Prose of William Blake ed.
    Geoffrey Keynes (1967).
Borrow, George Lavengro (1909 [3v. 1851]).
Borrow, George The Bible in Spain (Everyman, 1926
    [3v. 1843]).
Borrow, George The Romany Rye (1914 [2v. 1857]).
Bowles, William Lisle The Poetical Works of Milman,
    Bowles, Wilson, and Barry Cornwall (Paris, n.d.
    [1829]).
Burke, Edmund Reflections on the Revolution in France
    ed. Conor Cruise O'Brien (Harmondsworth, 1976
    [1790]).
Butler, Charles The Book of the Roman-Catholic Church
    2nd. ed. (1825 [1825]).
Carlyle, Thomas On Heroes, Hero-Worship, and the
    Heroic in History 3rd. ed. (1846 [1841]).
Carlyle, Thomas Past and Present (George Routledge &
    Sons, 1893 [1843]).
Chatterton, Thomas The Complete Works of Thomas
    Chatterton 2v. ed. Donald S. Taylor (Oxford at
    the Clarendon Press, 1971 [Rowley poems 1777,
    Miscellanies in Prose and Verse 1778]).
Chesterton, Gilbert K. A Short History of England
    (1917 [1917]).
Chesterton, Gilbert K. Alarms and Discursions 3rd.
    ed. (1924 [1910]).
Chesterton, Gilbert K. Chaucer (1962 [1932]).
Chesterton, Gilbert K. Lunacy and Letters Ist. ed.
    (1958).
Chesterton, Gilbert K. The Glass Walking-Stick and
    Other Essays Ist. ed. (1955).

Chesterton, Gilbert K. The New Jerusalem Ist. ed.
    (n.d. [1920]).
Chesterton, Gilbert K. The Resurrection of Rome Ist.
    ed. (n.d. [1930]).
Chesterton, Gilbert K. The Well and the Shallows
    2nd. impression (1935 [1935]).
Chesterton, Gilbert K. What's Wrong With the World
    8th.ed. (1910 [1910]).
Cobbett, William A History of the Protestant Reform-
    ation in England and Ireland 2v. (1829 [monthly
    parts 1824-6]).
Cobbett, William Cobbet's Weekly Political Register
    (Sept. 1822, Feb. 1829, Feb. 1834).
Coleridge, Samuel T. Coleridge's Miscellaneous
    Criticism ed. Thomas Raysor (1936).
Coleridge, Samuel T. Collected Letters of Samuel
    Taylor Coleridge ed. E.L. Griggs (Oxford, 1956).
Coleridge, Samuel T. On the Constitution of the
    Church and State Ist. ed. (1830) and v.X of The
    Collected Works of Samuel Taylor Coleridge ed.
    R.J. White (1976).
Coleridge, Samuel T. Table Talk (Bohn's ed. 1873).
Coleridge, Samuel T. The Complete Works of Samuel
    Taylor Coleridge ed. W.G.T. Shedd 7v. (New York,
    1854).
Coleridge, Samuel T. The Statesman's Manual v. VI
    Collected Works (1972).
Coulton, George G. Fourscore Years : An Autobiography
    (C.U.P., 1944).
Coulton, George G. Friar's Lantern Ist. ed. (1906).
Darley, George The Complete Poetical Works of George
    Darley ed. Ramsay Colles (Routledge [1908]).Ist.
    ed. Thomas à Becket1840.
De Vere, Aubrey Essays Chiefly Literary and Ethical
    Ist. ed. (1889).
De Vere, Aubrey Legends and Records of the Church and
    the Empire Ist. ed. (1887).
De Vere, Aubrey Legends of the Saxon Saints Ist. ed.
    (1879).
De Vere, Aubrey Mediaeval Records and Sonnets Ist.
    ed. (1893).
De Vere, Aubrey Recollections of Aubrey de Vere Ist.
    ed. (1897).
De Vere, Aubrey St. Thomas of Canterbury Ist. ed.
    (1876).
Digby, Kenelm Henry Compitum; or, The Meeting of the
    Ways at the Catholic Church Ist. ed. 7v.(1848-
    54).
Digby, Kenelm Henry Mores Catholici : or, Ages of
    Faith 11v. Ist. ed. (1831-42).
Digby, Kenelm Henry Morus (1826).

Digby, Kenelm Henry The Broad Stone of Honour : or,
    Rules for the Gentlemen of England 2nd.ed.
    (1823 [1822]).
Digby, Kenelm Henry The Broad Stone of Honour : or,
    the True Sense and Practice of Chivalry 5th.ed.
    5v. (1876-7).
Digby, Kenelm Henry The Broad Stone of Honour ...
    Morus 4th.ed. (1848).
Digby, Kenelm Henry The Broad Stone of Honour ...
    Tancredus 4th. ed. (1846).
Digby, Kenelm Henry The Temple of Memory 2nd. ed.
    (1875 [1874]).
Disraeli, Benjamin Coningsby Hughenden ed. (1882
    [3v. 1844]).
Disraeli, Benjamin Lothair Hughenden ed. (1882 [3v.
    1870]).
Disraeli, Benjamin Sybil Hughenden ed. (1882 [3v.
    1845]).
Disraeli, Benjamin Vivian Grey Hughenden ed. (1882
    [5v. 1826-7]).
Dixon, Richard W. History of the Church of England
    from the Abolition of the Roman Jurisdiction
    rev. 3rd. ed. 6v. (Oxford, 1895 [6v. 1878-
    1902]).
Dolben, Digby M. The Poems of Digby Mackworth Dolben
    rev. and enlarged ed. Robert Bridges (O.U.P.,
    1915 [1911]).
Dolben, Digby M. Uncollected Poems of Digby Mackworth
    Dolben ed. Martin Cohen (Reading, 1973).
Eastlake, Charles A History of the Gothic Revival ed.
    J. Mordaunt Crook (Leicester U.P., 1970),
    reprint in "The Victorian Library" ser. of Ist.
    ed. 1872 (Old Woking, Surrey).
Eliot, George Romola Ist. ed. 3v. (1863).
Eliot, George The Mill on the Floss Ist. ed. 3v.
    (Edinburgh, 1860).
Evans, Sebastian Brother Fabian's Manuscript and
    Other Poems Ist. ed. (1865).
Faber, Frederick Faber Poet and Priest, Selected
    Letters by Frederick William Faber 1833-1863 ed.
    Raleigh Addington (Glamorgan, 1974).
Faber, Frederick Poems, by Frederick William Faber,
    D.D.2nd.ed. (1857 [1856]).
Faber, Frederick Sights and Thoughts in Foreign
    Churches and Among Foreign Peoples Ist. ed.
    (1842).
Faber, Frederick Sir Lancelot Ist. ed. (1844).
Federer, Charles,ed. Yorkshire Chap-Books First
    Series (1889).
Francis, George H. "Literary Legislators (No.III):
    Lord John Manners" FM XXXV (Mar.1847) 321-39.

235

Freeman, E.A. Historical Essays 2nd. ed. (1872[1871])
Froude, James A. Short Studies on Great Subjects 4v.
    (1891 [2v. 1867]). Essay on Becket Ist.appeared
    Nineteenth Century I (June 1877)and was re-
    printed with alterations.
Froude, Richard H. "Old Times Compared With the
    Present" The British Magazine IV (1833).
Froude, Richard H. Remains of the Late Reverend
    Richard Hurrell Froude ed. John Henry Newman 4v.
    Ist. ed. (1838-9).
Froude, Richard H. St. Thomas Becket articles in The
    British Magazine II, III (1832-3).
Gasquet, Francis Henry VIII and the English Monast-
    eries 5th. ed. 2v. (1893 [1887]).
Gibbon, Edward The Decline and Fall of the Roman
    Empire abridged by D.M.Low (Harmondsworth, 1966
    [6v. 1776-1788]).
Hare, Julius C. (with A.W. Hare) Guesses at Truth by
    Two Brothers Ist. ser. (1847, 3rd. ed. [1827 -
    see NCBEL v.3, col. 1282]).
Hawker, Robert S. Cornish Ballads and Other Poems by
    R.S. Hawker Vicar of Morwenstow ed. C.E. Byles
    (1904 [Oxford, 1869, not ed. by Byles]).
Hawker, Robert S. Poetical Works of R.S. Hawker ed.
    Alfred Wallis (1899).
Hawker, Robert S. Stones Broken from the Rocks :
    Extracts from the Manuscript Note-books of
    Robert Stephen Hawker Vicar of Morwenstow, 1834
    -75 selected and arranged by E.R. Appleton, ed.
    C.E. Byles (Oxford, 1922).
Hazlitt, William The Spirit of the Age, v.XI The
    Complete Works ed. P.P. Howe (1932 [1825]).
Heine, Heinrich The Prose Writings of Heinrich Heine.
    Edited With an Introduction, by Havelock Ellis
    (London, n.d., "The Scott Library").
Hopkins, Gerard M. Further Letters of Gerard Manley
    Hopkins ed. Claude Colleer Abbott rev. ed.(1956)
Hopkins, Gerard M. Poems and Prose of Gerard Manley
    Hopkins ed. W.H. Gardner (Harmondsworth, 1978).
Hopkins, Gerard M. The Correspondence of Gerard
    Manley Hopkins and Richard Watson Dixon ed.
    Claude Colleer Abbott (Oxford, 1935).
Hopkins, Gerard M. The Journals and Papers of Gerard
    Manley Hopkins ed. Humphrey House, Graham Storey
    (O.U.P. London, 1959).
Houghton, Lord See Milnes, Richard Monckton.
Hurd, Richard An Introduction to the Prophecies
    Concerning the Christian Church, The Works v.V
    (1811).
Hurd, Richard Letters on Chivalry and Romance ed.
    Edith J. Morley (1911 [1762: expanded 1765]).

Jameson, Anna B. Legends of the Monastic Orders as
     Represented in the Fine Arts Ist. ed. (1850).
Jameson, Anna B. Sacred and Legendary Art 2v. (1890
     [2v. 1848]).
Johnson, Lionel Post Liminium : Essays and Critical
     Papers by Lionel Johnson (1911).
Johnson, Lionel The Complete Poems of Lionel Johnson
     ed. Iain Fletcher (1953).
Johnson, Samuel and Alexander Chalmers eds. The Works
     of the English Poets, From Chaucer to Cowper
     (1810).
Keble, John Occasional Papers and Reviews ed. E.B.
     Pusey Ist. ed. (Oxford & London, 1877).
Kingsley, Charles Hereward the Wake (1900 [2v.1866]).
Kingsley, Charles Hypatia Ist. ed. 2v. (1853).
Kingsley, Charles Literary and General Lectures and
     Essays (1890 [1880]).
Kingsley, Charles Poems (1902 [1872]).
Kingsley, Charles The Hermits (1878 [3 parts 1868]).
Kingsley, Charles The Roman and the Teuton Ist. ed.
     (Cambridge, 1864). "Why Should We Fear the
     Romish Priests?" FM XXXVII (Apr. 1848).
Kingsley, Charles Yeast 9th. ed. (1878 [first appear-
     ed in FM July-Dec. 1848; reprinted with correc-
     tions and additions 1851]). Also, Preface to 4th
     ed. of Yeast.
Kingsley, Fanny, ed. Charles Kingsley. His
     Letters and Memories of His Life 13th. ed. 2v.
     (1878 [1877]); also Iv. (1885).
Knox, Vicesimus Essays Moral and Literary 2v., 2nd.
     ed. (1779 [1778]).
Lindsay, A.W.C. (Lord) Sketches of the History of
     Christian Art 2v., 2nd. ed. (1885 [1847]).
Lingard, John The History of England 10v., 6th. ed.
     (1855 [3v. 1819, 8v. 1819-1830]).
Lisle, Ambrose Phillips de Letter to the Earl of
     Shrewsbury on the Re-establishment of the
     Hierarchy (1850). "Letters of Phillips de Lisle
     to Montalembert" DR. no. 463 (Ist.quarter,1954).
Lisle, Ambrose Phillips de Preface to The Diurnal of
     the Soul (1864).
Macaulay, Thomas B. Complete Works of Lord Macaulay
     12v. (1898).
Macaulay, Thomas B. History of England from the
     Accession of James the Second (1858 [v.1-2 1849,
     v. 3-4 1855, v.5 1861]).
Macaulay, Thomas B. Lord Macaulay's Essays and Lays
     of Ancient Rome "Popular Edition" (1893).
Maitland, Samuel R. Rev. of The Dark Ages in DR XVII
     (Sept. 1844).
Maitland, Samuel R. The Dark Ages Ist. ed. (1844).

Manners, Lord John A Plea for National Holidays 2nd.
    ed. (1843 [1842]).
Manners, Lord John England's Trust, and Other Poems
    Ist. ed. (1841).
Manners, Lord John The Monastic and Manufacturing
    Systems Ist. ed. (1843).
Masson, David "Pre-Raphaelitism in Art and Literat-
    ure" British Quarterly Review XVI (1852)
Maurice, Frederick D. "Preface" to Charles Kingsley's
    The Saint's Tragedy (1848).
Mill, John Stuart Autobiography of John Stuart Mill
    (New York, 1964 [1873]).
Mill, John Stuart The Spirit of the Age [1831] in
    Mill's Essays on Literature and Society ed.J.B.
    Schneewind (New York, 1965).
Milner, John, with T. Warton, J. Bentham, Grose
    Essays on Gothic Arthitecture (1802).
Milnes, Richard M. "Mr. D'Israeli's Tancred - the
    emancipation of the Jews" ER LXXXVI (Jul.1847)
    138-55.
Milnes, Richard M. The Poems of Richard Monckton
    Milnes 2v. (1838).
Montalembert, Charles de Count de Montalembert's
    Letters to a Schoolfellow 1827-1830 trans. C.F.
    Audley (1874). DR XVII (Sept. 1844) 241-52.
Montgomery, Robert Luther : or the Spirit of the
    Reformation 3rd. ed. rev. and corrected (1843
    [1842]).
Morris, William Introduction to J.M. Neale Good King
    Wenceslas (Birmingham, 1895).
Mosheim, John L. An Ecclesiastical History v.II (1774
    [Ist. English ed. 1756]).
Mozley, Thomas Rev. of Pugin's Contrasts, British
    Critic XXV (Oct. 1839).
Murry, John M. Things to Come (1938 [1928:mainly pub.
    in Adelphi]).
Neale, John Mason A Mirror of Faith. Lays and Legends
    of the Church in England (n.d. : c.1844).
Neale, John Mason Agnes de Tracy: A Tale of the Times
    of S Thomas of Canterbury Ist. ed. (1843).
Neale, John Mason Hierologus; or, The Church Tourists
    Ist. ed. (1843).
Neale, John Mason Letters of John Mason Neale ed.
    Mary Sackville Lawson (1910).
Neale, John Mason Mediaeval Preachers and Mediaeval
    Preaching (1873).
Newman, John Henry "Advertisement" to The Family of
    St. Richard, the Saxon (1844).
Newman, John Henry Apologia Pro Vita Sua ed. Martin
    J. Svaglic (1967 [1864]).
Newman, John Henry Essay on the Development of

Christian Doctrine (Harmondsworth, 1973 [1845]).
Newman, John Henry Historical Sketches v.III (1891
    [3v. 1872-3]).
Newman, John Henry Keble article in British Critic
    XXV (Apr. 1839).
Newman, John Henry Lectures on the Present Position
    of Catholics in England Ist. ed. (1851), 5th ed.
    (n.d.).
Newman, John Henry Letters and Correspondence of John
    Henry Newman 2v. ed. Anne Mozley Ist. ed.(1891).
Newman, John Henry Letters and Diaries of John Henry
    Newman chief ed. C.S. Dessain.
Newman, John Henry ed. Lives of the English Saints
    (1901).
Newman, John Henry Loss and Gain. The Story of a
    Convert (1848).
Newman, John Henry Prophetical Office of the Church
    Ist. ed. (1837).
Newman, John Henry Sermons Bearing on Subjects of the
    Day (1869 [1843]).
Newman, John Henry Sermons Preached on Various
    Occasions (1874 [1857]).
Newman, John Henry The Idea of a University (New York
    1959 [1852-9]).
Nichols, John Literary Anecdotes (1812).
Nicholson, John Airedale in ancient Times ... and
    other Poems (1825).
Nicholson, John Poems by John Nicholson ed. John
    James 2v. (Bingley, 1876).
Pater, Walter Appreciations (1901 [1889]).
Pater, Walter Miscellaneous Studies (1901 [1895]).
Pater, Walter The Renaissance (1963 [1895]).
Peacock, Thomas L. Nightmare Abbey, Crotchet Castle
    (Harmondsworth, 1969 [1818, 1831]).
Percy, Thomas Reliques of Ancient English Poetry 2v.
    (Everyman, 1926 [3v. 1765, 1767, 1775]).
Pinkerton, John ed. Select Scotish Ballads 2v. Ist.
    ed. (1783).
Pugin, Augustus Welby An Apology for the Revival of
    Christian Architecture in England "Victorian
    Library" reprint of 2nd.ed., Leicester U.P. (Old
    Woking, Surrey, 1969 [1843]).
Pugin, Augustus Welby Contrasts : or, a Parallel
    between the Noble Edifices of the Middle Ages,
    and Corresponding Buildings of the Present Day;
    Shewing the Present Decay of Taste Ist.ed.(1836).
Pugin, August Welby "Ecclesiastical Architecture in
    England" DR XII (Feb. 1842) 80-183.
Pugin, August Welby "Elevation of the Cathedral
    Church of St. Chad, Birmingham" DR X (May, 1841)
    301-48.

239

Pugin, Augustus Welby The True Principles and Revival
    of Christian Architecture (1853), comprising The
    True Principles of Pointed or Christian Archit-
    ecture [1841] and An Apology for the Revival of
    Christian Architecture in England.
Punch v.XIX.
Pusey, Edward B. Architectural article, British
    Magazine VIII (Nov. 1835) 579-90.
Reade, Charles Peg Woffington and Christie Johnstone
    (1927 [Christie Johnstone 1853]).
Reade, Charles The Cloister and the Hearth (1939
    [1861]).
Reiss, H.S., ed. The Political Thought of the German
    Romantics 1793-1815(Oxford, 1955).
Robertson, William History of the Reign of the
    Emperor Charles V in Works v.III(1840[3v.1769]).
Rogers, Henry "Recent Developments of Puseyism" ER
    LXXX (Oct. 1844).
Rushton, William "The Classical and Romantic Schools
    of English Literature" in Afternoon Lectures on
    Literature: a course under the presidency of
    Maziere Brady (1863).
Ruskin, John Ruskin in Italy. Letters to his Parents
    1845 ed. Harold Shapiro (Oxford, Clarendon
    Press, 1972).
Ruskin, John The Diaries of John Ruskin 1835-1847 ed.
    Joan Evans and John H. Whitehouse (Oxford,
    Clarendon Press, 1956).
Ruskin, John The Diaries of John Ruskin ... 1848-1873
    ed. Joan Evans and John H. Whitehouse (Oxford,
    Clarendon Press, 1958).
Ruskin, John The Library Edition, The Complete Works
    of John Ruskin ed. E.T. Cook and Alexander
    Wedderburn 39v. (1903-12) : "Angelico", Lecture
    on (1874) CW XXIII, "Cimabue", Lecture on (1874)
    CW XXIII, "Circular Respecting Memorial Studies
    of St.Mark's, Venice...." (1879-80) CW XXIV,
    Fors Clavigera (1871-73) CW XXVII, (1874-76) CW
    XXVIII, (1877-84) CW XXIX, Giotto and His Works
    in Padua CW XXIV, Lectures on Architecture and
    Painting (1853) CW XII, Letters II, 1870-1889
    CW XXXVII, "Lord Lindsay on the History of
    Christian Art"(1847) CW XII, "Mending the Sieve"
    (part of Valle Crucis)(1882) CW XXXIII, Modern
    Painters v.II (1846) CW IV, v.III (1856) CW V,
    v.V (1860) CW VII, Mornings in Florence (1875-7)
    CW XXIII, Praeterita (1885-9) CW XXXV, "Pre-
    Raphaelitism" (1853) CW XII, St. Mark's Rest
    (1877-84) CW XXIV, The Bible of Amiens (1880-5)
    CW XXXIII, The Pleasures of England (1884)CW
    XXXIII, The Seven Lamps of Architecture (1849)

CW VIII, The Stones of Venice v.I (1851) CW IX,
    v.II (1853) CW X, The Two Paths (1858-9) CW XVI,
    Valle Crucis (1882) CW XXXIII.
Russell, Charles William "Charitable institutions of
    Italy (Part I): Genoa" DR XIV (Feb.1843) 97-120.
Schlegel, Friedrich von Lectures on the History of
    Literature, Ancient and Modern (1859 [1815 -
    lectures given 1812]).
Scott, Sir Walter Ritson's Metrical Romances ER VII
    (Jan.1806) 387-413.
Scott, Sir Walter "Horace Walpole" [1820], in Sir
    Walter Scott On Novelists and Fiction ed. Ioan
    Williams (1968).
Scott, Sir Walter Ivanhoe Centenary Edition (Edinbur-
    gh, 1870-1 [3v.1820]).
Scott, Sir Walter Poetical Works ed. J. Logie
    Robertson (1904).
Scott, Sir Walter The Abbot (Edinburgh, 1886 [3v.
    1820]).
Scott, Sir Walter The Betrothed (Edinburgh, 1871
    [1825]).
Scott, Sir Walter The Fair Maid of Perth Centenary
    Edition (Edinburgh, 1870-1 [1828]).
Scott, Sir Walter The Journal of Sir Walter Scott ed.
    W.E.K. Anderson (Oxford, Clarendon Press, 1972).
Scott, William Bell Poems Ist. ed. (1854).
Smythe, George Historic Fancies 2nd.ed. (1844).
Southey, Robert Robert Southey: Journals of a Resid-
    ence in Portugal 1800-1801 and a Visit to France
    1838 ed. Adolfo Cabral (Oxford, Clarendon Press,
    1960).
Southey, Robert Sir Thomas More : or, Colloquies on
    the Progress and Prospects of Society 2v. Ist.
    ed. (1829).
Southey, Robert The Book of the Church 2v. Ist. ed.
    (1824).
Southey, Robert The Life and Correspondence of the
    Late Robert Southey ed. Charles Cuthbert Southey
    6v. (1850).
Southey, Robert The Poetical Works of Robert Southey
    10v. (1838-40).
Sterling, John Essays and Tales, by John Sterling
    ed. Juluis C. Hare 2v. (1848).
Tennyson, Alfred The Works of Alfred Tennyson (1889
    [Becket 1884]).
Tyrrell, George Medievalism (1909).
Vaughan, Robert A. Hours With the Mystics 4th. ed.
    (n.d. [2v. 1856]).
Walpole, Horace Anecdotes of Painting in England ed.
    Ralph N. Wornum 3v. (n.d. [1762-3, 1765 - see
    NCBEL v.2, 1589]).

Walpole, Horace Horace Walpole's Correspondence with
    the Rev. W.C. Cole Yale Edition ed. W.S.Lewis
    34v.
Warton, Thomas Observations on the Faerie Queene of
    Spenser (1762).
Warton, Thomas The History of English Poetry ed.
    Richard Price 4v. (1824 [4v. 1774,1778 & n.d.]).
Warton, Thomas The Poetical Works ed. Richard Mant
    (Oxford, 1802 [Poems: a New Edition 1777]).
Williams, Isaac The Baptistery, or The Way of Eternal
    Life 2nd. ed. (Oxford, 1844 [2v.1842-4]).
Williams, Isaac The Cathedral, or The Catholic and
    Apostolic Church in England 2nd. ed. (Oxford,
    1839 [1838]).
Wilson, John The Poetical Works of Milman, Bowles,
    Wilson and Barry Cornwall (Paris, n.d.[1829]).
Wiseman, Nicholas (Cardinal) "Catholicity in England"
    DR VIII (Feb. 1840).
Wiseman, Nicholas (Cardinal) "Christian Art" DR XXII
    (June, 1847) 486-515.
Wiseman, Nicholas (Cardinal) "Church Architecture of
    the Middle Ages" DR VII (Aug.1839) 250-3.
Wiseman, Nicholas (Cardinal) "Montalembert's St.
    Elizabeth" DR III (Oct.1837) 384-401.
Wiseman, Nicholas (Cardinal) "Pugin on Modern and
    Ancient" DR III (Oct.1837) 360-84.
Wordsworth, William Letters of William and Dorothy
    Wordsworth. The Later Years ed. Ernest de
    Selincourt (Oxford, 1939).
Wordsworth, William Wordsworth: Poetical Works ed.
    Thomas Hutchinson, rev. Ernest de Selincourt
    (1969).

SECONDARY TEXTS

Abbott, Claude Colleer The Life and Letters of George
    Darley Poet and Critic (1928).
Abrams, M.H. Natural Supernaturalism (New York,1971).
Abrams, M.H. The Mirror and the Lamp (1971).
Addington, Raleigh "Newman and the Benedictines" Pax
    v. LXIV no.332 (Spring/Summer 1974).
Alexander, Calvert The Catholic Literary Revival
    (Milwaukee, 1935).
Allen. B. Sprague Tides in English Taste (1619-1800)
    2v. (New York, 1958).
Altholz, J.The Liberal Catholic Movement in England.
    The Rambler and its contributors 1848-1864(1962).
Andrews, Keith The Nazarenes. A Brotherhood of German
    Painters in Rome (Oxford, Clarendon Press,1964).
Anson, Peter F. The Call of the Cloister (1956).
Aveling, J.C.H. The Handle and the Axe (1976).

BIBLIOGRAPHY

Baker, Joseph Ellis The Novel and the Oxford Movement
    (New York, 1965).
Baker, William J. "Hurrell Froude and the Reformers"
    Journal of Ecclesiastical History XXI no.3 (Jul.
    1970).
Barth, J. Robert The Symbolic Imagination : Coleridge
    and the Romantic Tradition (Princeton U.P.,1977).
Batho, Edith C. The Later Wordsworth (New York,1963).
Battiscombe, Georgina John Keble : A Study in Limit-
    ations (1963).
Baunard, Monsignor Louis Ozanam in His Correspondence
    (Dublin, 1925).
Beek, W.J.A.M. John Keble's Literary and Religious
    Contribution to the Oxford Movement (Nijmegan,
    1959).
Beers, Henry A. A History of English Romanticism in
    the Eighteenth Century (1926).
Beers, Henry A. A History of English Romanticism in
    the Nineteenth Century (1926).
Benn, Alfred W. History of English Rationalism in the
    Nineteenth Century (1906).
Bennet, J.A.W. Rev. of Chandler's Dream of Order,RES
    XXIII (1972) 376-78.
Blair, David Hunter John Patrick Third Marquess of
    Bute, K.T. (1921).
Blake, Robert Disraeli (1966).
Blankenagel, John C. "The Dominant Characteristics of
    German Romanticism" PMLA LV (1940).
Bond, Harold L. The Literary Art of Edward Gibbon
    (1960).
Bostram, Irene "The Novel and Catholic Emancipation"
    Studies in Romanticism II (1962-3).
Brendon, Piers Hurrell Froude and the Oxford Movement
    (1974).
Bright, Michael "A Reconsideration of A.W.N. Pugin's
    Architectural Theories" VS XXII (1979) 151-72.
Brilioth, Yngve The Anglican Revival : Studies in the
    Oxford Movement (1933).
Bullitt, John "Distinctions between Fancy and Imagin-
    ation in Eighteenth-Century English Criticism"
    Modern Language Notes LX (1945) 8-15.
Bump, Jerome "Hopkins' Imagery and Medievalist
    Poetics" VP XV (1977).
Bump, Jerome "Hopkins, Pater, and Medievalism" VNL L
    (Fall, 1976).
Burns, Wayne Charles Reade (New York, 1961).
Burrow J.W. "The Sense of the Past" in The Victorians
    ed. Laurence Learner (1978).
Burrows, Margaret F. Robert Stephen Hawker : A Study
    of His Thought and Poetry (Oxford, 1926).
Butterfield, Herbert The Whig Interpretation of

BIBLIOGRAPHY

Byles, C.E. The Life and Letters of R.S. Hawker (1905).

Calder, Grace J. The Writing of Past and Present : A Study of Carlyle's Manuscripts (1949).

Carnall, Geoffrey Robert Southey British Council Pamphlet (1964).

Carritt, E.F. A Calendar of British Taste, From 1600 to 1800 (n.d.).

Chadwick, Owen The Mind of the Oxford Movement(1960).

Chadwick, Owen The Secularization of the European Mind in the Nineteenth Century (Cambridge,London 1975).

Chadwick, Owen The Victorian Church 2v. (1966).

Chandler, Alice A Dream of Order : The Medieval Ideal in Nineteenth-Century English Literature (1971).

Chandler, Alice "Sir Walter Scott and the Medieval Revival" NCF XIX (1965).

Chapman, Raymond Faith and Revolt (1970).

Chapman, Ronald Father Faber (1961).

Chitty, Susan The Beast and the Monk. A Life of Charles Kingsley (1974).

Church, Richard W. The Oxford Movement (1909).

Clark, Kenneth The Gothic Revival (John Murray,1975).

Clausson, Nils "English Catholics and Roman Catholicism in Disraeli's Novels" NCF XXXIII(Mar.1979).

Cobban, Alfred Edmund Burke and the Revolt Against the Eighteenth Century (1962).

Collingwood, R.G. Ruskin's Philosophy (Chichester, 1971).

Collingwood, R.G. The Idea of History (Oxford, Clarendon Press, 1946).

Cook, Edward T. Studies in Ruskin (1890).

Cook, Edward T. The Life of John Ruskin 2v. 2nd. ed. (1912).

Cooper, Robyn "The Relationship between the Pre-Raphaelite Brotherhood and Painters before Raphael in English Criticism of the Late 1840s and 1850s VS XXIV no.4 (Summer 1981)405-438.

Coulson, Herbert H. "Medievalism in the Modern World" The Catholic Historical Review XXVI (1940-1).

Cruse, Amy The Victorians and Their Books (1962).

Crutwell, Patrick "Walter Scott" in The Pelican Guide to English Literature v.5 ed. Boris Ford (Harmondsworth, 1970).

DeLaura, David Hebrew and Hellene in Victorian England (Texas U.P.,Austin and London,1969).

Dellamora, Richard J. "The Revaluation of 'Christian' Art : Ruskin's Appreciation of Fra Angelico 1845-60" UTQ XLIII (1973-4) 143-50.

Douglas, Mary Natural Symbols : Explorations in

Cosmology (Harmondsworth, 1970).
Drummond, Andrew L. The Churches in English Fiction
    (Leicester, 1950).
Duncan, J.E. "The Anti-Romantic in Ivanhoe" in Walter
    Scott : Modern Judgements ed. D.D.Devlin (1968).
Duthie, D. Wallace The Church in the Pages of "Punch"
    (1912).
Elton, Oliver A Survey of English Literature 1830-
    1880 2v. (1927).
Elwin, Malcolm Charles Reade (1931).
Evans, Joan John Ruskin (New York/London, 1954).
Fairchild, Hoxie N. Religious Trends in English
    Poetry 5v. (1957-64).
Fairchild, Hoxie N. "Romanticism and the Religious
    Revival in England" Journal of the History of
    Ideas v.2 (1941) 330-38.
Fairchild, Hoxie N. "The Romantic Movement in
    England" PMLA LV (1940).
Fairchild, Hoxie N. The Romantic Quest (Philadelphia,
    1952).
Farmer, David H., ed. Benedict's Disciples (Leo-
    minster, 1980).
Farrell, John P. "Matthew Arnold and the Middle Ages:
    the Uses of the Past" VS XIII (Mar.1970) 319-38.
Ferguson, Wallace K. The Renaissance in Historical
    Thought : Five Centuries of Interpretation
    (Cambridge, Mass., 1948).
Ferrey, Benjamin Recollections of A.N. Welby Pugin
    (1861).
Finke, Ulrich German Painting from Romanticism to
    Expressionism (1974).
Frankl, Paul The Gothic : Literary Sources and Inter-
    pretations through Eight Centuries (Princeton,
    New Jersey, 1960).
Furst, Lilian Romanticism in Perspective (1969).
Gallaway, Francis Reason, Rule, and Revolt in English
    Classicism (New York, 1965).
Garside, P.D. "Scott, the Romantic Past and the
    Nineteenth Century" RES XXIII (1972).
Gay, Peter The Enlightenment : An Interpretation
    (1967).
Germann, Georg Gothic Revival in Europe and Britain :
    Sources, Influences and Ideas (1972).
Gilley, Sheridan "Charles Butler and Robert Southey's
    Book of the Church", unpublished paper (1976).
Girouard, Mark The Return to Camelot. Chivalry and
    the English Gentleman (Yale U.P. New Haven and
    London, 1981).
Gombrich, Ernst "The Turn of the Tide" The Listener
    CI no. 2599 (22 Feb. 1979).
Gooch, G.P. History and Historians in the Nineteenth

Century (1928).

Graves, Charles L. Mr. Punch's History of Modern England 3v. (1921).

Greenberg, Robert A. "Ruskin, Pugin and the Contemporary Context of 'The Bishop Orders His Tomb'" PMLA LXXXIV (1969) 1588-94.

Grennan, Margaret William Morris : Medievalist and Revolutionary (New York, 1945).

Grierson, Herbert The Background of English Literature. Classical and Romantic (1962).

Griggs, Earl Leslie Wordsworth and Coleridge (New York, 1962).

Guerard, Albert "Prometheus and the Aeolian Lyre" Yale Review XXXIII (1943).

Gwynn, Dennis R. Lord Shrewsbury, Pugin and the Gothic Revival (1946).

Hale, J.R. England and the Italian Renaissance (1963)

Halstead, John B. ed. Romanticism : Problems of Definition, Explanation, and Evaluation (Boston, 1968).

Hampson, Norman The Enlightenment (Harmondsworth, 1968).

Harris, R.W. Romanticism and the Social Order 1780-1830 (1969).

Harris, Wendell V. "The Gothic Structure of Ruskin's Praise of Gothic" UTQ XL (1970-71) 109-118.

Haskell, Francis Rediscoveries in Art : Some Aspects of Taste, Fashion and Collecting in England and France (1976).

Havens, Raymond D. The Mind of a Poet 2v. (Baltimore, 1941).

Havens, Raymond D. "Thomas Warton and the Eighteenth-Century Dilemma" Studies in Philology 25 (1928).

Heath-Stubbs, John The Darkling Plain (1950).

Hewison, Robert John Ruskin : The Argument of the Eye (Princeton, 1976).

Heyer, Friedrich The Catholic Church From 1648 to 1870 (1969).

Hill A.G. "A Medieval Victorian" TLS 5 Sept.1958,504.

Holland, Bernard Memoir of Kenelm Henry Digby (1919).

Holmes, J. Derek More Roman than Rome : English Catholicism in the Nineteenth Century (1978).

Holmes, J. Derek "Newman's Reputation and The Lives of the English Saints" Catholic Historical Review LI (Jan.1966).

Honour, Hugh Romanticism (1979).

Houghton, Walter E. "The Issue Between Kingsley and Newman" in Theology Today (Apr.1947), reprinted Victorian Literature : Selected Essays (New York, 1967) ed. Robert O. Preyer.

BIBLIOGRAPHY

Houghton, Walter E. The Victorian Frame of Mind 1830-
    1870 (Yale U.P., New Haven and London, 1974).
Hough, Graham The Last Romantics (1961).
Hough, Graham The Romantic Poets (1968).
House, Humphrey "Pre-Raphaelite Poetry" in All in Due
    Time (1955).
Hunt, John Dixon The Pre-Raphaelite Imagination,1848-
    1900 (1968).
Johnson, Edgar Sir Walter Scott 2v. (1970).
Johnston, Arthur Enchanted Ground (1964).
Kegel, Charles H. "Lord John Manners and the Young
    England Movement : Romanticism in Politics"
    Western Political Quarterly XIV (1961).
Ketton-Cremer, R.W. Horace Walpole (1964).
Ketton-Cremer, R.W. "The Elizabethan Walpole's" in
    Horace Walpole : Writer, Politician and Connoi-
    sseur ed. Warren Hunting Smith (1967).
Kitch, M.J. ed. Capitalism and the Reformation(1969).
Knoepflmacher, U.C.,G.B. Tennyson, eds. Nature and
    the Victorian Imagination (California U.P.,
    Berkeley/Los Angeles/London, 1977).
Knowles, David Thomas Becket (1970).
Knox, Ronald Enthusiasm : A Chapter in the History of
    Religion (1950).
Landow, George Rev. Chandler's Dream of Order,Modern
    Philology LXX (1972-3).
Landow, George The Aesthetic and Critical Theories of
    John Ruskin (Princeton, 1971).
LaValley, Albert Carlyle and the Idea of the Modern
    (1968).
Leslie, Shane Henry Edward Manning : His Life and
    Labours (1921).
Levine, Richard A. "Disraeli's Tancred and 'The Great
    Asian Mystery'" NCF XXII (1967-8).
Leys, M.D.R. Catholics in England 1559-1829 (Catholic
    Book Club ed., n.d.).
Liddon, Henry Parry Life of Edward Bouverie Pusey 4v.
    4th. ed. (1894).
Lough, A.G. The Influence of John Mason Neale (1962).
Lovejoy, Arthur O. "The First Gothic Revival and the
    Return to Nature" Modern Language Notes XLVII
    (1932) 419-46.
Lucas, F.L. The Decline and Fall of the Romantic
    Ideal (1963).
Mahoney, Thomas "Edmund Burke and Rome" The Catholic
    Historical Review XLIII (Jan. 1958).
Mandelbaum, Maurice History, Man and Reason (Balti-
    more and London, 1971).
Martin, B.W. "Wordsworth, Faber, and Keble" RES n.s.
    XXVI (1975) 436-42.
Martin, Robert B. The Dust of Combat.A Life of

<u>Charles Kingsley</u> (1959).

Masterson, Patrick <u>Atheism and Alienation</u> (Harmond-worth, 1973).

May, J. Lewis <u>Father Tyrrell and the Modernist Movement</u> (1932).

McCabe, Bernard "Disraeli and the 'Baronial Principle' : Some Versions of Romantic Medievalism" <u>VNL</u> XXXIV (Fall 1968) 7-13.

Merriman, James D. <u>The Flower of Kings. A Study of the Arthurian Legend in England Between 1485 and 1835</u> (Kansas U.P., Lawrence/Manhattan/Wichita, 1973).

Miller, Frances S. "The Historic Sense of Thomas Chatterton" <u>English Literary History</u> II (1944) 117-34.

Murphy, Howard R. "The Ethical Revolt Against Christian Orthodoxy in Early Victorian England" <u>The American Historical Review</u> LX (Jul. 1955).

Ollard, S.L. <u>A Short History of the Oxford Movement</u> (1915).

Osborne, John W. <u>William Cobbett</u> (New York, 1966).

Passmore, John <u>The Perfectibility of Man</u> (1970).

Patrick, James "Newman, Pugin, and Gothic" <u>VS</u> XXIV no.2 (Winter 1981) 188-96.

Pawley, Bernard, and Margaret Pawley <u>Rome and Canterbury Through Four Centuries</u> (1974).

Pevsner, Nikolaus <u>Some Architectural Writers of the Nineteenth Century</u> (Oxford, Clarendon Press, 1972).

Platzner, Robert L. and Robert D. Hume "Gothic Versus Romantic" <u>PMLA</u> LXXXVI (1971) 266-74.

Pope-Hennessy, Una <u>Canon Charles Kingsley</u> (1948).

Prickett, Stephen <u>Romanticism and Religion</u> (C.U.P. 1976).

Purcell, Edmund S. <u>An Appendix : in Which the Writings and Character of Augustus Welby Neale Pugin are considered in their Catholic Aspect</u> (1861) contained in Ferrey <u>Recollections of A.N.Welby Pugin.</u>

Purcell, Edmund S. <u>Life and Letters of Ambrose Phillips de Lisle</u> ed. and finished by Edwin de Lisle 2v. (1900).

Quennell, Peter <u>Romantic England : Writing and Painting 1717-1851</u> (1970).

Rance, Nicholas <u>The Historical Novel and Popular Politics in Nineteenth-Century England</u> (Plymouth 1975).

Reilly, M.Paraclita <u>Aubrey de Vere : Victorian Observer</u> (Dublin, London, 1956).

Renouf, Peter Le Page Rev. of Carlyle's <u>Past and Present</u> <u>DR</u> XV (Aug.1843) 182-200.

Rosenberg, John D. The Darkening Glass : A Portrait of Ruskin's Genius (1963).

Routh, H.V. Towards the Twentieth Century (C.U.P., 1937).

Rowley. Edwin N. Kenelm Henry Digby and the English Catholic Literary Revival (1942) unpublished thesis, St.John's University, New York.

Rowse, A.L. "Hawker of Morwenstow : A Belated Medieval" Essays and Studies n.s. XII (1959).

Saintsbury, George A Short History of English Literature (1898).

Saintsbury, George "The Young England Movement" in The Collected Essays and Papers of George Saintsbury 1875-1920 3v. (1923) v.III.

Sambrook, James A Poet Hidden. The Life of Richard Watson Dixon 1833-1900 (1962).

Sambrook, James William Cobbett (1973).

Sanders, Andrew The Victorian Historical Novel 1840-1880 (1978).

Schenk, H.G. The Mind of the European Romantics (1966).

Shea, Donald F. The English Ranke : John Lingard (New York, 1969).

Shuster, George N. The Catholic Spirit in Modern English Literature (New York, 1922).

Simmons, Jack Southey (1945).

Smith, A.L. "Richard Hurd's 'Letters on Chivalry and Romance'" English Literary History VI (1939).

Spacks, Patricia M. The Insistence of Horror (Cambridge, Mass., 1962).

Stanton, Phoebe B. The Gothic Revival and American Church Architecture (Baltimore, 1968).

Stanton, Phoebe B. "The Sources of Pugin's Contrasts" in Concerning Architecture : Essays on Architectural Writers and Writing presented to Nikolaus Pevsner ed. John Summerson (1968).

Steegman, John Victorian Taste : A Study of the Arts and Architecture from 1830 to 1870 (1970).

Stewart, Herbert L. A Century of Anglo-Catholicism (1929).

St. Louis, Ralph F. The Middle Ages as a Political and Social Ideal in the Writings of Edmund Burke, Samuel Taylor Coleridge, Thomas Carlyle and John Ruskin (1972) unpublished thesis, Nebraska University, listed Dissertation Abstracts Index v.33, no.7 : 3600A-0IA (1973).

Storr, Vernon F. The Development of English Theology in the Nineteenth Century 1800-1860 (1913).

Svaglic, Martin J. "Religion in the Novels of George Eliot" Journal of English and Germanic Philology LIII (1954).

Swain, Joseph W. Edward Gibbon the Historian (1966).
Tawney, Richard H. Religion and the Rise of Capital-
      ism.
Taylor, Ronald, ed. The Romantic Tradition in Germany
      : An Anthology (1970).
Tennyson, Charles Alfred Tennyson (1949).
Tennyson, G.B. Victorian Devotional Poetry, The
      Tractarian Mode (Harvard U.P., Cambridge, Mass.,
      London, 1981).
Tennyson, Hallam Alfred Lord Tennyson : A Memoir by
      His Son 2v. (1924).
Thorlby, Anthony, ed. The Romantic Movement (1966).
Thorpe, Clarence De Witt "Coleridge on the Sublime"
      in Wordsworth and Coleridge : Studies in honour
      of George McLean Harper ed. Earl Leslie Griggs
      (New York, 1962).
Trappes-Lomax, Michael Pugin. A Mediaeval Victorian
      (1932).
Turner, Paul Tennyson (1976).
Unrau, John "A Note on Ruskin's Reading of Pugin"
      English Studies XLVIII 335-7.
Unrau, John "Ethics and Architecture : Some
      Precursors of Pugin and Ruskin" Notes and
      Queries CCXTX (1974) 174-5.
Unrau, John "Ruskin's Uses of the Adjective 'Moral'"
      English Studies LII (1971) 339-47.
Varma, Devendra P. The Gothic Flame (New York, 1966).
Vaughan, William Romantic Art (1978).
Walker, Hugh The Literature of the Victorian Era
      (C.U.P., 1921).
Ward, A.W., A.R. Waller, eds. Cambridge History of
      English Literature (1913).
Ward, Wilfrid Aubrey de Vere (1904).
Ward, Wilfrid The Life and Times of Cardinal Wiseman
      2v. (1897).
Watkin, E.I. Catholic Art and Culture (1947).
Watkin, E.I. Roman Catholicism in England from the
      Reformation to 1950 (1958).
Weatherby, Harold L. Cardinal Newman in His Age. His
      Place in English Theology and Literature
      (Nashville, 1973).
Weisinger, H. "The Middle Ages and the Late Eight-
      eenth-Century Historians" PQ XXVII (1948).
Weiskel, Thomas The Romantic Sublime (Baltimore and
      London, 1976).
Weiss, John Conservatism in Europe 1770-1945 (1977).
Wellek, René A History of Modern Criticism : 1750-
      1950. The Romantic Age (1955).
Whibley, Charles Lord John Manners and His Friends
      2v. (1925).
White, James F. The Cambridge Movement : The

Ecclesiologists and the Gothic Revival (Cambridge, 1962).

Willey, Basil _Nineteenth-Century Studies_ (Harmondsworth, 1969).

Willey, Basil _The Seventeenth-Century Background_ (1957).

Williams, Raymond _Culture and Society 1780-1950_ (Harmondsworth, 1971).

Willoughby, L.A. "On Some German Affinities with the Oxford Movement" _MLR_ XXIX (1934).

INDEX